kingsway

classical music's premier recording venue

discography
compiled by
john hunt

kingsway
classical music's premier recording venue

John Hunt

© John Hunt 2019

ISBN 978-1-901395-36-5

Travis & Emery Music Bookshop
17 Cecil Court
London
WC2N 4EZ
United Kingdom.
Tel. (+44) (0) 20 7240 2129.
newpublications@travis-and-emery.com

CONTENTS

Introduction/*page 7*

The discography 1925-1984/*page 11*

Index of conductors/*page 383*

Guide to record prefixes/*page 393*

KINGSWAY: CLASSICAL MUSIC'S PREMIER RECORDING VENUE

The heyday of the recording industry in Great Britain coincides with that of a Methodist church hall in Central London, where many of the recordings still today enjoying classic status were produced. The time span involved covers the onset of electrical (microphone) recording, leading on to the introduction of magnetic tape and the long-playing record, first in monophonic but eventually stereophonic sound.

It was the purpose-built organ of the West London Central Mission, a Methodist chapel located just off London's Kingsway (hence the name Kingsway Hall), that first attracted the attention of the marketing people at the Gramophone Company in the mid 1920s. By the time that the electrical process was fully established, enabling a full symphony orchestra to be captured with some fidelity, the record makers no longer wanted to rely exclusively for a venue on the capital's main concert hall (Queens Hall). Although in due course both HMV and Decca were to construct their own studios (Abbey Road and West Hampstead respectively), they were constantly attracted back to the mellow warmth which was inherent in Kingsway's sonic quality. The partnership

introduction/continued

was to continue uninterrupted for both main record companies, as well as for many smaller ones, for almost sixty years, notwithstanding the fact that the vast public appetite for LP records meant that many other church and civic halls in the Greater London area were also used. Detailed information about Kingsway and its various vicissitudes over the decades, culminating in its closure and eventual demolition, can be found in a series of articles written by Gordon Drury in 2014 for the periodical *Classic Record Collector*.

The initial impetus for this discography came from a collector friend of mine who specialises in audiophile LPs from the 1950s-1970s. A vast number of these records originated in the Kingsway acoustic, and because of this I have concentrated exclusively on first issue record numbers throughout. For the LP era, however, I have added some subsequent LP re-issues which are considered to retain the depth and bloom of the original pressings. What in my view must be excluded are editions like most of the Decca Eclipse label (with exceptions), where that company proceeded to disfigure its excellent mono catalogue with fake (electronic) stereo re-processing.

introduction/concluded

Readers will need to look elsewhere for current availability of a particular recording in its CD format, as they will also for full casts of operas and other works involving multiple soloists. To have embraced all the data would have doubled the size of the volume.

Scarcely a name of note in the pantheon of twentieth-century conductors is missing from the Kingsway gallery, whilst the list of composers conducting their own works is impressive: Edward Elgar, Samuel Barber, Aram Khachaturian, Benjamin Britten, Ernest Bloch, Alan Rawsthorne, Paul Hindemith, Lennox Berkeley and Michael Tippett, to name just a few.

Reproduced overleaf is the playbill for the Philharmonia Orchestra's very first public concert in 1945: it is nowadays almost totally forgotten that, as well as being a venue for religious and political gatherings, Kingsway Hall was in its earlier years a much valued concert auditorium.

My thanks for help with the preparation goes to John Baker, John Hancock and Malcolm Walker.

John Hunt 2019

KINGSWAY HALL
KINGSWAY, W.C.2

PHILHARMONIA
CONCERT SOCIETY
(Walter Legge and Victor Schuster)

AUTUMN, 1945

PHILHARMONIA ORCHESTRA
(Leader: Leonard Hirsch)

Sir THOMAS BEECHAM
Bart.

REGINALD KELL

Mozart Concert

Saturday October 27, at 3 p.m.

Programme 6d.

IBBS & TILLETT,
124, Wigmore Street, W.1

0001/1925-1930/recordings for which precise details could not be verified

e.stanley roper (organ solo)
elgar imperial march; dubois cantilene nuptiale

herbert dawson (organ solo)
widor marche pontificale

reginald goss-custard (organ solo)
widor toccata from the organ symphony; watling menuet antique; goss-custard chelsea fayre; wolstenholme question and answer; walford davies solemn melody

0002/31 december 1925 & 21 january 1926/hmv sessions
herbert dawson (organ solo)
elgar idylle; easthorpe martin evensong/B 2263
elgar idylle was re-recorded in saint margarets westminster

0003/3 february 1926/hmv session
herbert dawson (organ solo)
christ the lord is risen today; all people that on earth do dwell/B 2274

0004/7 july 1926/hmv session
henry ley (organ solo)
handel concerto in g; purcell tunes and ayres/C 1314

0005/27 august 1926/hmv session
g.d.cunningham (organ solo)
bach toccata and fugue BWV 565/C 1291
mendelssohn finale from organ sonata no 1/B 2522

0006/15 september-25 october 1926/hmv sessions
london symphony orchestra/albert coates/
*philharmonic choir/*soloists
holst jupiter from the planets/D 1129
wagner tannhäuser overture/D 1138-1139
beethoven symphony 3/D 1158-1163
*beethoven symphony 9/D 1164-1171
tchaikovsky symphony 6/D 1190-1194
borodin prince igor overture/D 1210
wagner meistersinger overture/D 1260
humperdinck hänsel und gretel overture/D 1261
holst mercury from the planets; first dance from
the perfect fool/D 1308
strauss don juan/D 1309-1310
weber oberon overture/D 1311
wagner tanz der lehrbuben from die meistersinger/D 1319
holst uranus from the planets/D 1384
holst mars from the planets/D 2006
wagner lohengrin act three prelude/unpublished
orchestra described for these sessions as "the symphony orchestra"; last side of tchaikovsky symphony 6 was re-made in january 1927; recording of beethoven symphony 9 was completed in queens hall

0007/27 september 1926/hmv session
reginald goss-custard (organ solo)
wolstenholme romanze; lemare madrigals/C 1345

0008/3-16 december 1926/hmv sessions
reginald goss-custard (organ solo)
wolstenholme allegretto in e flat/B 2536
coleridge-taylor three fours waltz/B 2725

0009/4-6 january 1927/hmv sessions
london symphony orchestra/albert coates
beethoven prometheus overture/D 1163
wagner meistersinger act three prelude/D 1219
prokofiev selection from love of 3 oranges/D 1259
respighi fontane di roma/D 1429-1430
rimsky-korsakov selection from legend of kitesh/unpublished
wagner lohengrin prelude/unpublished
wagner frau sonne sendet from götterdämmerung/unpublished
wagner waldweben from siegfried/unpublished

0010/9 march 1927/vocalion sessions
festival symphony orchestra/adrian boult
weber der freischütz overture/K 05299
wagner der fliegende holländer overture/K 05296

0011/27-30 may 1927/hmv sessions
london symphony orchestra/albert coates/soloists
wagner schläfst du gast? & der männer sippe from
die walküre/D 1321
wagner raste nur hier & hinweg flieh die entweihte
from die walküre/D 1325
wagner death of tristan from tristan und isolde/unpublished
wagner ich sah das kind from parsifal/unpublished

0012/23-26 august 1927/hmv sessions
london symphony orchestra/albert coates/soloists
mozart symphony 41; der schauspieldirektor
overture/D 1359-1362
wagner sink hernieder nacht der liebe from
tristan/D 1414-1415
wagner seit er von dir geschieden from
götterdämmerung/D 1576
wagner schweigt eures jammers & starke scheite
(part one) from götterdämmerung/D 1586
wagner seit ewigkeiten from parsifal/D 1651
D 1414 was re-recorded later in berlin

0013/18-25 october 1927/hmv sessions
london symphony orchestra/albert coates/soloists
strauss till eulenspiegels lustige streiche/D 1418-1419
stravinsky petrushka/D 1521-1524
borodin polovtsian dances from prince igor/D 1528

0014/5-10 january 1928/hmv sessions
london symphony orchestra/albert coates/soloists
wagner spottet nur zu & wotan gemahl erwache
from das rheingold/D 1546
wagner ich sah das kind from parsifal/D 1651-1652

0015/19 january 1928/hmv session
london symphony orchestra/geoffrey toye
delius brigg fair/D 1442-1443
delius in a summer garden/D 1696-1697
delius on hearing the first cuckoo in spring/E 505

0016/15-16 february 1928/hmv sessions
london symphony orchestra/albert coates/*chorus
rimsky-korsakov selection from tsar sultan/D 1491
stravinsky selection from the firebird/D 1510
wagner faust overture/D 1631
humperdinck dream pantomime from hänsel und gretel/ES 556
*borodin polovtsian dances from prince igor/unpublished
recording of ES 556 was completed in january 1929

0017/28 march 1928/hmv sessions
new symphony orchestra/edward elgar/beatrice harrison
elgar cello concerto/D 1507-1509
recording completed in june 1928

0018/29 march 1928/spanish hmv session
london cello school/john barbirolli
casals sardana; mozart-barbirolli der hölle rache from
die zauberflöte/AF 207 (spain)/C 10060 (Italy)

0019/11 and 28 may 1928/hmv sessions
orchestra/john barbirolli/frida leider
mozart or sai chi l'onore from don giovanni; gluck divinites du styx frm alceste/D 1547
wagner träume from wesendonk-lieder/DB 1553
beethoven abscheulicher from fidelio/unpublished
recording of abscheulicher transferred to queens hall

0020/10-18 october 2018/hmv sessions
london symphony orchestra/albert coates/soloists
strauss tod und verklärung; handel-elgar overture in d minor/D 1525-1527
bach-elgar fantasy and fugue in c minor/D 1560
liszt les preludes/D 1616-1617
tchaikovsky romeo and Juliet overture; glinka ruslan and lyudmila overture/ES 481-483
wagner dich teure halle from tannhäuser/unpublished
wagner euch lüften die mein klagen from lohengrin/unpublished
wagner mild und leise from tristan und isolde/unpublished

0021/19-20 december 1928
london symphony orchestra/edward elgar
elgar wand of youth first suite; minuet from beau brummel/D 1636-1638
elgar wand of youth second suite/D 1649-1650
elgar contrasts/unpublished

0022/january-june 1929/hmv sessions
essie ackland/organ and piano accompaniments
popular ballads/B 2964, B 3128 and B 3203

0023/18-22 march, 6-23 april and 14-31 may 1929/hmv sessions
london symphony orchestra/albert coates/
"philharmonic choir/soloists
*bach mass in b minor/C 1710-1726
wagner sink hernieder nacht der liebe from tristan/D 1723-1724

0024/15 april 1929/hmv session
orchestra/john barbirolli/maartje offers
bach du lieber heiland from matthäus-passion/DB 1286
elgar where corals lie from sea pictures/DB 1761
elgar sabbath morning at sea from sea pictures/unpublished

0025/21 october and 4 november 1929/hmv sessions
essie ackland/reginald goss-custard (organ)
popular ballada and religious arias/B 3339 and B 3460

0026/22-23 october 1929/hmv sessions
london symphony orchestra/albert coates/*artur rubinstein
*brahms piano concerto 2/D 1746-1750
wagner lohengrin act three prelude/D 1815
mussorgsky gopak from sorochinsky fair/D 1934

0027/5-7 november 1929/hmv sessions
london symphony orchestra/albert coates
borodin symphony 2/DB 1554-1556
rimsky-korsakov may night overture/D 1744
rimsky-korsakov le coq d'or prelude/D 1745
dvorak carnival overture/D 1796
liadov eight russian folksongs; musical snuffbox/D 1811-1812
rimsky-korsakov capriccio espagnol/D 1861-1862
borodin steppes of central asia/D 1885

0028/11 november 1929/hmv session
london symphony orchestra/landon ronald/*misha levitzki
*liszt piano concerto 1/D 1775-1776
stanford irish rhapsody 4/unpublished (recording incomplete)

0029/13-14 november 1929/hmv sessions
london symphony orchestra/malcolm sargent/mark hambourg
beethoven piano concerto 3/C 1865-1868
orchestra described for these sessions as "symphony orchestra"

0030/20 november 1929/hmv session
orchestra/john barbirolli/fernando autori
rossini la calumnia from il barbiere di siviglia; gounod vous qui faites l'endormie from faust/C 1842
gounod le veau d'or from faust/unpublished

0031/3 december 1929/hmv sessions
london symphony orchestra/landon ronald/
***victor hely-hutchinson**
tchaikovsky theme and variations from third suite;
chant sans paroles op 2 no 3/C 1798-1800
*hely-hutchinson noel fantasy from carol symphony/C 1968
orchestra described for C 1968 as "royal opera orchestra"

0032/11 december 1929/hmv session
london symphony orchestra/john barbirolli
luigini ballet russe/C 1927
grieg symphonic dance op 64 no 4/C 1928
wallace maritana overture/C 1948-1949
orchestra described for this session as "royal opera orchestra"

0033/16 december 1929/hmv session
london symphony orchestra/malcolm sergent
mendelssohn ruy blas overture/C 1815
sibelius finlandia/C 1827
schubert rosamunde overture/C 1873-1874
orchestra described for this session as "symphony orchestra"

0034/23 january and 17 february 1930/hmv sessions
reginald goss-custard (organ)/marguerite carlton
songs and ballads/B 3311 and C 2101

0035/4-6 february 1930/hmv sessions
london symphony orchestra/malcolm sargent/soloists
sullivan hms pinafore/D 1844-1852
orchestra described for this recording as "orchestra"

0036/11 march 1930/hmv session
orchestra/lawrance collingwood/walter widdop
english ballads/D 1833

0037/8-11 april 1930/hmv sessions
london symphony orchestra/landon ronald/*john barbirolli
schumann-glazunov carnaval/D 1840-1842
*glazunov bacchanale from the seasons; ballabile from les ruses d'amour/C 1930
orchestra described for C 1930 as "royal opera orchestra"

0038/1 may 1930/hmv session
london symphony orchestra/albert coates/soloists
wagner grüss gott mein junker & abendlich glühend from die meistersinger/EJ 567-568

0039/21-23 may 1930/hmv sessions
london symphony orchestra/eugene goossens
franck le chasseur maudit; chabrier marche joyeuse/C 2016-2017
mendelssohn hebrides overture/unpublished
orchestra described for this session as "royal opera orchestra"

0040/28 may 1930/hmv session
de groot (violin)/herbert dawson (organ)
berceuse; a perfect day/B 3512

0041/29 may 1930/hmv sessions
london symphony orchestra/john barbirolli/lauritz melchior
meyerbeer o paradis from le prophete; leoncavallo vesti
la giubba from pagliacci/EJ 582
wagner dir töne lob from tannhäuser; allmächtiger vater
from rienzi/EJ 583
de greef old flemish folksong/unpublished

0042/2 june 1930/hmv session
london symphony orchestra/eugene goossens
rossini-respighi selection from la boutique fantasque/C 1996
auber le cheval de bronze overture/C 1997
orchestra described for this session as "royal opera orchestra"

0043/20 june-3 july 1930/hmv sessions
london symphony orchestra/vincenzo bellezza
rossini tancredi overture/C 1998
rossini italiana in algeri overture/C 1999
mascagni le maschere overture/C 2018
respighi ancient airs and dances second suite/C 2345-2346
massenet gavotte and menuet/B 3544
puccini suor angelica intermezzo; mascagni danza delle quecas from iris/S 10223 (italy)
montemezzi amor di 3 tre act three intermezzo; wolf-ferrari gioelli della madonna intermezzo/S 10224 (italy)
marinuzzi suite siciliana/S 10226 (italy)
van westenhout ronde d'amour and mabelle/unpublished

0044/15 and 18 september 1930/hmv sessions
london symphony orchestra/edward elgar
elgar in the south overture/D 1665-1667
elgar crown of india suite; pomp and circumstance march 5/D 1899-1900
recording of D 1900 was completed in september 1930

0045/17 september 1930/hmv session
london symphony orchestra/landon ronald
svendsen carnival in paris/DB 1759-1760
edward german welsh rhapsody/D 1939-1940

0046/18 and 23 september 1930/hmv sessions
london symphony orchestra/john barbirolli
gounod selection from faust/C 2055
bizet selection from carmen/C 2056
handel concerto grosso op 6 no 4/unpublished
orchestra described for these sessions as "royal opera orchestra"

0047/24 september and 1-8 october 1930/hmv sessions
london symphony orchestra/malcolm sergent/
*chorus/*soloists
*sullivan patience/D 1909-1918
handel overture & pastoral symphony from messiah/C 2071
dvorak slavonic dances op 46 nos 1 and 3/C 2149
raff cavatina/C 2176
auber zanetta overture/C 2183
beethoven movements from moonlight & pathetique sonatas/C 2234
sullivan selection from princess ida/C 2236
orchestra described for D 1909-1918 as "orchestra", for C 2176, C 2234 and C 2246 as "new light symphony orchestra" and for C 2149 and C 2183 as "royal opera orchestra"; recording of D 1909-1918 completed in november 1930

0048/9-10 and 14 october 1930/hmv sessions
london symphony orchestra/albert coates
liszt mephisto waltz 1/D 1928
tchaikovsky francesca da rimini/D 1929-1930
liszt hungarian rhapsody 1/D 1931
stravinsky selection from le chant du rossignol/D 1932
tchaikovsky marche slave/D 1933
rimsky-korsakov procession of the nobles from mlada/D 1934
liadov kikimora/E 565

0049/28 october 1930/hmv session
london symphony orchestra/lawrance collingwood/soloists
wagner das süsse lied verhallt from lohengrin/D 2020
wagner geliebter komm from tannhäuser/
EX 29 01693 (unpublished on 78rpm)

0050/17 and 21 november 1930/hmv sessions
london symphony orchestra/piero coppola
lalo le roi d'ys overture and andantino/L 863-864 (france)
massenet scenes alsaciennes/L 901-902 (france)

0051/20-22 november 1930/hmv sessions
london symphony orchestra/edward elgar
elgar symphony 1/D 1944-1949

0052/5 december 1930/hmv session
john mccormack/herbert dawson (organ)/*string quintet
ave maria; *the perfect prayer/DA 1177

0053/29-30 december 1930/hmv sessions
london symphony orchestra/albert coates/vladimir horowitz
rachmaninov piano concerto 3/DB 1486-1490

0054/7 january 1931/hmv session
mayfair orchestra/ray noble
an alpine fantasy/C 2103

0055/8-9 january 1931/hmv sessions
london symphony orchestra/john barbirolli/artur rubinstein
mozart piano concerto 23/DB 1491-1493
chopin piano concerto 2/DB 1494-1497

0056/21-23 february 1931/hmv sessions
london symphony orchestra/lawrance collingwood/
erno von dohnanyi
dohnanyi variations on a nursery song/D 2054-2056
london symphony orchestra/erno von dohnanyi
dohnanyi second movement from ruralia hungarica/D 2056

0057/5-23 march and 13-14 april 1931/hmv sessions
london symphony orchestra/malcolm sargent/soloists
sullivan selection from the yeomen of the guard/B 3799-3804
sullivan selection from the pirates of penzance/B 3846-3851
sullivan selection from the gondoliers/B 3866-3871

0058/17 april 1931/hmv session
london symphony orchestra/lawrance collingwood
wagner motifs 1-48 of the ring cycle/C 2237

0059/18 april 1931/hmv session
london symphony orchestra/albert coates
mussorgsky night on bare mountain/D 2010

0060/5 may 1931/hmv session
**london symphony orchestra/lawrance collingwood/
lauritz melchior**
loewe fredericus rex/unpublished

0061/9, 12 and 21 may 1931/hmv sessions
london symphony orchestra/robert heger/soloists
wagner extracts from siegfried/D 1836-1837 and DB 1578-1583
wagner abendlich glühend from meistersinger/D 2000

0062/11 and 16 may 1931/hmv sessions
london symphony orchestra/john barbirolli/soloists
loewe fredericus rex; hill das herz am rhein/DA 1224
wagner winterstürme from die walküre/DA 1227
haydn schon eilt der frohe ackersmann from the seasons;
mendelssohn herr gott abraham from elijah/DB 1564
wagner morgenlich leuchtend from meistersinger/DB 1858
wagner selig wie die sonne from meistersinger/D 2002

0063/23 may and 4 june 1931/hmv sessions
london symphony orchestra/edward elgar
elgar nursery suite/D 1998-1999
elgar bavarian dance 3/DB 1167

0064/23 may 1931/hmv session
london symphony orchestra/lawrance collingwood/
*lauritz melchior
wagner motifs 49-90 from the ring cycle/C 2238
*wagner am stillen herd from meistersinger/DB 1227

0065/6-8 june 1931/hmv sessions
london symphony orchestra/max steinmann/feodor chaliapin
dargomitzky miller's aria and mad scene from rusalka;
glinka the happy day from ruslan and lyudmila/DB 1530-1531
mussorgsky coronation & death scenes from
boris godunov/DB 1532

0066/20 and 28 june 1931/hmv sessions
orchestra/john barbirolli/beniamino gigli
tosti addio; sullivan the lost chord/DB 1526
massenet fuyez douce image from manon/DA 1216

0067/24-29 june 1931/hmv sessions
london symphony orchestra/eugene goossens
tchaikovsky polonaise from evgeny onegin/DB 1760
delibes mazurka & czardas from coppelia/B 9341
lalo le roi d'ys overture/B 9342
tommasini selection from the good-humoured ladies/C 2272
bach-goossens suite in g/C 2273
massenet scenes pittoresques/unpublished

0068/25 september 1931/hmv session
jeannette macdonald/ray noble (organ)
songs and ballads/B 3952-3953

0069/25 and 29 september 1931/hmv sessions
orchestra/john barbirolli/richard crooks
religious songs/DB 1798 and DA 1288
london symphony orchestra/john barbirolli
mascagni cavalleria rusticana intermezzo/C C 2292
wagner selection from tannhäuser/C 2293

0070/19 october 1931/hmv session
dennis diehl (boy soprano)/dr rhodes (organ)
religious arias/B 4071

0071/27-29 october 1931/hmv sessions
london symphony orchestra/leo blech
grieg norwegian dances/DB 1668-1669
mendelssohn meeresstille glückliche fahrt overture/DB 1671-1672
weber oberon overture/DB 1675
mozart selection from les petits riens/DB 1676
mendelssohn saltarello from symphony 4/DA 1263
auber le domino noir overture/DA 1264

0072/5 november 1931/hmv session
de groot (violin)/herbert dawson (organ)
softly awakes my heart; serenata/B 4070
english ballad arrangements/B 4185

0073/16 december 1931/hmv session
dennis middleton (boy soprano)/herbert dawson (organ)
handel arias/B 4133

0074/20 february 1932/hmv session
london symphony orchestra/albert coates/
*george thalben-ball (organ)
*handel cuckoo and the nightingale/DA 1261
bach-holst fugue BWV 577/DA 1327
rimsky-korsakov dance of the tumblers/DB 1698

0075/4 march 1932/hmv session
iwan davies (boy soprano)/herbert dawson (organ)
handel arias/B 4108

0076/29 april 1932/hmv session
london symphony orchestra/chorus/einar nilson
humperdinck selection from das mirakel/C 2429

0077/27 may 1932/hmv session
john mccormack/herbert dawson (organ)
hymn to christ the king/GEMM 274 (not on 78rpm)

0078/19-21 september 1932/hmv sessions
london philharmonic orchestra/royal choral society/
malcolm sargent
handel messiah choruses; haydn creation choruses/
C 2489, C 2513 and C 2548

0079/17 february 1933/hmv session
george thalben-ball (organ solo)
grieg peer gynt suite 1 (arrangement)/B 4484-4485

0080/6 april 1933/hmv session
herbert dawson (organ solo)
elgar organ sonata 2/B 4422-4423

0081/20-21 july 1933/hmv sessions
london philharmonic orchestra/john barbirolli
quilter a childrens overture/C 2603
tchaikovsky swan lake suite/2619-2620
auber fra diavolo overture/C 2644

0082/29 august 1933/hmv session
london philharmonic orchestra/edward elgar
elgar elegy for strings/DB 1939
elgar serenade for strings/DB 2132-2133

0083/7 march 1935/hmv session
london philharmonic orchestra/landon ronald
elgar coronation march/DB 2437
edward german coronation march and hymn/DB 2438

0084/October 1935/hmv session
london philharmonic orchestra/john barbirolli/ina souez
bach cantata arias/unpublished

0085/16 april 1937/hmv session
bbc symphony orchestra/adrian boult
meyerbeer coronation march from le prophete;
elgar imperial march/DB 3163
walton crown imperial/DB 3164

0086/9 july 1937/hmv session
light orchestra/walter goehr
selections from famous ballet scores/C 2914-2915 & C 2925

0087/15-16 july 1937/hmv sessions
london philharmonic orchestra/eugene goossens
schumann-glazunov carnaval/C 2916-2918
grieg peer gynt suite 1/C 2933-2934
borodin polovtsian dances/C 3048-3049
recording of peer gynt suite was completed at
abbey road studios

0088/19 july 1937/columbia session
london philharmonic orchestra/efrem kurtz
tchaikovsky swan lake waltz; delibes naila waltz/DX 787
delibes selection from coppelia/DX 797
delibes selection from sylvia/DX 817

0089/23 september 1937/hmv private session
london philharmonic orchestra/malcolm sargent/soloists
songs by nettlefold

0090/27 september 1937/hmv and columbia sessions
london philharmonic orchestra/antal dorati
erlanger les cent baisers/C 3098-3099
dargomitzky danses slaves et tziganes from rusalka/DX 804

0091/2-5 november 1937/hmv sessions
london philharmonic orchestra/walter goehr
marches by sousa/C 2957
kings of the waltz/C 2962
themes of offenbach and johann strauss/C 2963
weber aufforderung zum tanz/unpublished

0092/20 july and 9 august 1938/columbia sessions
london philharmonic orchestra/antal dorati
tchaikovsky swan lake suite/DX 869-872/DX 8132-8135
chabrier cotillon suite/DX 877-878

0093/12 september 1938/hmv session
**london philharmonic orchestra/warwick braithwaite/
webster booth**
arias by puccini and bizet/C 3030 and B 8803

0094/16 september 1938/columbia session
london philharmonic orchestra/efrem kurtz
offenbach-rosenthal gaite parisienne/DX 883-884
mozart-seitz l'epreuve d'amour/DX 897

0095/11 october 1938/hmv sessions
busch chamber players/adolf busch/*rudolf serkin
mozart serenata notturna K239/DA 1673-1674
*mozart piano concerto 14/DB 3960-3962

0096/21 october 1938/hmv sessions
**london philharmonic orchestra/george szell/
benno moiseiwitsch**
beethoven piano concerto 5/C 3043-3047/C 7517-7521

0097/24 november 1938/hmv session
london philharmonic orchestra/constant lambert
auber le cheval de bronxe overture/C 3061
auber les diamants de la couronne overture/C 3071

0098/13-15 december 1938 & 18 january 1939/
columbia sessions
london philharmonic orchestra/thomas beecham
schubert symphony 5/LX 785-788/LX 8424-8427
mozart symphony 36/LX 797-800/LX 8435-8438
haydn symphony 104/LX 856-858/LX 8469-8471
*recording of haydn symphony completed in february
and july 1939*

0099/10 february 1939/hmv session
sadlers wells orchestra/constant lambert
tchaikovsky sleeping beauty suite/C 3081-3083/C 7525-7527

0100/11 february 1939/hmv session
**london philharmonic orchestra/malcolm sargent/
fritz kreisler**
mozart violin concerto 4/unpublished

37

0101/28 february 1939/hmv session
london philharmonic orchestra/warwick braithwaite/
webster booth
sacred arias by handel and mendelssohn/C 3087 & C 3098

0102/12 april 1939/columbia session
london philharmonic orchestra/thomas beecham
grieg peer gynt suite/LX 838-839
recording completed in july 1939

0103/8 may 1939/hmv session
sadlers wells orchestra/constant lambert
rossini ballet music from william tell/B 8900-8901
meyerbeer selection from les patineurs/C 3105

0104/23 june 1939/hmv session
london philharmonic orchestra/thomas beecham
sibelius pelleas et melisande suite/DB 3892-3893
mozart adagio from divertimento K131/unpublished
recording of sibelius completed in july 1939

0105/28 june 1939/hmv session
london philharmonic orchestra/constant lambert
offenbach orfee aux enfers overture/C 3110
meyerbeer coronation march from le prophete;
chabrier marche joyeuse/C 3112

0106/4-7 july 1939/hmv and columbia sessions
london philharmonic orchestra/thomas beecham
sibelius en saga/DB 3889
mozart symphony 35/LX 851-853
first movement of mozart recorded previously in abbey road studios

0107/25 july 1939/hmv session
webster booth/herbert dawson (organ)
sullivan the lost chord; handel largo/C 3130

0108/27 july 1939/columbia session
london philharmonic orchestra/antal dorati
boccherini-francaix scuola di ballo/DX 944-945
stravinsky pas de deux from baiser de la fee/DX 949

0109/27 july 1939/hmv private session
london philharmonic orchestra/charles hambourg/ elsie suddaby
works by nettlefold

0110/20 october 1939/hmv session
herbert dawson (organ)/choir/soloists
sacred arias/unpublished

0111/26 october 1939/hmv session
orchestra/warwick braithwaite/webster booth
songs by tosti, liszt and freire/B 9009 and C 3139

0112/27 october 1939/hmv session
orchestra/choir/isidore godfrey/soloists
sullivan selections from the mikado and the gondoliers/
C 3128 and C 3151

0113/28 october 1939/hmv sssion
**london philharmonic orchestra/wynn reeves/
choir/soloists**
arias by bach-gounod, bizet, handel and liddle/
B 8990 and C 3130

0114/2 november 1939/hmv session
**sadlers wells orchestra/warwick braithwaite/
choir/soloists**
works by mascagni, offenbach and handel/
C 3126 and C 3129

0115/8 december 1939/hmv session
sadlers wells orchestra/warwick braithwaite/dennis noble
arias by rossini, leoncavallo, verdi and gounod/
C 3141 and C 3157

0116/13 december 1939/hmv session
webster booth/herbert dawson (organ)
bless this house; danny boy/B 9022

0117/21 december 1939/hmv sessions
london philharmonic orchestra/constant lambert/*sadlers wells orchestra/*warwick braithwaite/*soloists
*selections from carmen and aida/C 3143
weinberger polka anf fugue from schwanda
the bagpiper/C 3148-3149
chabrier danse slave from le roi malgre lui/C 3218

0118/26-29 february 1940/columbia sessions
london philharmonic orchestra/felix weingartner
liszt les preludes/LX 877-878
mozart symphony 39/LX 881-883/LX 8483-8485
brahms academic festival overture/LX 886
liszt mephisto waltz 1; beethoven ruinen von athen overture/LX 897-898
brahms symphony 2/LX 899-903/LX 8492-8496

0119/23 may 1940/hmv sessions
orchestra/walter goehr/webster booth
operetta arias/B 9058 and B 9069

0120/6 november 1940/hmv session
webster booth/herbert dawson (organ)
star of bethlehem; the holy city/C 3196

0121/9 may 1941/hmv session
webster booth/gerald moore (piano)
the lord's prayer; when big ben chimes/B 9201

0122/11 june 1941/hmv session
webster booth/bertram harrison (organ)
o come all ye faithful; a perfect day/B 9507

0123/18 june 1941/columbia session
joan hammond/harry blech (violin)/
bertram harrison (organ)
panis angelicus; ave maria/DX 1023

0124/5 august 1941/columbia session
Isobel baillie/arnold goldsborough (organ)
purcell blessed virgin's expostulation/DX 1031
handel i know that my redeemer liveth/unpublished

0125/24 june 1942/hmv session
kentucky minstrels/leslie woodgate
choral songs/C 3298 and C 3313

0126/15 october 1943/columbia session
Isobel baillie/bertram harrison (organ)
arias by bach/DX 1133

0127/8 june 1944/decca sessions
national symphony orchestra/sidney beer/
*moura lympany
tchaikovsky symphony 5/AK 1032-1036
debussy prelude a l'apres-midi d'un faune/K 1037
delius irmelin prelude/K 1836
*grieg piano concerto/unpublished

0128/3 and 11-12 october 1944/decca sessions
national symphony orchestra/sidney beer
bizet l'arlesienne suite 1; puccini manon lescaut
intermezzo/K 1278-1280
wagner rhine journey and funeral march from
götterdämmerung/K 1284-1285

0129/4-5 october 1944/decca sessions
national symphony orchestra/anatole fistoulari
weber-berlioz aufforderung zum tanz/K 1108
berlioz marche hongroise from la damnation de faust;
gliere russian sailors' dance from the red poppy/K 1281
tchaikovsky marche slave/K 1282

0130/10 october 1944/decca session
national symphony orchestra/eric coates
coates four centuries suite/K 1272-1273

0131/10-13 october 1944/decca sessions
national symphony orchestra/anatole fistoulari
suppe pique dame overture/K 1283
bizet carmen suites 1 and 2/K 1286-1288
recordings completed in november 1944

0132/31 october 1944/decca session
national symphony orchestra/boyd neel
saint-saens danse macabre/K 1289
wolf-ferrari gioelli della madonna intermezzi 1 and 2

0133/1 november 1944/decca session
national symphony orchestra/anatole fistoulari
tchaikovsky oprichnik overture/K 1291

0134/2 november 1944/decca session
national symphony orchestra/victor olof
chabrier espana/K 1292
suppe morgen mittag und abend in wien overture/K 1293

0135/15 november 1944/decca session
national symphony orchestra/eric coates
coates three elizabeths suite/K 1109-1110

0136/16 november and 5 december 1944/decca sessions
national symphony orchestra/anatole fistoulari
ponchielli dance of the hours from la gioconda/K 1119
beethoven symphony 7/K 1221-1225
delibes selection from coppelia ballet music/K 1294
recording of beethoven symphony completed in january 1945

0137/6 and 13-14 december 1944/decca sessions
national symphony orchestra/boyd neel/*kathleen long
*mozart piano concerto 15/K 1121-1123
*faure ballade/K 1130-1131
elgar three bavarian dances/AK 1295-1296
figaro and cosi overtures/K 1297

0138/12 december 1944/decca session
national symphony orchestra/anatole fistoulari
schubert symphony 8/K1114-1116

0139/13 december 1944/decca session
**national symphony orchestra/malcolm sargent/
clifford curzon**
tchaikovsky piano concerto 1/unpublished

0140/15 december 1944/decca session
national symphony orchestra/heinz unger
mendelssohn hebrides overture/K 1120
mendelssohn athalie overture/K 1298

0141/2-3 january 1945/decca sessions
national symphony orchestra/malcolm sargent
beethoven symphony 5/K 1126-1129
tchaikovsky symphony 4/K 1226-1230

0142/10-12 january 1945/decca sessions
national symphony orchestra/boyd neel/*soloists
*arias by saint-saens, puccini & gounod/K 1200 & K 1201
thomas raymonda overture/K 1299
suppe leichte kavallerie overture/K 1300

0143/17 and 26 january 1945/decca sessions
national symphony orchestra/*london symphony orchestra/anatole fistoulari
schubert rosamunde entr'acte & ballet music/K 1304
*schubert rosamunde overture/K 1406

0144/18-20 january 1945/decca sessions
national symphony orchestra/stanford robinson
tchaikovsky nutcracker suite/K 1142-1144
tchaikovsky evgeny onegin polonaise & waltz/K 1301
offenbach orfee aux enfers overture/K 1302

0145/19 january 1945/decca session
national symphony orchestra/karl rankl
rossini il barbiere di siviglia overture/K 1125
weber euryanthe overture/K 1154

0146/25-27 january 1945/decca sessions
national symphony orchestra/victor olof
sibelius valse triste; jaernefelt praeludium/K 1149
nicolai lustigen weiber overture/K 1303

0147/8-9 february 1945/decca sessions
national symphony orchestra/sidney beer/*victor olof
tchaikovsky swan lake suite/K 1308-1309
*rossini william tell overture/K 1310-1311
berlioz carnaval romain overture/K 1312

0148/8 and 23 february 1945/decca sessions
national symphony orchestra/albert coates
tchaikovsky romeo and Juliet; rimsky-kprsakov dance
of the tumblers from snow maiden/K 1305-1307

0149/14-15 february 1945/decca sessions
national symphony orchestra/karl rankl
brahms symphony 4/K 1231-1235
beethoven egmont overture/K 1313

0150/22 february 1945/decca session
london symphony orchestra/victor olof
dvorak slavonic dances 1 and 2/K 1124
auber masaniello overture/K 1314

0151/23 february 1945/decca session
national symphony orchestra/walter goehr
mozart symphony 39/K 1236-1238

0152/7-8 march 1945/decca sessions
london symphony orchestra/clarence raybould/
*john hargreaves
*verdi arias from rigoletto/K 1203
humperdinck hänsel und gretel overture/K 1315

0153/7-9 march 1945/decca sessions
national symphony orchestra/karl rankl
beethoven symphony 1/K 1239-1242
dvorak carnival overture/K 1316

0154/9 march 1945/decca session
london symphony orchestra/warwick braithwaite
elgar pomp and circumstance marches 1-4/K 1140-1141

0155/14 march 1945/decca sessions
national symphony orchestra/sidney beer/moura lympany
grieg piano concerto/K 1134-1137
mendelssohn capriccio brilliant/K 1191

0156/16-17 march 1945/decca sessions
london symphony orchestra/albert coates/*walter goehr
mussorgsky night on bare mountain/K 1317-1318
*grieg peer gynt suite 1/K 1319-1320

0157/21 march 1945/decca session
national symphony orchestra/walter goehr
liszt hungarian rhapsody 2/K 1321

0158/22 march 1945/decca session
national symphony orchestra/warwick braithwaite
sibelius finlandia/K 1150
weber oberon overture/K 1322

0159/24 march 1945/decca session
national symphony orchestra/boyd neel
mozart die entführung aus dem serial overture/K 1323

0160/11-13 april 1945/decca sessions
national symphony orchestra/albert coates
tchaikovsky symphony 6/K 1243-1248
recording completed in july 1945

0161/13 april 1945/decca sessions
national symphony orchestra/victor olof/*heinz unger
rossini tancredi overture/K 1324
auber le cheval de bronze overture/K 1325
*mendelssohn ruy blas overture/K 1326
*schubert overture in the Italian style/K 1327

0162/26-28 april 1945/decca sessions
national symphony orchestra/basil cameron/
*ida haendel
*saint-saens introduction and rondo capriccioso/K 1171
rimsky-korsakov capriccio espagnol/K 1328-1329
*tchaikovsky violin concerto/K 1444-1447
recording of tchaikovsky completed in february 1946

0163/13 may 1945/decca session
london symphony orchestra/albert coates
mussorgsky gopak from sorochinsky fair/K 1318
rimsky-korsakov introduction and bridal procession
from le coq d'or/K 1330

0164/16 may 1945/decca sessions
london symphony orchestra/anatole fistoulari/
moura lympany
khachaturian piano concerto/K 1145-1148

0165/18 may 1945/decca session
national symphony orchestra/london symphony orchestra/warwick braithwaite/soloists
arias by rimsky-korsakov, mussorgsky and schubert/
K 1172 and K 1272

0166/28-29 may 1945/decca sessions
london mozart orchestra/anthony collins
mozart symphony 33; march K334/K 1249-1251

0167/18 june 1945/decca session
boyd neel orchestra/boyd neel/frederick grinke
mozart violin concerto 5/K 1266-1271

0168/11-13 july 1945/decca sssions
national symphony orchestra/karl rankl/*heinz unger
dvorak symphony 9/K 1357-1361
*mendelssohn symphony 4/K 1370-1373

0169/24 july 1945/decca session
national symphony orchestra/warwick braithwaite/moura lympany
saint-saens piano concerto 2/K 1161-1163

0170/25 july 1945/decca sessions
new symphony orchestra/karl rankl
schubert symphony 4/K 1252-1255
smetana bartered bride overture/K 1331

0171/27 july 1945/decca session
national symphony orchestra/sidney beer
ravel mother goose suite/K 1342-1343

0172/10 august 1945/hmv session
**philharmonia chamber orchestra/maurice miles/
heddle nash**
arias by handel/C 3454 and 7EG 8681

0173/15-24 august 1945/hmv sessions
london philharmonic orchestra/thomas beecham
borodin prince igor overture; berlioz marche
troyenne/DB 6237-6238
berlioz hunt and storm from les troyens/DB 6241
beethoven symphony 4/DB 6280-6283
mendelssohn symphony 5/DB 6316-5319
handel-beecham great elopement suite/DB 9667-9668
these recordings were completed in october-december 1945

0174/5-6 september 1945/decca sessions
national symphony orchestra/enrique jorda
falla el amor brujo/AK 1332-1334
falla dances from el sombrero de 3 picos/AK 1335-1336

0175/6-7 september 1945/decca sessions
national symphony orchestra/anatole fistoulari/
*walter goehr
thomas mignon overture/K 1116
*delius on hearing the first cuckoo in spring/K 1341

0176/11 september 1945/decca sessions
national symphony orchestra/heinz unger
beethoven symphony 3/K 1256-1262

0177/12-16 september 1945/decca sessions
national symphony orchestra/enrique jorda/*ida haendel
dukas l'apprenti sorcier; debussy prelude to
la demoiselle elue/K 1175-1176
turina danzas fantasticas/K 1337-1338
*lalo symphonie espagnole/unpublished

0178/22-23 september 1945/decca sessions
national symphony orchestra/malcolm sargent/
ida haendel
dvorak violin concerto/K 1377-1380

0179/26 september 1945/decca session
national symphony orchestra/enrique jorda/
clifford curzon
falla nights in the gardens of spain/K 1158-1160

0180/1 october 1945/hmv session
instrumental ensemble/victor hely-hutchinson/soloists
hely-hutcinson hymns/C 3464-3465

0181/2 october 1945/decca session
national symphony orchestra/boyd neel
elgar in the south overture/unpublished

0182/3 october 1945/columbia session
london symphony orchestra/eric coates
coates three bears fantasy/DX 1217
coates concert waltz from dancing night/DX 2345

0183/10 october 1945/decca session
national symphony orchestra/basil cameron
dvorak symphony 8/K 1263-1267

0184/11 october 1945/decca session
national symphony orchestra/sidney beer/*luton ladies choir
*debussy trios nocturnes/K 1344-1346
strauss don juan/K 1347-1348

0185/17-24 october 1945/hmv sessions
london philharmonic orchestra/thomas beecham/*soloists
mozart die entführung aus dem serail overure/DB 6251
tchaikovsky waltz from evgeny onegin/DB 6266
*wagner einzug der götter from rheingold/unpublished
strauss schleiertanz from salome/unpublished
rimsky-korsakov may night overture/unpublished

0186/7-8 november 1945/decca sessions
national symphony orchestra/malcolm sargent
elgar enigma variations; pomp and circumstance
march 5/K 1351-1354

0187/13 november 1945/decca session
national symphony orchestra/anatole fistoulari/
nicholas orloff
tchaikovsky piano concerto 1/K 1167-1170

0188/27 november 1945/decca sessions
national symphony orchestra/malcolm sergent
beethoven symphony 4/K 1384-1387
bbc theatre orchestra/stanford robinson
edward german henry Viii dances/K 1356

0189/28-29 november 1945 & 9 january 1946/
decca sessions
national symphony orchestra/reginald goodall
tchaikovsky 1812 overture/K 1349-1350
beethoven coriolan overture/unpublished
beethoven leonore 1 overture/unpublished

0190/12 december 1945/decca sessions
**national symphony orchestra/boyd neel/
clifford curzon/*malcolm sargent**
mozart piano concerto 23/K 1394-1396
*rossini semiramide overture/K 1475-1476

0191/12-13 december 1945/decca sessions
bbc theatre orchestra/stanford robinson
johann strauss die fledermaus overture/K 1362
offenbach barcarolle from les contes d'hoffmann;
mascagni cavalleria rusticana intermezzo/K 1363
delibes sylvia ballet suite/K 1364-1365

0192/9 january 1946/decca session
national symphony orchestra/enrique jorda
haydn symphony 88/AK 1472-1474

0193/10 january 1946/decca session
london symphony orchestra/anatole fistoulari/
***oda slobodskaya**
mendelssohn war march of the priests from athalie/K 1373
mendelssohn wedding march from sommernachtstraum/K 1380
*tchaikovsky letter scene from evgeny onegin/LXT 5663
(unpublished on 78rpm)

0194/17 january 1946/decca session
mantovani and his concert orchestra
london fantasia/K 1173

0195/17-18 january 1946/columbia sessions
philharmonia orchestra/reginald Jacques/
walter susskind/soloists
selection of opera and oratorio arias/unpublished

0196/24-30 january 1946/columbia sessions
philharmonia orchestra/constant lambert/
*walter susskind
borodin steppes of central asia/DX 1449
*rimsky-korsakov baba yaga/DX 1485-1486
glinka jota aragonesa/unpublished
*dvorak cunning peasant overture/unpublished
*dvorak scherzo capriccioso/unpublished
(recording incomplete)

0197/5 february 1946/decca session
national symphony orchestra/muir mathieson/
chorus/eileen joyce
baraza from men of two worlds/K 1174

0198/7 february 1946/decca sessions
london symphony orchestra/malcolm sargent
schubert symphony 9/AK 1459-1464

0199/12-13 and 19 february 1946/decca sessions
london philharmonic orchestra/ernest ansermet
stravinsky petrushka/K 1388-1392

0200/27 february 1946/decca sessions
london symphony orchestra/malcolm sargent/
*kathleen ferrier
*arias by handel and gluck/K 1466
handel pastoral symphony from messiah/K 1499
haydn symphony 98; handel arrival of the
queen of sheba/K 1500-1503

0201/28 february 1946/decca sessions
london symphony orchestra/malcolm sargent/
moura lympany
beethoven piano concerto 4/K 1467-1470

0202/11-13 march 1946/decca sessions
london philharmonic orchestra/basil cameron
herold zampa overture/K 1453
rossini william tell overture/K 1454-1455
grieg peer gynt suite 2/K 1456-1457
auber les diamants de la couronne overture/K 1458

0203/13 march 1946/decca session
london philharmonic orchestra/malcolm sargent
holst the perfect fool ballet music/K 1561-1562

0204/25 march 1946/hmv session
arthur grumiaux/gerald moore (piano)
mozart violin sonata 32/unpublished

0205/2 april 1946/decca session
london philharmonic orchestra/franz andre
franck le chasseur maudit/K 1485-1486
liszt mephisto waltz 1/unpublished

0206/3 april 1946/decca sessions
london symphony orchestra/anatole fistoulari
chopin-douglas les sylphides ballet suite/K 1487-1488
auber fra diavolo overture/K 1489
rossini italiana in algeri overture/K 1490
schubert marche militaire/unpublished

0207/8 april 1946/decca session
bbc theatre orchestra/stanford robinson
luigini ballet egyptien/K 1477-1478

0208/9-10 april 1946/decca sessions
london philharmonic orchestra/gregor fitelberg
tchaikovsky symphony 3/K 1479-1483
wagner meistersinger overture/K 1484

0209/11-12 april 1946/decca sessions
national symphony orchestra/*london symphony orchestra/enrique jorda
rimsky-korsakov russian easter overture/K 1522-1523
*mozart symphony 36/K 1538-1540

0210/17 and 24 may 1946/decca sessions
bbc theatre orchestra/stanford robinson
tchaikovsky sleeping beauty suite/K 1524-1525
johann strauss frühlingsstimmen/K 1526

0211/23-24 may 1946/decca session
london philharmonic orchestra/victor de sabata
sibelius en saga/K 1504-1506

0212/4 june 1946/decca session
national symphony orchestra/victor olof/campoli
paganini first movement from violin concerto 1/
K 1822-1823

0213/6 june 1946/decca session
**london symphony orchestra/anatole fistoulari/
marian nowakowski**
borodin komchak's aria from prince igor; song of the
volga boatmen/GEM 0152 (unpublished on 78rpm)

0214/7 june 1946/decca session
london symphony orchestra/malcolm sargent
scarlatti-tommasini good-humoured ladies suite/K 1497-1498
handel messiah overture/K 1499

0215/19 june 1946/columbia session
**philharmonia orchestra/george weldon/isobel baillie/
harry mortimer**
haydn auf starkem fittiche from the creation/DX 1392
handel aria from judas maccabeus/unpublished
clarke trumpet voluntary/unpublished

0216/24 june 1946/decca session
london philharmonic orchestra/erich leinsdorf
tchaikovsky theme & variations from suite 3/AK 1987-1988

0217/25 june 1946/decca session
london symphony orchestra/muir mathieson
parker seascope from western approaches; alwyn
calypso music from the rake's progress/K 1544
vaughan williams epilogue from forty-ninth parallel/
LA 48 (usa only)

0218/8-13 july 1946/decca sessions
london philharmonic orchestra/erich leinsdorf/*eileen joyce
*rachmaninov piano concerto 2/K 1545-1549
weber der freischütz overture/K 1589
sibelius symphony 5; alla marcia from karelia/AK 2193-2196

0219/9-12 july 1946/decca sessions
london symphony orchestra/*national symphony orchestra/piero coppola
grieg symphonic dances 1, 2 and 4/K 1869-1870
*schumann symphony 1/AK 2151-2154

0220/26 september 1946/decca session
orchestra/charles groves/soloists
mendelssohn arias from elijah/K 1557
elgar selection from starlight express/K1995

0221/22-23 october 1946/decca sessions
london philharmonic orchestra/*national symphony orchestra/karl rankl/*paul schoeffler
strauss der rosenkavalier waltzes/AK 2053-2054
*wagner wahnmonolog from meistersinger/K 1573

0222/23-25 october 1946/decca sessions
london symphony orchestra/muir mathieson
warrack men of arnhem march from theirs is the glory;;
benjamin Jamaican song and rumba/K 1571
greenwood waltz into jig from hungry hill/K 1579
bax quiet interlude & gay march from malta qc/LA 48 (usa only)
jacob ferry flight from maintenance command; rawsthorne
prisoners march from the captive heart/unpublished

0223/24 october 1946/decca session
london symphony orchestra/karl rankl/soloists
mozart sarastro arias from die zauberflöte/K 1851
bach cantata 53/K 2228

0224/12 november 1946/decca session
london philharmonic orchestra/eduard van beinum
tchaikovsky francesca da rimini/unpublished

0225/14 november 1946/decca session
london symphony orchestra/muir mathieson
williams the last waltz from edge of the world/K 1579
addinsell wrvs march; bliss vision of leonard from
conquest of the air/unpublished

0226/15 november 1946/decca session
london symphony orchestra/enrique jorda
falla dances from el sombrero de 3 picos; mussorgsky khovantschina prelude/AK 1796-1797

0227/27-29 november 1946/decca sessions
london philharmonic orchestra/eduard van beinum/
*eugenia zareska
*mahler lieder eines fahrenden gesellen/K 1624-1625
haydn symphony 100/AK 1808-1810
side one of mahler was remade in december 1947

0228/10 december 1946/decca session
london philharmonic orchestra/ernest ansermet
stravinsky firebird suite/K 1574-1576

0229/12 december 1946/decca sessions
national symphony orchestra/boyd neel/
*james whitehead
mozart don giovanni overture/unpublished
*boccherini cello concerto/unpublished

0230/31 december 1946/decca sessions
london philharmonic orchestra/julius harrison
marches by saint-saens, elgar, halfvorsen and meyerbeer/LK 4020

0231/1 january 1947/decca session
bbc theatre orchestra & chorus/stanford robinson
choruses by gounod/K 1599

0232/1 january 1947/decca session
london philharmonic orchestra/karl rankl/
paul schoeffler
verdi iago arias from otello/K 1664

0233/13 january 1947/decca session
mantovani orchestra and chorus
selection from the noel coward musical "pacific 1860*/
K 1590-1595

0234/13-14 january 1947/decca sessions
london philharmonic orchestra/jean martinon/
monique haas
mozart piano concerto 20/unpublished

0235/17 and 22 january 1947/decca sessions
london symphony orchestra/muir mathieson/
janine micheau
rossini una voce poco fa from barbiere di siviglia/K 1650
bizet comme autrefois from les pecheurs de perles/K 1672
gounod waltz song from romeo et juliette/unpublished

0236/5-7 february 1947/decca sessions
london philharmonic orchestra/basil cameron
sibelius tapiola/AK 2214-2215

0237/24-26 february and 1 march 1947/columbia sessions
philharmonia orchestra/alceo galliera
dvorak symphony 9/DX 1399-1403/DX 8275-8279
debussy prelude a l'apres-midi/DX 1381

0238/7 march and 30 april 1947/decca sessions
bbc theatre orchestra/walter goehr
smetana dance & polka from bartered bride/K 1667

0239/15 march 1947/decca session
national symphony orchestra/roger desormiere
bizet jeux d'enfants; chabrier habanera/K 1845-1846

0240/19 march 1947/columbia session
philharmonia orchestra/ernest irving
berners nicholas nickleby film music/DX 1362

0241/23 april 1947/columbia session
philharmonia orchestra/walter susskind/
leon goossens
marcello oboe concerto in d minor/DX 1389-1390
scarlatti oboe concerto in f/DX 8347-8348

0242/30 april 1947/decca session
london symphony orchestra/stanford robinson/soloists
mussorgsky nursery scene from boris godunov/K 1601

0243/1 may 1947/decca sessions
london symphony orchestra/muir mathieson
ireland film score for the overlanders/K 1602
bbc theatre orchestra/walter goehr
smetana the moldau/K 1912-1913

0244/13-14 may 1947/decca sessions
london philharmonic orchestra/jean martinon/
*****eugenia zareska**
ravel le tombeau de couperin/AK 1838-1839
*tchaikovsky final aria from maid of orleans/K 2087

0245/15 may 1947/decca session
national symphony orchestra/roger desormiere
debussy marche ecossaise/K 2095
bizet patrie overture/K 2105-2106

0246/16 may 1947/decca session
london philharmonic orchestra/karl rankl/*eugenia zareska
dvorak scherzo capriccioso/LA 101 (usa only)
*tchaikovsky none but the lonely heart/unpublished

0247/21-22 may 1947/columbia sessions
philharmonia orchestra/alceo galliera/*dennis brain
*strauss horn concerto 1/DX 1397-1398
wagner tannhäuser overture/unpublished

0248/27 may 1947/decca session
new symphony orchestra/royalton kisch/eugene conley
puccini cavaradossi arias from tosca/M 656

0249/27 may 1947/hmv session
royal philharmonic orchestra/thomas beecham
sibelius symphony 6/DB 6640-6642
recording completed in july, september & november 1947

0250/29-30 may 1947/hmv sessions
halle orchestra/john barbirolli
humperdinck hänsel und gretel overture/C 3623
elgar introduction and allegro/C 3669-3670
elgar bavarian dance 2/C 3695

0251/2-6 june 1947/decca sessions
london philharmonic orchestra/charles munch
roussel le festin de l'araignee/K 1695-1696
bizet symphony in c: danse bohemian from
la jolie fille de perth/K 1781-1784
roussel suite in F/AX 317-318
faure pelleas et melisande suite/EDA 58 (usa only)
schumann symphony 4/EDA 61 (usa only)

0252/22-23 and 29 june 1947/decca sessions
southern philharmonic orchestra/fritz stiedry/
glyndebourne festival chorus/soloists
gluck orfeo ed euridice, abridged version/AK 1656-1662

0253/30 june-4 july 1947/decca sessions
jacques orchestra/reginald Jacques/
bach choir/soloists
bach mathäus-passion/AK 2001-2021
recording completed in may and september 1948;
an abridged version also issued on AK 1673-1679

0254/1-3 july 1947/decca sessions
london philharmonic orchestra/carlo zecchi/*clara haskil
*beethoven piano concerto 4/K 1944-1947
rossini la scala di seta overture/K 2123
pizzetti la pisanella suite/unpublished

0255/30-31 july 1947/decca sessions
national symphony orchestra/karl rankl/ida haendel
dvorak violin concerto/K 1744-1747

0256/31 july 1947/decca session
kingsway symphony orchestra/camarata
one fine day; softly awakes my heart/K 1771

0257/27-28 august 1947/columbia sessions
philharmonia orchestra/malcolm sargent/soloists
haydn now heaven in fullest glory from
the seasons/DX 1407
elgar the sun goeth down from the kingdom/DX 1445
dvorak where art thou from the spectre's bride/DX 1471
arias by haydn and dyson/unpublished

0258/1 and 13 september 1947/hmv sessions
philharmonia orchestra/lawrance collingwood/soloists
arias by leoncavallo, puccini and giordano/
B 9705, C 3720 and C 3995

0259/2-3 september 1947/decca sessions
national symphony orchestra/royalton kisch/
*moura lympany
*liszt piano concerto 1/AK 1834-1836
haydn symphony 92/AK 2201-2203

0260/5 september 1947/decca session
**london symphony orchestra/anatole fistoulari/
eileen joyce**
mendelssohn piano concerto 1/K 1687-1688

0261/8-9 september 1947/decca sessions
new symphony orchestra/eric coates
london suite & london again suite/AK 2072-2074

0262/15 and 23 september 1947/columbia sessions
philharmonia orchestra/alceo galliera/leon goossens
strauss oboe concerto/DX 1444-1446

0263/18-19 september 1947/decca sessions
london philharmonic orchestra/george enescu
schumann symphony 2/AK 1748-1752
mendelssohn scherzo from the octet/unpublished

0264/23-24 september 1947/columbia sessions
philharmonia orchestra/alceo galliera/*dennis brain
mussorgsky khovantschina act 5 prelude/DX 1507
franck les eolides/unpublished
*strauss horn concerto 2/unpublished

0265/29 september 1947/decca session
**national symphony orchestra/clemens krauss/
paul schoeffler**
mozart figaro arias from le nozze di figaro/M 613

0266/29 september-6 october 1947/decca sessions
**orchestre des concerts du conservatoire de paris/
charles munch/*ernest ansermet**
mendelssohn symphony 5/K 1715-1718
prokofiev symphony 1/K 1756-1757
debussy Iberia from images; berceuse heroique/
K 1763-1765
*ravel la valse/AK 1867-1868
beethoven symphony 8/K 1933-1935

0267/7-9 october 1947/decca sessions
london symphony orchestra/clemens krauss
brahms academic festival overture/K 1726
brahms haydn variations/K 2107-2108

0268/8 october 1947/decca session
**london symphony orchestra/royalton kisch/
moura lympany**
schumann piano concerto/K 1884-1887

0269/13 october 1947/decca session
**orchestra des concerts du conservatoire de paris/
enrique jorda**
liszt les preludes/AK 1733-1734

0270/14 october 1947/decca sessions
london symphony orchestra/josef krips/*hilde gueden
mozart symphony 39/K 1829-1831
*mozart arias from don giovanni & figaro/K 1861
*puccini arias from boheme & gianni schicchi/M 614

0271/14-17 october 1947/decca sessions
london philharmonic orchestra/ernest ansermet/
***london philharmonic choir**
*stravinsky symphony of psalms/AK 1753-1755
mussorgsky pictures at an exhibition/EDA 90 (usa only)

0272/17 october 1947/decca session
national symphony orchestra/josef krips
johann strauss an der schönen blauen donau/K 1725

0273/21 october 1947/hmv sessions
halle orchestra/john barbirolli
elgar enigma variations/C 3693-3695

0274/28 october 1947/decca session
london symphony orchestra/royalton kisch/
*moura lympany
*mendelssohn rondo brillant/K 1806
sinigaglia le baruffe chiozzotte overture/K 1807

0275/29 october 1947/decca session
national symphony orchestra/royalton kisch
mozart symphony 32/K 2200

0276/4-5 november 1947/decca sessions
eiar symphony orchestra turin/alberto erede/
*mario rossi
beethoven leonore 3 overture/K 1849-1850
*mendelssohn symphony 4; vivaldi andante from
l'olimpiade/AK 1974-1977
*weber preciosa overture/K 2184
ravel valses nobles et sentimentales/AK 2207-2208
vivaldi concerto RV 269/LK 3004 (unpublished 78rpm)

0277/7 november 1947/decca session
london symphony orchestra/gaston poulet/
christian ferras
elizalde violin concerto/K 1777-1779

0278/2 december 1947/decca session
kingsway symphony orchestra/camerata
musetta's waltz song; they call me mimi/K 1816

0279/16 december 1947/decca session
london philharmonic orchestra/eduard van beinum
arnold beckus the dandipratt overture/K 1848

0280/18-20 december 1947/decca sessions
london philharmonic orchestra/clemens krauss/
*london philharmonic choir/*kathleen ferrier
*brahms alto rhapsody/K 1847-1848
strauss tod und verklärung/AK 1892-1894

0281/22 december 1947/columbia session
philharmonia orchestra/george weldon/
harry mortimer
clarke trumpet voluntary/unpublished

0282/22-23 december 1947/decca sessions
london philharmonic orchestra/basil cameron
sibelius symphony 2/AK 2127-2131

0283/31 december 1947-3 january 1948/decca sessions
london philharmonic orchestra/hans knappertsbusch
wagner rienzi overture; lohengrin act 3 prelude/K 1820-1821
wagner meistersinger suite/AK 2209-2210
wagner tannhäuser overture & venusberg/AK 2211-2213

0284/20-25 february 1948/decca sessions
london philharmonic orchestra/erich kleiber
beethoven symphony 6/K 1824-1828
josef strauss sphärenklänge waltz/K 1924
johann strauss zigeunerbaron overture/K 1954
dvorak carnival overture/K 1989
beethoven recording completed in may 1948

0285/20-25 march 1948/decca sessions
london philharmonic orchestra/wilhelm furtwängler
brahms symphony 2/K 1875-1879

0286/31 march 1948/decca session
london philharmonic orchestra/carl schuricht
schumann manfred overture; weber abu
hassan overture/LA 115 (usa only)

0287/5-8 april 1948/decca sessions
london symphony orchestra/josef krips
schubert rosamunde overture/K 2071
schubert symphony 6/AK 2119-2122

0288/7-10 april 1948/decca sessions
new symphony orchestra/Josef krips/*anton dermota
johann strauss kaiserwalzer/K 1874
johann strauss accelerationen waltz/K 1936
johann strauss rosen aus dem süden.K 1986
*mozart dies bildnis from die zauberflöte; dalla sua pace from don giovanni/K 2125
johann strauss perpetuum mobile; annenpolka/M 621

0289/9 april 1948/decca session
london philharmonic orchestra/sergiu celibidache
mozart symphony 25/AK 2197-2199
recording completed in december 1948

0290/16 april 1948/columbia session
philharmonia orchestra/walter susskind/hans hotter
bach cantata 82/unpublished

0291/23 april 1948/decca session
mantovani and his concert orchestra
concerto in jazz/K 1881

0292/29 april 1948/decca sessions
kingsway symphony orchestra/victor olof
godard berceuse de jocejyn; lalo naila intermezzo
and pas de deux/M 667
brahms hungarian dance 5; mozart turkish march/M 668
khachaturian sabre dance; rubinstein toreador
et andalouse/F 8922
wagner wedding march from lohengrin; mendelssohn
wedding march from sommernachtstraum/unpublished

0293/12 may 1948/decca sessions
london symphony orchestra/malcolm sargent/
royal choral society/soloists
handel hallelujah chorus from messiah; plague chorus
from israel in egypt/K 2132
handel he spake the word from israel in egypt/K 2133
handel he gave them hailstones & he sent a thick darkness
from israel in egypt/K 2134
handel arias/K 2135, K 2137 and K 2138
handel zadok the priest/K 2136

0294/24-31 may 1948/columbia sessions
philharmonia orchestra/paul kletzki
brahms hungarian dances 5 & 6/LX 1252
wagner siegfried idyll/LX 1296-1297
sibelius valse triste/LX 1309
sibelius en saga/unpublished

0295/26-28 may 1948/columbia sessions
philharmonia orchestra/walter susskind/
elisabeth schwarzkopf
mozart exsultate jubilate/LX 1196-1197
bach cantata 51/SBT 2172 (unpublished on 78rpm)

0296/27 may 1948/hmv session
philharmonia orchestra/walter susskind/kirsten flagstad
arias & songs by gluck, purcell & grieg/DB 6913 & DA 1904

0297/4 june 1948/hmv session
philharmonia orchestra/walter susskind/
george thalben-ball
handel organ concerto op 7 no 3/C 3814-3816/C 7741-7743

0298/9 june 1948/decca session
mantovani and his concert orchestra
the dream of olwen; skyscraper fantasy/K 1911

0299/17 june 1948/decca sessions
royal opera orchestra and chorus/karl rankl
choruses from zauberflöte and rigoletto/M 624
choruses from trovatore, carmen & pagliacci/unpublished

0300/29 june 1948/decca session
new symphony orchestra/eric coates
works by coates/LA 43 (usa only)

0301/5-9 july 1948/decca sessions
london philharmonic orchestra/sergiu celibidache
tchaikovsky symphony 5/AK 2036-2041

0302/10 july 1948/decca session
london philharmonic orchestra/carl schuricht
beethoven coriolan overture/K 2079

0303/19-28 july 1948/decca sessions
new promenade orchestra/isidore godfrey/
d'oyly carte opera chorus/soloists
sullivan trial by jury/AK 2248-2251
sullivan hms pinafore/AK 2261-2268

0304/19 august and 11 september 1948/decca sessions
mantovani and his concert orchestra
swedish rhapsody; dedication/K 1962
winter melody; poem to the moon/K 1998

0305/6 october 1948/decca session
london symphony orchestra/mansel thomas
grace williams fantasy on welsh nursery tunes/
AK 1999-2000

0306/23 november 1948/decca session
mantovani and his concert orchestra
italian festival/K 2170

0307/1-2 december 1948/columbia sessions
philharmonia orchestra/malcolm sargent
elgar pomp and circumstance marches 1 & 4/DX 1561
bizet l'arlesienne suite 2/DX 1605-1606
wagner einzug der götter & walkürenritt/DX 1607

0308/15 december 1948/decca session
london philharmonic orchestra/jean martinon
chabrier suite pastorale/AK 2239-2240/AX 390-391

0309/28-29 december 1948/decca sessions
london philharmonic orchestra/sergiu celibidache
tchaikovsky nutcracker suite/AK 2148-2150
parts of the recording were remade in july 1949

0310/10-12 january 1949/decca sessions
london symphony orchestra/clemens krauss
dvorak slavonic dances op 46 nos 5 & 8/K 2233
beethoven fidelio overture/K 2241
wagner karfreitagszauber from parsifal/K 2242-2243
wagner tristan prelude & liebestod/K 2245-2246
dvorak slavonic dance op 46 no 3/K 28222 (germany)
brahms hungarian dances 1 & 3/F 9301

0311/4-5 february 1949/decca sessions
london philharmonic orchestra/eduard van beinum
elgar wand of youth suite 1/AK 2190-2192
mendelssohn hebrides overture/K 2237

0312/7 february 1949/decca session
new promenade orchestra/george scott-wood
london caprice; serenade & elegy/K 2236

0313/14-16 february 1949/columbia sessions
london symphony orchestra/malcolm sargent/
isobel baillie
handel from mighty kings from
judas maccabaeus/DX 1559
handel lusinghe piu care from alessandro/
HLM 7013 (unpublished on 78rpm)

0314/1-4 april 1949/decca sessions
london symphony orchestra/josef krips/chorus/soloists
mussorgsky death scene from boris godunov/K 2229
arias from manon & les pecheurs de perles/K 2291
arias from faust & la sonnambula/K 2328
mussorgsky song of the flea/unpublished

0315/5-6 april 1949/decca sessions
london philharmonic orchestra/josef krips
haydn symphony 104/AX 287-289

0316/5-7 and 14 april 1949/decca sessions
london symphony orchestra/josef krips/*new promenade orchestra/*hans may/hilde gueden
mozart symphony 41; figaro overture/AX 392-395
puccini arias from la boheme/X 302
*operetta arias/M 666
mozart arias from cosi fan tutte/M 38114 (switzerland)
mozart arias from figaro & don giovanni/unpublished
mozart andante from cassation K63/unpublished

0317/25 april 1949/decca sessions
london philharmonic orchestra/erich kleiber
mozart symphony 40; handel minuet from berenice/AX 448-450

0318/30 april 1949/hmv session
halle orchestra/john barbirolli
elgar serenade in e minor/B 9778-9779

0319/may 1949/decca sessions
new symphony orchestra/oscar straus
from strauss to strauss/K 2269
straus ein walzertraum overture; march from
der tapfere soldat/K 2331

0320/may 1949/decca sessions
new symphony orchestra/*queens hall light orchestra/eric coates
coates three bears fantasy/K 2280
coates three men suite; dance of the orange
blossoms from jester at the wedding/AK 2436-2437
*coates waltz from the three bears; rediffusion
march from music everywhere/F 9157

0321/1-2 may 1949/decca sessions
london philharmonic orchestra/eduard van beinum/ *alfredo campoli
*mendelssohn violin concerto/AX 290-292
brahms haydn variations/AX 299-300
beethoven leonore 1 overture/X 311

0322/13-15 may 1949/decca sessions
london philharmonic orchestra/eduard van beinum/
*anthony pini
elgar elegy for strings/K 2190
elgar cockaigne overture/AX 296-297
*elgar cello concerto/AX 46-419

0323/20-31 may 1949/decca sessions
new symphony orchestra/alberto erede/eugene conley
arias by bizet and gounod/K 2326
puccini arias from la boheme & turandot/X 402
arias by flotow and donizetti/X 433

0324/26 may-2 june 1949/decca sessions
new promenade orchestra/hans may/erna sack
la serenata; la vilanelle/K 2328
christmas fantasia/K 2382
la danza; handel largo/K 2383

0325/27 may 1949/decca session
new symphony orchestra/royalton kisch/erna sack
delibes bell song from lakme/K 2384

0326/20 june 1949/hmv sessions
philharmonia orchestra/walter susskind/moura lympany
turina rapsodia sinfonica/C 3913
franck variations symphoniques/C 7784-7785

0327/16 july 1949/decca session
new symphony orchestra/eric coates
works by coates/K 2280 and AK 2436-2437

0328/29 july 1949/decca sessions
**new promenade orchestra/isidore godfrey/
d'oyly carte opera chorus/soloists**
sullivan the pirates of penzance/AK 2315-2325
recording completed in august 1949

0329/25 august 1949/decca session
new promenade orchestra/alberto erede
respighi ancient airs and dances suite 1/unpublished

0330/29-31 august 1949/decca sessions
london philharmonic orchestra/georg solti
verdi la forza del destino overture/X 298
haydn symphony 103/AX 333-335

0331/30-31 august 1949/decca sessions
**new symphony orchestra/alberto erede/
giuseppe valdengo**
leoncavallo prologue from i pagliacci/X 303
verdi arias from rigoletto/X 304
arias by gounod and thomas/X 364

0332/12-13 september 1949/decca sessions
**london philharmonic orchestra/george szell/
clifford curzon**
beethoven piano concerto 5/K 2281-2285/AX 282-286

0333/4 october 1949/columbia sessions
**wiener philharmoniker/bruno walter/
kathleen ferrier**
mahler kindertotenlieder/LX 8939-8941

0334/6-8 october & 1-3 november 1949/decca sessions
**jacques orchestra/reginald Jacques/cantata
singers/soloists**
bach cantata 67/AX 347-348
bach cantata 11/AX 399-401
bach cantatas 140 and 147/K 2292

0335/14-15 october 1949/decca sessions
london philharmonic orchestra/ernest bloch/
london philharmonic choir/soloists
bloch sacred service/AX 377-382

0336/1 november 1949/decca session
london philharmonic orchestra/ernest bloch/
zara nelsova
bloch schelomo/LA 226 (usa only)

0337/3 november 1949/decca session
queens hall light orchestra/robert farnon
haydn wood soliloquy; kabalevsky galop from
the comedians/F 9295

0338/18-30 november 1949/columbia and
hmv sessions
philharmonia orchestra/herbert von karajan/
*boris christoff
balakirev symphony 1/LX 1323-1328/LX 8746-8751
roussel symphony 4/LX 1348-1351/LX 8763-8766
bartok music for strings percussion & celesta/
LX 1371-1374/LX 8781-8784
*verdi ella giammai m'amo from don carlo/DB 21007
*mussorgsky varlaam;s song from boris godunov/
DB 21097
*gounod vous qui faites l'endormie from faust/
unpublished

0339/6 december 1949/decca session
london philharmonic orchestra/nicolai malko/
frank phillips
prokofiev peter and the wolf/AX 356-358

0340/9 and 15 december 1949/decca sessions
london philharmonic orchestra/basil cameron
grieg peer gynt suite 1/AX 421-422
grieg peer gynt suite 2/LK 4008 (unpublished on 78rpm)

0341/29 december 1949 & 2 february 1950/hmv sessions
halle orchestra/john barbirolli
elgar cockaigne overture/DB 9633-9634
elgar dream children 1/DB 21594

0342/17-18 january 1950/decca sessions
london symphony orchestra/royalton kisch
haydn symphony 99/AX 340-342
smetana bartered bride overture/K 2332

0343/26-27 january 1950/decca sessions
new symphony orchestra/malcolm sargent/
ruggiero ricci
tchaikovsky violin concerto/AX 336-339

0344/31 january-2 february 1950/decca sessions
new symphony orchestra/don gillis
gillis symphony 7/LA 2227 (usa only)
gillis symphony 5 and a half; the alamo/
LM 4510 (unpublished on 78rpm)
gillis the man who invented music; portrait of a
frontier town/LK 4014 (unpublished on 78rpm)

91

0345/3-4 february 1950/decca sessions
london philharmonic orchestra/anthony collins
bizet carmen suite/AK 2353-2354
falla el amor brujo suite/LXT 2518 (unpublished on 78rpm)

0346/8-10 february 1950/decca sessions
new symphony orchestra/warwick braithwaite/
ellabelle davies
verdi tu che la vanita from don carlo/X 469
english songs/M 653 and M 665

0347/11-13 february 1950/decca sessions
london philharmonic orchestra/eduard van beinum
bizet l'arlesienne suite 1/AK 2385-2387
elgar wand of youth suite 2/AX 465-466

0348/21-25 february 1950/columbia sessions
philharmonia orchestra/alceo galliera
rossini la gazza ladra overture/DX 1680
rossini il barbiere di siviglia overture/DX 1690
beethoven symphony 7/DX 1697-1701/DX 8359-8363

0349/22 february 1950/columbia sessions
royal philharmonic orchestra/thomas beecham
mozart symphony 41; march K249/LX 1337-1340

0350/22-24 march 1950/columbia sessions
philharmonia orchestra/constant lambert/
***anthony bernard/*hans hotter**
*bach cantata 82/LX 1290-1292/LX 8719-8721
suppe morgen mittag und abend in wien/DX 1665
waldteufel les patineurs waltz/DX 1674
waldteufel estudianita waltz/DX 1693
suppe pique dame overture/DX 1746

0351/29-30 march 1950/columbia sessions
philharmonia orchestra/george weldon
handel largo from serse/DX 1670
walford davies solemn melody/DX 1681
handel minuet from berenice; boccherini menuetto/
SEL 5507 (unpublished on 78rpm)

0352/11 april 1950/decca session
london philharmonic orchestra/eduard van beinum
borodin polovtsian dances/AX 531-532
beethoven die weihe des hauses overture/
LW 5016 (unpublished on 78rpm)

0353/14 april 1950/decca session
london philharmonic orchestra/anthony collins
humperdinck fream pantomime from
hänsel und gretel/X 414
strauss first waltz sequence from der rosenkavalier/
LK 4017 (unpublished on 78rpm)

0354/17-22 april 1950/decca sessions
london symphony orchestra/josef krips
johann strauss wiener blut waltz/X 415
weber euryanthe overture/X 462
brahms symphony 4/AX 482-486
johann strauss wein weib und gesang; tritsch-tratsch
polka; johann strauss father piefke und pufke/
LM 4530 (unpublished on 78rpm)
schubert symphony 8/LX 3012 (unpublished on 78rpm)

0355/18 and 24 april 1950/columbia sessions
royal philharmonic orchestra/thomas beecham
haydn symphony 93/LX 1361-1363
mendelssohn sommernachtstraum overture/LX 1438
mozart symphony 38/LX 1517-1519
chabrier espana/LX 1592
handel-beecham faithful shepherd suite/
33CX 1105 (unpublished on 78rpm)
haydn symphony completed in june 1950 and
handel-beecham in september 1950

0356/1-5 may 1950/decca sessions
london philharmonic orchestra/eduard van beinum
mozart symphony 35/AX 467-468
handel water music suite/AX 495-496
mozart cosi fan tutte overture/unpublished

0357/31 may-1 june 1950/columbia sessions
royal philharmonic orchestra/thomas beecham
arnell punch and the child/LX 1391-1393
mendelssohn hebrides overture/CFL 1021
mendelssohn was completion of a recording started earlier in abbey road studios

0358/18-22 july 1950/decca sessions
london symphony orchestra/ernest ansermet/
*ellen ballon
rossini-respighi la boutique fantasque/
K 23123-23126 (germany)
*chopin piano concerto 2/X 53075-53078 (germany)

0359/21 july 1950/decca session
mantovani and his orchestra/soloists
selection from noel coward's "ace of clubs"/K 2370

0360/14 september 1950/columbia session
philharmonia orchestra/constant lambert
waldteufel pomona waltz/DX 1713
waldteufel sur la plage waltz/DX 1755

0361/25-26 september 1950/decca sessions
new symphony orchestra/alberto erede
donizetti don pasquale overture/K 23089
rossini italiana in algeri overture/K 23127
catalani la wally act 3 prelude; verdi nabucco
overture; puccini manon lescaut intermezzo/
LK 4038 (unpublished on 78rpm)
rossini la cenerentola overture; verdi vespri
siciliani overture/unpublished

0362/27 september 1950/columbia session
philharmonia orchestra/constant lambert
walton façade suite; chabrier-lambert
ballabile/DX 1734-1736

0363/28 september 1950/columbia sessions
royal philharmonic orchestra/thomas beecham
rossini il cambiale di matrimonio overture/LX 1458
sibelius scenes historiques/33C 1018
(unpublished on 78rpm)
sibelius recording completed later in
abbey road studios

0364/4 october 1950/hmv session
philharmonia orchestra/anatole fistoulari/mirimi del pozo
arias by bellini and donizetti/C 4237

0365/5-7 october 1950/hmv sessions
philharmonia orchestra/issay dobrowen/*boris christoff
rimsky-korsakov russian easter overture/C 7916-7917
*arias by mussorgsky & rimsky-korsakov/DB 21305

0366/6 october 1950/columbia session
philharmonia orchestra/peter gellhorn/
elisabeth schwarzkopf
bach cantata 51/LX 1334-1336

0367/11-14 october 1950/columbia sessions
philharmonia orchestra/alceo galliera/glyndebourne
festival chorus/*igor markevitch
debussy la mer/DX 1726-1728/DX 8369-8371
debussy trios nocturnes/DX 1754 and DX 1782
(sirenes not published on 78rpm)
*brahms haydn variations/unpublished

0368/17-19 october 1950/hmv sessions
halle orchestra/john barbirolli
tchaikovsky selection from swan lake/DB 9549-9550
bizet l'arlesienne suite/DB 9656-9657

0369/18-19 october 1950/columbia sessions
philharmonia orchestra/alceo galliera/
elisabeth schwarzkopf
arias from madama butterfly and la traviata/LX 1370
arias from fidelio and carmen/LX 1410
arias from la boheme and turandot/LB 110

0370/30-31 october 1950/decca sessions
london symphony orchestra/malcolm sargent/
max rostal
bartok violin concerto 2/K 23104-23108 (germany)

0371/9 november 1950/decca session
new symphony orchestra/richard blareau/
mado robin
arias by delibes, benedict, rossini & debussy/LX 3037

0372/14-15 november 1950/decca sessions
london philharmonic orchestra/georg solti
beethoven symphony 4/LXT 2564

0373/11 december 1950/decca sessions
new symphony orchestra/samuel barber/*zara nelsova
*barber cello concerto/LX 3048
barber medea ballet/LX 3049
barber symphony 2/LX 3050

0374/18 december 1950/columbia session
philharmonia orchestra/james robertson/jean watson
arias by handel and gluck/DX 1721
verdi arias from il trovatore and un ballo
in maschera/DB 2912

0375/1951/bartok records sessions
**new symphony orchestra/tibor serly/franco autori/
emmanuel vardi/jean pougnet/william primrose**
bartok miraculous mandarin/BR 301
bartok-serly mikrokosmos suite; two portraits/BR 303
bartok dance suite/BR 304
bartok two images for orchestra/BR 305
bartok violin rhapsodies 1 and 2/BR 307
bartok viola concerto/BR 309

0376/9 january-1 february 1951/columbia sessions
royal philharmonic orchestra/thomas beecham
rimsky-korsakov coq d'or suite/33CX 1087
(unpublished on 78rpm)
haydn symphony 103/33CX 1104
(unpublished on 78rpm)
schubert symphony 8/LX 8942-8944
schubert recording completed in may and july 1951

0377/16 and 27 january 1951/decca sessions
london symphony orchestra/josef krips/ilse hollweg
arias by mozart and strauss/LX 3054

0378/24-27 january 1951/hmv sessions
philharmonia orchestra/igor markevitch
verdi luisa miller overture/C 4097
tchaikovsky nutcracker suite/C 4133-4135/C 7885-7887
verdi la battaglia di legnano overture/C 4181
brahms haydn variations/C 7856-7857
tchaikovsky recording was remade later in
abbey road studios

0379/13-15 february 1951/decca sessions
london philharmonic orchestra/jean martinon
overtures by offenbach/LXT 2590
overtures by boieldieu, adam & herold/LXT 2606

0380/19 february 1951/decca session
new symphony orchestra/richard blareau/
*mado robin
*arias by mozart and verdi/LX 3037
debussy childrens corner suite/unpublished

0381/6 march 1951/hmv session
philharmonia orchestra/anatole fistoulari/
boris christoff
arias by gluck and verdi/RLS 735
(unpublished on 78rpm)

0382/9 march 1951/columbia sessions
royal philharmonic orchestra/thomas beecham
mozart symphony 31/33CX 1038
(unpublished on 78rpm)
franck le chasseur maudit/LX 8813-8814
mozart recording completed later in
abbey road studios

0383/6 and 10 april 1951/decca sessions
london philharmonic orchestra/georg solti
overtures by suppe/LXT 2589

0384/11-12 april 1951/decca sessions
new symphony orchestra/anatole fistoulari/
julius katchen
rachmaninov piano concerto 2/AX 535-539

0385/17-18 april 1951/decca sessions
new symphony orchestra/royalton kisch/
*alfredo campoli
*bruch violin concerto 1/AX 558-560
cimarosa il matrimonio segreto overture/K 23201
gluck iphigenie in aulis overture/K 23246
gluck alceste overture/K 27231
cimarosa gli orazi ed I currazi overture/LX 3063
(unpublished on 78rpm)

0386/24 april and 16 may 1951/hmv sessions
philharmonia orchestra/stanford robinson/
joan hammond
puccini in questa reggia from turandot/DA 1988
massenet dis-moi que je suis belle from thais/DA 1997
massenet il est doux from herodiade/unpublished

0387/8 may 1951/decca session
london philharmonic orchestra/jean martinon/
moura lympany
saint-saens piano concerto 2/LX 3064

0388/18 may 1951/columbia session
royal philharmonic orchestra/thomas beecham
beethoven symphony 8/33CX 1039
(unpublished on 78rpm)
recording completed later in abbey road studios

0389/20 may 1951/hmv session
philharmonia orchestra/anatole fistoulari/
margherita carosio
verdi sempre libera from la traviata/DB 21306
bellini ah quante volte from capuleti e montecchi/
DB 21336

0390/23 may and 14-16 june 1951/hmv sessions
philharmonia orchestra/leopold stokowski
rimsky-korsakov scheherazade/ALP 1339

0391/5 june 1951/hmv session
philharmonia orchestra/anatole fistoulari/
joan hammond
rossini sombre forets from william tell; massenet
pleurez mes yeux from le cid/HLM 7042
(unpublished on 78rpm)

0392/6-11 june 1951/columbia sessions
philharmonia orchestra/herbert von karajan/walter gieseking
beethoven piano concerto 4/LX 1443-1446/LX 8831-8834
grieg piano concerto/LX 1503-1506/LX 8888-8891
mozart piano concerto 23/LX 1510-1513/LX 8894-8897
franck variations symphoniques/LX 8937-8938
beethoven piano concerto 5/33CX 1010
(unpublished on 78rpm)

0393/8 june 1951/hmv session
royal opera orchestra/reginald goodall/walter midgely
arias by meyerbeer and flotow/unpublished

0394/2 july 1951/decca sessions
new symphony orchestra/enrique jorda/*clifford curzon
dvorak symphony 9/LXT 2608
*falla nights in the gardens of spain/K 28599-28601

0395/6 july 1951/columbia session
philharmonia orchestra/issay dobrowen/ludwig weber
wagner titurel der fromme held from parsifal/LX 1441
wagner gnade höchstes heil from parsifal/LX 1442
wagner gar viel und schön from tannhäuser/LWX 449
wagner mein herr und gott from lohengrin/unpublished

0396/7-10 july 1951/hmv and columbia sessions
philharmonia orchestra/issay dobrowen/*carla martinis
grieg symphonic dance 1/C 4142
tchaikovsky polonaise & waltz from evgeny onegin/C 4190
mozart le nozze di figaro overture/unpublished
*opera arias by verdi/LX 1463, LX 1536 and LX 1548

0397/5-7 september 1951/columbia sessions
philharmonia orchestra/paul kletzki
brahms hungarian dances 1, 2 & 3/LX 8926 & LX 8935
mussorgsky night on bare mountain; glinka
ruslan and lyudmila overture/LX 8951-8952
berlioz overtures/33CX 1003/XLP 30014
(unpublished on 78rpm)

0398/15-16 october 1951/decca sessions
london symphony orchestra/anatole fistoulari/
clifford curzon
grieg piano concerto/LXT 2657/LXT 5165

0399/29-30 october 1951/decca sessions
london symphony orchestra/malcolm sargent/
clifford curzon
rawsthorne piano concerto 2/LX 3066

0400/5-8 november 1951/hmv sessions
london symphony orchestra/malcolm sargent/
gioconda de vito
mendelssohn violin concerto/BLP 1008
(unpublished on 78rpm)

0401/6-9 november 1951/columbia sessions
philharmonia orchestra/george weldon
mascagni cavalleria rusticana intermezzo; tchaikovsky
sleeping beauty waltz/DX 1807
humperdinck hänsel und gretel dream
pantomime/DX 1811
berlioz marche hongroise; mendelssohn war march
of the priests/DX 1818
offenbach orfee aux enfers overture/DX 1823

0402/20-26 november 1951/decca sessions
london philharmonic orchestra/georg solti
haydn symphony 102/LXT 2984

0403/21-22 november 1951/decca sessions
london symphony orchestra/josef krips/zara nelsova
dvorak cello concerto/LXT 2727

0404/28 november 1951/columbia session
philharmonia orchestra/walter susskind
mozart le nozze di figaro overture/DX 8405
mendelssohn hebrides overture/unpublished

0405/28 november-4 december 1951/columbia sessions
philharmonia orchestra/herbert von karajan
strauss till eulenspiegels lustige streiche/LX 8908-8909
strauss don juan/LX 8920-8921
sibelius symphony 5/33CX 1047 (unpublished on 78rpm)
handel water music suite/unpublished

0406/5-7 december 1951/parlophone and columbia sessions
philharmonia sessions/wilhelm schüchter
rimsky-korsakov capriccio espagnol; ippolitov-ivanov caucasian sketches; tchaikovsky marche slave/PMD 1003
opera preludes by bizet, leoncavallo, mascagni and wolf-ferrari/PMD 1022
mussorgsky dance of the persian slaves from khovantschina/DX 1862
beethoven march from egmont/unpublished

0407/17-19 december 1951 & 2-4 january 1952/decca sessions
london symphony orchestra/Josef krips/
*alfredo campoli
*beethoven violin concerto/LXT 2674
mozart overtures/LXT 2684
mozart symphonies 31 and 39/LXT 2689

0408/2 january 1952/hmv session
london symphony orchestra/robert irving
grieg peer gynt suite 2/C 7902-7903

0409/8-11 january 1952/decca sessions
london philharmonic orchestra/adrian boult
vaughan williams symphony 2/LXT 2693
tchaikovsky hamlet overture/LXT 2696

0410/15-17 and 23 january 1952/hmv sessions
philharmonia orchestra/vilem tausky/joan hammond
arias by dvorak and tchaikovsky/DB 21451
verdi tu che la vanita from don carlo/DB 21510
rossini sombre forets from william tell/DB 21549
verdi willow song & ave maria from otello/DB 21558
offenbach elle a fui from les contes d'hoffmann/
HLM 7042 (unpublished on 78rpm)
verdi o patria mia from aida/unpublished

0411/18-22 january 1952/decca sessions
**london philharmonic orchestra/adrian boult/
ruggiero ricci**
beethoven violin concerto/LXT 2570

0412/21-30 january and 28 march 1952/decca sessions
**london symphony orchestra/anatole fistoulari/
alfredo campoli**
tchaikovsky swan lake (abridged)/LXT 2681-2682

0413/18-19 february 1952/hmv sessions
philharmonia orchestra/rudolf schwarz/
gioconda de vito/amadeo baldoni
brahms double concerto/BLP 1028

0414/21-22 february 1952/decca sessions
london symphony orchestra/anthony collins
sibelius symphony 1/LXT 2694/ACL 170

0415/24-29 february & 19 march 1952/decca sessions
london philharmonic orchestra/eduard van beinum
beethoven coriolan & egmont overtures/LW 5015
beethoven leonore 3 overture/LW 5016
beethoven fidelio overture/LW 5018
beethoven prometheus ballet music/LXT 2741

0416/2 april 1952/decca session
london philharmonic orchestra/adrian boult
tchaikovsky 1812 overture/LXT 2696/ACL 10

0417/18-21 april 1952/columbia sessions
philharmonia orchestra/wilhelm schüchter/leonie rysanek/
sigurd bjoerling
strauss das war sehr gut from arabella/LX 1559
wagner die frist ist um from der fliegende holländer/LX 1562
wagner traft ihr das schiff from der fliegende holländer/LX 1573
wagner wie aus der ferne from der fliegende holländer/
33C 1035 (unpblished on 78rpm)

0418/26 april-8 may 1952/columbia sessions
philharmonia orchestra/herbert von karajan
handel water music suite/LX 8945-8946
beethoven symphony 7/33CX 1035 (unpublished on 78rpm)
brahms symphony 1/33CX 1053 (unpublished on 78rpm)
stravinsky jeu de cartes/XLP 60003 (unpublished on 78rpm)
tchaikovsky symphony 5/unpublished
mozart divertimento 15/unpublished
recordings of handel, stravinsky and brahms works
completed in july 1952

0420/27-29 may 1952/decca sessions
new symphony orchestra/anthony collins/
moura lympany
rachmaninov piano concerto 3/LXT 2701

0421/4-7 june 1952/hmv sessions
philharmonia orchestra/wilhelm schüchter/geraint jones
handel organ concerti op 4 nos 2 & 4/DLP 1037
handel organ concerti op 7 nos 2 & 4/DLP 1052

0422/7 june 1952/hmv session
philharmonia orchestra/walter susskind/leon goossens
vaughan williams oboe concerto/SH 243
(unpublished on 78rpm)
bach oboe concerto BWV1055/unpublished
vaughan williams recording was completed in september 1952

0423/9-25 june 1952/hmv sessions
philharmonia orchestra/wilhelm furtwängler/
royal opera chorus/soloists
wagner starke scheite from götterdämmerung/ALP 1016
wagner tristan und isolde/ALP 1030-1035/HQM 1001-1005
mahler lieder eines fahrenden gesellen/ALP 1270

0424/1-5 july 1952/columbia sessions
philharmonia orchestra/john pritchard/
elisabeth schwarkopf
mozart arias from don giovanni & le nozze di figaro/
33CX 1069
mozart ach ich fühl's from zauberflöte/unpublished

0425/7-10 july 1952/columbia sessions
philharmonia orchestra/paul kletzki
berlioz le carnaval romain overture/LX 1574
schubert selection from rosamunde/33CX 1157
tchaikovsky serenade for strings/33CX 1164
bizet l'arlesienne suite 1/unpublished

0426/14-16 july 1952/decca sessions
london symphony orchestra/robert irving
massenet ballet music from le cid; meyerbeer les patineurs/LXT 2746/ACL 62

0427/29-31 july 1952/columbia sessions
philharmonia orchestra/herbert von karajan
sibelius finlandia/LX 1593
tchaikovsky nutcracker suite/33CX 1033
these recordings were completed in december 1952

0428/3-5 september 1952/hmv sessions
philharmonia orchestra/rafael kubelik/*solomon
mozart die zauberflöte overture/ALP 1109
*brahms piano concerto 1/ALP 1172
mendelssohn die schöne melusine overture/unpublished

0429/9-10 and 15-16 september and 3 october 1952/
columbia sessions
philharmonia orchestra/john pritchard/elisabeth schwarzkopf/*hampstead & royal opera choruses
mozart arias from idomeneo & le nozze di figaro/33CX 1069
*stille nacht heilige nacht; the first nowell/LB 131
*o come all ye faithful/9029 595517 (unpublished on 78rpm)
mozart exsultate jubilate; mi tradi from
don giovanni/unpublished

0430/7-8 october 1952/decca sessions
london philharmonic orchestra/adrian boult/ kathleen ferrier
sacred arias by bach and handel/LXT 2757

0431/31 october-1 november 1952/decca sessions
london philharmonic orchestra/anatole fistoulari/ moura lympany
khachaturian piano concerto/LXT 2762/ACL 42

0432/3-7 november 1952/hmv sessions
philharmonia orchestra/andre cluytens/*solomon
*beethoven piano concerto 2/BLP 1024
*beethoven piano concerto 4/BLP 1036
chabrier espana/9029 588669 (unpublished on 78rpm)

0433/11-12 november 1952/decca sessions
london philharmonic orchestra/georg solti
kodaly dances of galanta; bartok dance suite/LXT 2771

0434/14-15 november 1952/decca sessions
london symphony orchestra/georg solti
mendelssohn symphony 3/LXT 2762/ACL 149

0435/18-19 november & 31 december 1952-1 january
1953/parlophone sessions
philharmonia orchestra/wilhelm schüchter
dohnanyi ruralia hungarica suite; kodaly
hary janos suite/PMC 1017
turina danzas fantasticas; granados danzas
espanolas 2, 5 and 6/PMD 1018

0436/19 november-1 december 1952/columbia sessions
philharmonia orchestra/herbert von karajan
beethoven symphony 3/33CX 1046
tchaikovsky swan lake & sleeping bauty suites/33CX 1065
mozart symphony 35/unpublished
bartok concerto for orchestra/unpublished

0437/26-27 november 1952/decca sessions
london symphony orchestra/josef krips
schumann symphony 4/LXT 2887
mozart le nozze di figaro overture/unpublished

0438/3 december 1952/hmv session
**philharmonia orchestra/anatole fistoulari/
kirsten flagstad**
handel I know that my redeemer liveth from
messiah/SBT 1018 (unpublished on 78rpm)
gluck divinites du styx from alceste/unpublished

0439/4-6 december 1952/columbia sessions
philharmonia orchestra/issay dobrowen
rimsky-korsakov tsar sultan & coq d'or suites/33SX 1010
saint-saens bacchanale from samson et dalila/DX 1898

0440/12-13 december 1952/decca sessions
**london philharmonic orchestra/adrian boult/
margaret ritchie**
vaughan williams symphony 3/LXT 2787/ACL 311

0441/15-16 december 1952/hmv sessions
philharmonia orchestra/anatole fistoulari
grieg holberg suite; wolf-ferrari gioielli della
madonna intermezzo/unpublished

0442/5-7 january 1953/decca sessions
london symphony orchestra/malcolm sargent
elgar enigma variations; purcell suite from the
dramatic music/LXT 2786/ACL 55
*cd reissue of this lp on the retrospective label incorrectly
describes orchestra as london philharmonic*

0443/19-24 january 1953/columbia sessions
philharmonia orchestra/alceo galliera
overtures by rossini & verdi/33SX 1006 & 33SX 1009
tchaikovsky capriccio italien/33SX 1013/MFP 2087

0444/28-31 january & 6 february 1953/hmv sessions
philharmonia orchestra/nicolai malko
herold zampa overture/C 4227
beethoven coriolan overture/C 4232
tchaikovsky symphony 4/CLP 1045
beethoven leonore 3 & prometheus overtures/DLP 1061
tchaikovsky 1812 overture/DLP 1069/MFP 2034
borodin polovtsian dances and march/DLP 1092

0445/6-9 february 1953/columbia sessions
**philharmonia orchestra/fritz rieger/
witold malcuzynski**
brahms piano concerto 1/33CX 1048

0446/23-25 february 1953/decca sessions
london symphony orchestra/anthony collins
delius brigg fair; on hearing the first cuckoo in spring; song of summer; walk to the paradise garden/LXT 2788

0447/25-27 february and 2-6 march 1953/hmv sessions
philharmonia orchestra/rudolf schwarz/gioconda de vito
brahms violin concerto/ALP 1104/MFP 2003

0448/26-27 february 1953/decca sessions
london symphony orchestra/robert irving
lambert horoscope suite/LXT 2791

0449/2 march and 27 april 1953/decca sessions
london symphony orchestra/malcolm sargent
elgar pomp and circumstance marches 1 & 4; imperial march; walton orb and sceptre; bax coronation march/LXT 2793/ACL 137

0450/3-5 march 1953/decca sessions
london philharmonic orchestra/eduard van beinum/
alfredo campoli/*jan damen
lalo symphonie espagnole/LXT 2801/ACL 124
*sibelius violin concerto/LXT 2813

0451/10 and 27 march 1953/decca sessions
london symphony orchestra/robert irving
walton façade suite/LXT 2791

0452/12-17 march 1953/decca sessions
london symphony orchestra/josef krips
mozart symphony 40; haydn symphony 92/LXT 2819

0453/13-25 march and 1 april 1953/hmv sessions
philharmonia orchestra/walter susskind/
joan hammond
operatic arias by beethoven, mozart, bruch,
weber, massenet, korngold, cilea, boito,
saint-saens, berlioz and verdi/ALP 1076 & BLP 1073

0454/16 march 1953/hmv session
glyndebourne festival orchestra/vittorio gui
mozart symphony 39/ALP 1155

0455/18-21 march 1953/columbia sessions
philharmonia orchestra/william walton
walton orb and sceptre march; crown imperial march;
portsmouth point overture; sheep may safely graze
from the wise virgins/33C 1016

0456/23-25 march 1953/decca sessions
ndr-sinfonie-orchester hamburg/hans schmidt-isserstedt
tchaikovsky symphony 5/LXT 2758/ACL 3
dvorak symphony 7/LXT 2807
brahms selection from the hungarian dances; dvorak
selection from the slavonic dances/LXT 2814/ACL 23

0457/26-27 march 1953/decca sessions
london symphony orchestra/josef krips/wilhelm kempff
schumann piano concerto/LXT 2806

0458/30 march 1953/hmv session
philharmonia orchestra/anatole fistoulari
grieg holberg suite and herzenswunden from
elegiac melodies/ALP 1570
recordings completed in july and december 1953

0459/1-9 april 1953/hmv sessions
philharmonia orchestra/adrian boult/*wilhelm furtwängler/yehudi menuhin
mendelssohn violin concerto in d minor/ALP 1085
*beethoven violin concero/ALP 1100
*beethoven violin romances 1 & 2/ALP 1135/HLM 7015
vivaldi violin concerto op 6 no 8/LHMV 16 (usa only)
bach violin concerto BWV1041/unpublished

0460/10-15 april 1953/columbia sessions
philharmonia orchestra/alceo galliera/*nicolai gedda
*operatic arias by massenet, bizet, gounod, donizetti, flotow, cilea, auber, tchaikovsky, ponchielli and verdi/33CX 1130
liszt les preludes/33SX 1013/MFP 2087
rossini-respighi la boutique fantasque/33S 1009

0461/16-21 april 1953/columbia sessions
philharmonia orchestra/otto ackermann/ bbc chorus/soloists
lehar die lustige witwe/33CX 1051-1052/SXDW 3045
lehar das land des lächelns/33CX 1114-1115/SXDW 3044
arias by lortzing/C 70407 (germany)

0462/27 april and 4 & 12 may 1953/decca sessions
jennifer vyvyan/ernest lush (piano)
recital of english song/LXT 2797

0463/4-5 may 1953/hmv sessions
philharmonia orchestra/robert irving
tchaikovsky selection from swan lake/CLP 1018

0464/11-12 may 1953/decca sessions
london symphony orchestra/anthony collins
sibelius symphony 2/LXT 2815/ACL 34

0465/15 and 21-22 may 1953/hmv sessions
philharmonia orchestra/guido cantelli
brahms symphony 1/ALP 1152/ENC 116/XLP 30023
schumann symphony 4/BLP 1044/ENC 122/XLP 30030

0466/11-12 june 1953/hmv sessions
philharmonia orchestra/robert irving
arnold homage to the queen/CLP 1011
arnold eight english dances/CLP 1172

0467/15-24 june 1953/columbia sessions
philharmonia orchestra/paul kletzki
wagner tristan prelude and liebestod; tannhäuser overture and venusberg/33CX 1129
ravel bolero; smetana bartered bride overture/33CX 1164
barber adagio for strings/LX 1595

0468/19-20 june 1953/columbia sessions
philharmonia orchestra/herbert von karajan
tchaikovsky symphony 5/33CX 1133
beethoven egmont overture/33CX 1136
beethoven coriolan overture/33CX 1227

0469/27 june-16 july 1953/columbia sessions
philharmonia orchestra/herbert von karajan/loughton and bancroft's choirs/soloists
humperdinck hänsel & gretel/33CX 1096-1097/EX 769 2931

0470/30 june 1953/columbia sessions
philharmonia orchestra/george weldon
elgar enigma variations/33SX 1024/MFP 2093

0471/2-3 july 1953/hmv sessions
london symphony orchestra/gaston poulet/ yehudi menuhin
saint-saens violin concerto 3/ALP 1241/EX 29 08643

0472/4-22 july 1953/columbia sessions
philharmonia orchestra/herbert von karajan
bartok concerto for orchestra/33CX 1054
debussy la mer; ravel rapsodie espagnole/33CX 1099
beethoven symphony 6/33CX 1124
sibelius symphony 4; tapiola.33CX 1125
beethoven leonore 3 overture/33CX 1136
tchaikovsky symphony 4/33CX 1139
chabrier espana; waldteufel les patineurs/33CX 1235
strauss tod und verklärung/RLS 7715
sousa stars and stripes; el capitan/unpublished

0473/21-23 july 1953/decca sessions
new symphony orchestra/anatole fistoulari
johann strauss-dorati graduation ball/LXT 2848
minkus pas de deux from don quichotte/LW 5084

0474/17-19 august 1953/columba sessions
philharmonia orchestra/paul kletzki/andre gertler
berg violin concerto/33C 1030

0475/24-28 august 1953/columbia sessions
philharmonia orchestra/herbert von karajan/
*walter gieseking
*mozart piano concerto 24/33CX 1526
*schumann piano concerto/33C 1033
beethoven symphony 5/unpublished
mozart symphony 41/unpublished (incomplete)

0476/september 1953/bartok records sessions
new symphony orchestra/walter susskind/
chorus/soloists
bartok the wooden prince/BR 308
bartok bluebeard's castle/BR 310-311
bartok cantata profana/BR 312

0477/2 september 1953/columbia session
london mozart playes/harry blech/irmgard seefried
mozart concert arias K582 & K583/LX 1596
mozart ruhe sanft from zaide/EX 29 05983

0478/7-8 september 1953/hmv sessions
philharmonia orchestra/otto ackermann/solomon
mozart piano concerto 15/ALP 1194/RLS 726

0479/14-15 september 1953/hmv & columbia sessions
**philharmonia orchestra/anthony bernard/
yehudi menuhin/gioconda de vito**
bach double violin concerto BWV1043/BLP 1046
philharmonia orchestra/george weldon
holst saint paul suite/33S 1100

0480/1-6 october 1953/columbia sessions
**philharmonia orchestra/alceo galliera/elisabeth
schwarzkopf/rolando panerai**
baritone arias by verdi, leoncavallo, giordano
and rossini/33C 1052
verdi madamigella valery? from traviata/EX 29 10753
verdi ave maria from otello/unpublished

0481/2-8 october 1953/columbia sessions
**philharmonia orchestra/alceo galliera/mattiwilda
dobbs/rolando panerai**
operatic arias by verdi, bellini, rimsky-korsakov,
delibes and massenet/33CX 1305
dvorak symphony 9/33SX 1025

0482/9 october 1953/columbia session
philharmonia orchestra/george weldon
elgar cockaigne overture; pomp and circumstance
marches 1 and 4/33SX 1024
recordings completed in november 1953

0483/12-14 and 19-22 october 1953/decca sessions
london symphony orchestra/josef krips/clifford curzon
mozart piano concerti 23 and 24/LXT 2867

0484/19 october 1953/decca session
london symphony orchestra/anatole fistoulari/raffaele arie
arias and songs by rimsky-korakov, kenemann and traditional/LW 5104

0485/20-21 october 1953/decca sessions
london symphony orchestra/anthony collins
delius paris; in a summer garden; summer night on the river/LXT 2899/ACL 245

0486/27-28 october 1953/decca sessions
london symphony orchestra/josef krips
mendelssohn symphony 4/LXT 2887/ACL 90

0487/10 november 1953/decca sessions
london symphony orchestra/anatole fistoulari/ alfredo campoli
saint-saens introduction & rondo capriccioso; havanaise/LW 5085/ACL 64

0488/11 november 1953/decca session
new symphony orchestra/anatole fistoulari
weber-berlioz aufforderung zum tanz/LW 5084

0489/12-16 & 21-23 november 1953/columbia sessions
philharmonia orchestra/herbert von karajan/
*dennis brain
beethoven symphony 1/33CX 1136
*mozart horn concerti 1-4/33CX 1140/ASD 1140
beethoven symphony 4/33CX 1278
beethoven symphony 2/unpublished

0490/24 november 1953/decca sessions
london philharmonic orchestra/adrian boult/
zara nelsova
lalo cello concerto/LXT 2906/ACL 244

0491/1-11 december 1953/decca sessions
london philharmonic orchestra/adrian boult/
*zara nelsova
*saint-saens cello concerto 1/LXT 2906/ACL 244
vaughan williams symphony 4/LXT 2909/ACL 315
vaughan williams symphony 5/LXT 2910/ACL 311
vaughan williams symphony 6/LXT 2911/ACL 289
vaughan williams symphony 7/LXT 2912/ACL 291

0492/28 december 1953-1 january 1954/decca sessions
london philharmonic orchestra/adrian boult/
london philharmonic choir/soloists
vaughan williams symphony 1/LXT 2907-2908/ACL 247-248
vaughan williams the wasps suite/LW 5277/ACL 248

0493/4-13 january 1954/decca sessions
london philharmonic orchestra/adrian boult/
london philharmonic choir/soloists
handel messiah/LXT 2721-2724/ACL 118-120
vaughan williams job/LXT 2937/ACL 313

0494/7 january 1954/hmv session
philharmonia orchestra/john pritchard/yehudi menuhin
mozart violin concerto 5/ALP 1281

0495/15-16 january 1954/decca sessions
new symphony orchestra/eugene goossens/peter pears
britten les illuminations/LXT 2941
recording completed in march 1954

0496/26-28 january 1954/columba sessions
philharmonia orchestra/arthur bliss
bliss suite from miracle in the gorbals; music for strings/
33CX 1205/HQM 1009

0497/29 january-5 february & 12-17 february 1954/
columbia sessions
philharmonia orchestra/paul kletzki/johanna martzy
brahms violin concerto/33CX 1165
philharmonia orchestra/paul kletzki/*bbc chorus/*soloists
borodin symphony 2/33CX 1167
*mendelssohn sommernachtstraum incidental music/
33CX 1174/XLP 30035
tchaikovsky manfred symphony/33CX 1189/XLP 30015

0498/8-10 february 1954/decca sessions
**london philharmonic orchestra/jean martinon/
kathleen long**
faure ballade; francaix piano concertino/LXT 2963/ACL 257
london philharmonic orchestra/jean martinon/peter katin
liszt totentanz; mendelssohn capriccio brilliant;
rondo brilliant/LXT 2932/ACL 156

0499/18-19 february 1954/decca sessions
**london philharmonic orchestra/adrian boult/
*friedrich gulda**
*chopin piano concerto 1/LXT 2925/ACL 94
elgar chanson de matin; chanson de nuit/X 574

0500/22-25 february 1954/decca sessions
london symphony orchestra/anthony collins
elgar falstaff/LXT 2940/ACL 316
sibelius symphony 7/LXT 2960/ACL 181
sibelius symphony 4/LXT 2962/ACL 184

0501/5 march 1954/hmv session
philharmonia orchestra/wilhelm schüchter/
dietrich fischer-dieskau
wagner tannhäuser: als du in kühnem sange; blick ich umher; o du mein holder abendstern/7ER 5033

0502/15 march 1954/decca session
new symphony orchestra/eugene goossens
bridge sally in our alley; cherry ripe/45-71071

0503/17 march 1954/columbia session
philharmonia orchestra/paul kletzki
mendelssohn ruy blas overture; heimkehr aus der fremde overture/SEL 1525
mendellsohn hebrides overture/unpublished

0504/22-23 march & 1 april 1954/columbia sessions
philharmonia orchestra/rudolf schwarz/
denis matthews
mozart piano concerti 12 and 14/33SX 1031
mozart piano concerto 27/33S 1032
mozart piano concerto 23/33S 1039

0505/21-22 april 1954/decca sessions
london symphony orchestra/georg solti
mozart symphonies 25 and 38/LXT 2946

0506/23 april-3 may 1954/decca sessions
london philharmonic orchestra/georg solti/*london philharmonic choir/*william mcalpine
kodaly peacock variations; *psalmus hungaricus/LXT 2878
haydn symphony 100/LXT 2984

0507/27-29 april 1954/hmv sessions
philharmonia orchestra/robert irving
delibes selection from sylvia/CLP 1058

0508/5-6 may 1954/decca sessions
london symphony orchestra/anthony collins
sibelius symphony 3/LXT 2960/ACL 181
sibelius pohjola's daughter/LXT 2962/ACL 184

0509/10-12 may 1954/decca sessions
london philharmonic orchestra/adrian boult/ julius katchen
rachmaninov paganini rhapsody; dohnanyi nursery variations/LXT 2862/LXT 5374/ACL 65

0510/11 may 1954/columbia session
philharmonia orchestra/arthur bliss
bliss welcome to the queen/DX 1912

0511/17-21 may 1954/decca sessions
london symphony orchestra/malcolm sargent/
bbc chorus
holst the planets/LXT 2871/ACL 26

0512/18-31 may 1954/columbia sessions
philharmonia orchestra/otto ackermann/
chorus/soloists
johann strauss wiener blut/33CX 1186-1187/SXDW 3042
johann strauss eine nacht in venedig/
33CX 1224-1225/SXDW 3043
johann strauss der zigeunerbaron/
33CX 1329-1330/SXDW 3046
recordings of nacht in venedig and zigeunerbaron
completed in september 1954

0513/1-3 june 1954/decca sessions
london philharmonic orchestra/adrian boult/
mischa elman
tchaikovsky violin concerto/LXT 2970/ACL 26

0514/1-9 june 1954/hmv sessions
philharmonia orchestra/guido cantelli
falla el sombrero de 3 picos suite; dukas l'apprenti
sorcier; debussy prelude a l'après-midi/ALP 1207
debussy le martyre de saint sebastien/ALP 1228

0515/2-4 june 1954/decca sessions
london symphony orchestra/anatole fistoulari/
wilhelm kempff
liszt piano concerti 1 and 2/LXT 5025/ACL 58

0516/9-15 june 1954/columbia sessions
philharmonia orchestra/wolfgang sawallisch/
*johanna martzy
dvorak symphony 8; scherzo capriccioso/33SX 1034
*mozart violin concerto 3; mendelssohn
violin concerto/SBT 1483

0517/10 june 1954/columbia session
philharmonia orchestra/arthur bliss/
bbc chorus/soloists
bliss song of welcome/370 5642/228 9452

0518/14 june 1954/hmv session
london symphony orchestra/john barbirolli/philip catelinet
vaughan williams tuba concerto/BLP 1078/HQM 1016

0517/22-23 june 1954/decca sessions
london symphony orchestra/anatole fistoulari/
felicia blumenthal
paderewski fantaisie polonaise; tavares piano concerto/
LXT 2975

0518/30 june-7 july 1954/columbia sessions
philharmonia orchestra/herbert von karajan/*soloists
berlioz symphonie fantastique/33CX 1206
*strauss ariadne auf naxos/33CX 1292-1294/RLS 760

0519/13 july 1954/columbia session
philharmonia orchestra/herbert von karajan
mozart cosi fan tutte
commencement only of a recording subsequently
transferred to abbey road studios

0520/22-24 july 1954/columbia sessions
philharmonia orchestra/herbert von karajan
opera intermezzi/33CX 1265
bizet carmen preludes acts 2 and 3; beethoven
weihe des hauses overture/unpublished

0521/28-30 july 1954/decca sessions
**london symphony orchestra/benjamin britten/
julius katchen**
britten diversions for piano & orchestra/LXT 2981/ACL 314

0522/13-14 september 1954/hmv sessions
philharmonia orchestra/guido cantelli
debussy la mer/ALP 1228

0523/15-16 september 1954/decca sessions
**london symphony orchestra/anthony collins/
friedrich gulda**
mozart piano concerto 14; strauss burleske/LXT 5013

0524/18-24 september 1954/decca sessions
**london philharmonic orchestra/josef krips/
london philharmonic choir/soloists**
mendelssohn elijah/LXT 5000-5002/ACL 220-222

0525/24 and 29 september 1954/columbia sessions
philharmonia orchestra/alan rawsthorne
rawsthorne practical cats/33C 1044

0526/25 september 1954/columbia session
philharmonia orchestra/otto ackermann
smetana from bohemia's woods and fields from
ma vlast/33C 1042

0527/27-29 september & 6 october 1954/
columbia sessions
philharmonia orchestra/lovro von matacic/soloists
strauss scenes from arabella/33CX 1226/33CX 1897

0528/october-november 1954/decca sessions
new symphony orchestra/isidore godfrey/
d'oyly carte chorus/soloists
sullivan princess ida/LK 4092-4093

0529/4-7 october 1954/decca sessions
london symphony orchestra/anatole fistoulari/soloists
scenes from werther & damnation de faust/LXT 5034

0530/5-9 october 1954/columbia sessions
philharmonia orchestra/otto klemperer/*dennis brain
brahms haydn variations; hindemith nobilissima
visione/33CX 1241
mozart symphonies 29 & 41/33CX 1257
*hindemith horn concerto/unpublished (incomplete)
items from these sessions completed in november 1954

0531/12-13 october 1954/columbia sessions
philharmonia orchestra/lovro von matacic
bruckner symphony 4/33CX 1274-1275
recording completed in december 1954

0532/19-21 october 1954/decca sessions
london philharmonic orchestra/adrian boult
walton portsmouth point overture; siesta; scapino
overture; bach-walton wise virgins suite/LXT 5028
vaughan williams old king cole ballet/LW 5151
elgar three bavarian dances/LW 5174

0533/28 october-2 november 1954/decca sessions
london philharmonic orchestra/adrian boult/
*alfredo campoli
*elgar violin concerto/LXT 5014/ACL 312
holst the perfect fool suite; bax tintagel; butterworth
on the banks of green willow; a shropshire lad/LXT 5015
arnold eight english dances/LW 5166

0534/5-12 november 1954/columbia sessions
philharmonia orchestra/herbert von karajan/
*kurt leimer
beethoven symphony 5/33CX 1266
ballet music from the operas/33CX 1327
*leimer 2 piano concerti/WCX 1508 (germany)

0535/17 november-4 december 1954/columbia sessions
philharmonia orchestra/otto klemperer
bach 4 orchestral suites/33CX 1239-1240
beethoven leonore 1-3 & fidelio overtures/33CX 1270

0536/24 november-4 december 1954/columbia sessions
philharmonia orchestra/aram khachaturian/*david oistrakh
*khachaturian violin concerto/33CX 1303
khachaturian gayaneh suite/33C 1041
khachaturian masquerade suite; in memoriam/33C 1043

0537/1-2 december 1954/decca sessions
london philharmonic orchestra/stanford robinson/
***winifred attwell**
*grieg piano concerto/LF 1206/ACL 1026
balfour gardiner shepherd's fennel dance/unpublished

0538/6-7 december 1954/hmv sessions
philharmonia orchestra/john pritchard/*anatole
fistoulari/yehudi menuhin
*vieuxtemps violin concerto 5/ALP 1241
mozart violin concerto 4/ALP 1281

0539/11-18 december 1954/columbia sessions
philharmonia orchestra/lovro von matacic/
*michael rabin
orchestral works by balakirev/33CX 1280
*glazunov violin concerto; paganini
violin concerto 1/33CX 1281
balakirev overture on russian themes/33CX 1420

0540/20-21 december 1954/hmv sessions
philharmonia orchestra/john pritchard
haydn symphony 80; notturno in c; mozart
serenata notturna K239/CLP 1061

0541/10-11 january 1955/decca sessions
new symphony orchestra/peter maag
mozart serenade K203/LXT 5074

0542/17 january 1955/hmv sessions
bbc symphony orchestra/malcolm sargent
tchaikovsky symphony 5/ALP 1236

0543/18-21 january 1955/columbia sessions
philharmonia orchestra/paul kletzki
suppe leichte kavallerie & morgen mittag
und abend in wien overtures/SEL 1529
johann strauss sphärenklänge/SEL 1535
herold zampa & nicolai lustigen weiber
overtures/SEL 1541
suppe pique dame overture; mussorgsky dance of
the persian slaves from khovantschina/SEL 1542
suppe schöne galathea overture; glinka
kamarinskaya/SEL 1603
weinberger polka & fugue from schwanda/
unpublished

0544/25-27 january 1955/decca sessions
london symphony orchestra/anthony collins
sibelius symphony 5/LXT 5083/ACL 226
sibelius symphony 7/LXT 5084/ACL 319

0545/7-11 february 1955/hmv sessions
philharmonia orchestra/nicolai malko
prokofiev symphonies 1 & 7/CLP 1044/SXLP 30437
prokofiev love of 3 oranges suite/CLP 1060/SXLP 30437
tchaikovsky nutcracker suite/CLP 1060/ESD 7115

0546/14-15 february 1955/decca sessions
new symphony orchestra/robert irving
gluck-mottl & gretry-lambert ballet suites/LXT 5063

0547/14 and 18 february 1955/decca sessions
**london symphony orchestra/anthony collins/
ruggiero ricci**
paganini violin concerti 1 and 2/LXT 5075

0548/21-25 february 1955/decca sessions
london philharmonic orchestra/georg solti
kodaly hary janos suite; bartok music for strings,
percussion and celesta/LXT 5059
rossini barbiere & italiana overtures/LW 5207

0549/1-2 march 1955/decca sessions
**london philharmonic orchestra/ernest ansermet/
zara nelsova**
bloch schelomo; voice in the wilderness/LXT 5062

0550/15-19 march 1955/columbia sessions
philharmonia orchestra/alceo galliera
strauss tod und verklärung; tchaikovsky
romeo and Juliet/33CX 1328
respight impressioni brasliane; fontane di roma/
33CX 1339
rimsky-korsakov capriccio espagnol/33CX 1356

0551/18 march 1955/hmv session
**philharmonia orchestra/lawrance colligwood/
gwen catley/denis dowling**
verdi duets from rigoletto/unpublished

0552/22-23 march 1955/hmv sessions
**london symphony orchestra/dino fedri/
beniamino gigli**
carlini questo foulard/7ER 5515
leo ave maria; volonnino luntano luntano/HLM 7151
popular italian songs/3C053 54010

0553/22-25 march 1955/hmv sessions
philharmonia orchestra/efrem kurtz
shostakovich symphony 10/ALP 1322
shostakovich age of gold suite; barber
souvenirs ballet/BLP 1080

0554/24 march 1955/hmv sessions
philharmonia orchestra/malcolm sargent
tchaikovsky theme & variations from suite 3/ALP 1372

0555/18-20 april 1955/columbia sessions
philharmonia orchestra/william walton/soloists
walton scenes from troilus and cressida/33CX 1313
walton façade suites 1 and 2/unpublished

0556/21-25 april and 9-11 may 1955/decca sessions
london philharmonic orchestra/jean martinon/
*georg solti/*mischa elman
*beethoven violin concerto/LXT 5068
lalo namouna ballet suite/LXT 5114
weinberger polka & fugue from schwanda/CEP 532

0557/26-30 april 1955/columbia sssions
philharmonia orchestra/herbert von karajan/
chorus/soloists
johann strauss die fledermaus/33CX 1309-1310

0558/4-5 may 1955/decca sessions
new symphony orchestra/josef krips/mischa elman
mozart violin concerti 4 and 5/LXT 5078

0559/9-11 may 1955/decca sessions
london philharmonic orchestra/louis de froment/
irma kolassi
chausson poeme de l'amour et de la mer/LX 3150

0560/16 may 1955/columbia session
royal philharmonic orchestrat/thomas beecham
handel solomon
only a small section of the work was recorded:
main sessions were held in abbey road studios

0561/17-29 may 1955/columbia sessions
philharmonia orchestra/herbert von karajan
brahms haydn variations; schubert symphony 8/33CX 1349
brahms symphony 2/33CX 1355/SXLP 30513
brahms symphony 4/33CX 1362/SXLP 30505
beethoven symphony 8/33CX 1392
johann strauss pizzicato polka & künstlerleben/33CX 1393
mozart symphony 35; divertimento 15/33CX 1511
tchaikovsky symphony 6/unpublished
certain works in these sessions were completed in
july 1955

0562/2-3 june 1955/decca sessions
london symphony orchestra/anthony collins
sibelius night ride and sunrise/LXT 5083/ACL 319
sibelius pelleas and melisande suite/LXT 5084/ACL 228
sibelius karelia overture/LW 5209/ACL 319

0563/20-28 june 1955/hmv sessions
london philharmonic orchestra/adrian boult/
*yehudi menuhin
*sibelius violin concerto/ALP 1350/EX 29 08643
elgar in the south overture/ALP 1359
elgar pomp and circumstance marches 1-5/ALP 1379

0564/27-29 june 1955/decca sessions
london philharmonic orchestra/adrian boult/
*clifford curzon
*rachmaninov piano concerto 2/LXT 5178/ACL 322
prokofiev love of 3 oranges suite/LXT 5119/ACL 159
rachmaninov recording completed in december 1955

0565/4-9 july 1955/columbia sessions
philharmonia orchestra/herbert von karajan
beethoven symphony 2/33CX 1227
philharmonia promenade concert/33CX 1335
sibelius symphonies 6 & 7/33CX 1341/SXLP 30430 (no 7)
works by the strauss family/33CX 1393
reznicek donna diana overture/unpublished

0566/16-21 july 1955/columbia sessions
philharmonia orchestra/paul kletzki
sibelius symphony 1/33CX 1311
sibelius symphony 2/33CX 1332/SAX 2280
sibelius symphony 3/35315 (usa only)
sibelius en saga/unpublished

0567/25 july 1955/hmv sessions
london philharmonic orchestra/adrian boult
works by j.c.bach, stamitz, monn and haydn/HLP 18-19
recorded for the "history of music in sound"

0568/3-18 august 1955/hmv sessions
philharmonia orchestra/guido cantelli
mendelssohn symphony 4; schubert symphony 8/
ALP 1325/SH 290
mozart ein musikalischer spass/ALP 1461/XLP 30034
brahms symphony 3/BLP 1083/XLP 30030/SH 315
debussy nuages & fetes from 3 nocturnes/
BLP 1089/XLP 30042
ravel daphnis et chloe second suite/unpublished

0569/1-2 september 1955/decca sessions
london symphony orchestra/pierino gamba
5 rossini overtures/LXT 5137/ACL 198

0570/19 september 1955/columbia session
philharmonia orchestra/malcolm arnold
arnold tam o'shanter overture; english dances
3 & 5/SED 5521

0571/20 september 1955/hmv sessions
london philharmonic orchestra/adrian boult
elgar nursery suite/ALP 1359
elgar froissart overture; dream children/ALP 1379

0572/22-23 september 1955/hmv sessions
philharmonia orchestra/nicolai malko
borodin symphonies 2 and 3/CLP 1075/XLP 30010
**philharmonia orchestra/malcolm sargent/chorus/
arda mandikian**
ibert suite elisabethiane/2564 634121

0573/3-7 october 1955/columbia sessions
philharmonia orchestra/otto klemperer
beethoven symphony 3/33CX 1346
beethoven symphony 7/33CX 1379
beethoven symphony 5/33C 1051

0574/11-12 october 1955/columbia sessions
philharmonia orchestra/herbert von karajan
mussorgsky pictures at an exhibition/33CX 1421/SAX 2261
recording completed in june 1956

0575/24-25 october 1955/decca sessions
london philharmonic orchestra/jean martinon
johann strauss-desormiere le beau danube; rossini
william tell ballet music/LXT 5149/ACL 158

0576/9-11 november 1955/decca sessions
london philharmonic orchestra/arthur bliss/
alfredo campoli
bliss violin concerto; theme & cadenza/LXT 5166/ACL 317

0577/15-17 november 1955/decca sessions
london philharmonic orchestra/anatole fistoulari/
mado robin
arias by proch, dell'aqua, arditi, alyebyev & ravel/
LW 5238 and LW 5239
ravel vocalise/unpublished

0578/23-24 november 1955/decca sessions
london symphony orchestra/arthur bliss
bliss colour symphony; introduction and allegro/
LXT 5170/ACL 239

0579/25-29 november 1955/columbia sessions
philharmonia orchestra/otto ackermann/*eugene malinin
*rachmaninov piano concerto 2/33CX 1369
haydn symphony 100/unpublished
philharmonia orchestra/otto ackermann/leonid kogan/
***elizaveta gilels**
bach violin concerto BWV1042; *double violin
concerto BWV 1043/33CX 1373
tchaikovsky serenade melancholique/unpublished

0580/26 november-5 december 1955/hmv sessions
philharmonia orchestra/glauco curiel/joan hammond
operatic arias by verdi and puccini/ALP 1407 & BLP 1086

0581/14-15 december 1955/decca sessions
london philharmonic orchestra/adrian boult/
***clifford curzon**
*franck variations symphoniques/
LXT 5547/SXL 2173/JB 104
holst scherzo for an unfinished symphony/unpublished

0582/15-16 december 1955/decca sessions
london symphony orchestra/pierino gamba/
julius katchen
tchaikovsky piano concerto 1; liszt hungarian fantasia/
LXT 5164/ACL 163

0583/17-19 december 1955/columbia sessions
philharmonia orchestra/otto klemperer
brahms symphony 1/unpublished (incomplete)

0584/20-22 december 1955/columbia sessions
philharmonia orchestra/paul kletzki/johanna martzy
mendelssohn violin concerto; beethoven violin
romances 1 and 2/33CX 1497

0585/5-10 january 1956/columbia sessions
philharmonia orchestra/henry krips
waltzes by waldteufel/33SX 1048/SCX 3251/CFP 40305
overtures by suppe/33SX 1053/SCX 3256
orchestra described on these recordings as
philharmonia promenade orchestra

0586/11-16 january 1956/hmv & columbia sessions
philharmonia orchestra/lovro von matacic
glazunov raymonda ballet suite/CLP 1843
tchaikovsky hamlet; the storm/
33CX 1420/CLP 1843 (the storm)
bruckner overture in g minor; scherzo in d minor/
3548 (usa only)

0587/17-18 january 1956/decca sessions
london symphony orchestra/anthony collins
tchaikovsky francesca da rimini; capriccio italien/
LXT 5186/ACL 258

0588/24-27 january 1956/hmv sessions
london philharmonic orchestra/adrian boult
robert simpson symphony 1/BLP 1092/HQM 1010

0589/25-26 january 1956/hmv sessions
royal opera orchestra/robert irving
silver jubilee tribute to sadlers wells ballet/CLP 1070

0590/31 january-1 february 1956/decca sessions
**london philharmonic orchestra/peter maag/
jennifer vyvyan**
recital of mozart arias/LW 5247

0591/2-3 february 1956/decca sessions
london philharmonic orchestra/adrian boult
tchaikovsky symphony 3/LXT 5297
recording completed in november 1956

0592/7-15 february 1956/hmv sessions
philharmonia orchestra/eugene goossens
scriabin poeme de l'extase; reverie; albeniz
iberia suite/ALP 1470
rimsky-korsakov coq d'or suite; russian easter festival
overture; balakirev islamey/ALP 1490/ASD 262

0593/9-10 february 1956/decca sessions
london symphony orchestra/anthony collins/peter katin
mendelssohn piano concerti 1 & 2/LXT 5201/ACL 169

0594/16-18 february 1956/hmv sessions
philharmonia orchestra/nicolai malko
overtures by borodin, glinka, mendelssohn
and suppe/CLP 1110
dvorak symphony 9/CLP 1125/MFP 2004

0595/20-22 february 1956/hmv sessions
philharmonia orchestra/malcolm sargent
dvorak symphonic variations/ALP 1372/
XLP 20065/SXLP 20065

0596/21-22 february 1956/decca sessions
**london philharmonic orchestra/adrian boult/
mischa elman**
bruch violin concerto 1; wieniawski
violin concerto 2/LXT 5222

0597/24 february-1 march 1956/hmv & columbia sessions
philharmonia orchestra/nicolai malko/*david oistrakh
rimsky-korsakov snow maiden suite; ivan the terrible
overture; mendelssohn ruy blas overture/CLP 1110
*taneyev suite de concert/33CX 1390

0598/27 february-1 march 1956/hmv sessions
philharmonia orchestra/anatole fistoulari
tchaikovsky the tempest fantasy/ALP 1582/SXLP 30101
glazunov stenka razin/SXLP 30119
recordings completed in july 1956 & march 1957

0599/29 february-3 march 1956/columbia sessions
philharmonia orchestra/alceo galliera/
david oistrakh/pierre fournier
brahms double concerto/33CX 1487/SAX 2264

0600/12-14 march 1956/columbia sessions
philharmonia orchestra/george weldon
popular orchestral works/33SX 1054/MFP 2037
grainger irish tune; delibes pizzicato from sylvia/
SED 5547

0601/13 march 1956/columbia session
philharmonia orchestra/walter susskind
grieg peer gynt suites 1 & 2/33SX 1057/SXLP 30105

0602/15-16 march 1956/columbia sessions
philharmonia orchestra/malcolm sargent/
pierre fournier
schumann cello concerto; tchaikovsky rococo
variations/33CX 1407/SAX 2282

0603/24-26 march 1956/hmv sessions
royal philharmonic orchestra/robert irving
immortal pas de deux/CLP 1239/CSD 1286

0604/9-10 april 1956/decca sessions
new symphony orchestra/paul bonneau/
gerard souzay
arias from french opera/LXT 5269

0605/18-19 april and 10 may 1956/columbia sessions
philharmonia orchestra/george weldon
tchaikovsky sleeping beauty/33SX 1095-1096/
CFPD 4458
national anthem arranged by walton (2 versions)/
unpublished

0606/27-28 april & 9 may 1956/columbia sessions
philharmonia orchestra/walter susskind/elisabeth schwarzkopf/*grace hofmann
operatic arias by weber & wagner/33CX 1658/SAX 2300
weber ozean du ungeheuer from oberon; *wagner lohengrin act 2 scene 2/unpublished

0607/9-24 may 1956/columbia sessions
royal philharmonic orchestra/thomas beecham/ beecham choral society/soloists
mozart die entführung aus dem serial/
33CX 1402-1403/SAX 2427-2429

0608/28 may-5 june 1956/hmv sessions
philharmonia orchestra/guido cantelli
mozart symphony 29/ALP 1461/ENC 122/XLP 30034
beethoven symphony 7/ALP 1472/ASD 254/CFP 103
beethoven symphony 5 (movements 2-4)/ALP 1535
ravel daphnis et chloe second suite/BLP 1089

0609/4 june 1956/hmv session
royal philharmonic orchestra/charles mackerras
burkhard der schuss von der kanzel overture;
reznicek donna diana overture/7EP 7037

0610/12 june 1956/hmv session
philharmonia orchestra/rudolf kempe
mozart symphony 39/unpublished (incomplete)

0611/18-29 june 1956/columbia sessions
philharmonia orchestra/herbert von karajan/
*chorus/*soloists
tchaikovsky symphony 6/33CX 1377/SXLP 30534
*verdi falstaff/33CX 1410-1412/SAX 2254-2256

0612/2-3 july 1956/decca sessions
london philharmonic orchestra/anatole fistoulari/
ruggiero ricci
khachaturian violin concerto/LXT 5259

0613/6 and 30 july 1956/hmv sessions
glyndebourne festival orchestra/john pritchard/
*glyndebourne festival chorus/soloists
mozart idomeneo
the bulk of this recording was made at abbey road studios

0614/11-17 july 1956/columbia sessions
philharmonia orchestra/walter susskind/janos starker
milhaud cello concerto 1; prokofiev
cello concerto/33CX 1425
dvorak cello concerto; faure elegie/33CX 1477/SAX 2263
dohnanyi konzertstück/33CX 1595

0615/19-25 july 1956/columbia sessions
philharmonia orchestra/otto klemperer
mozart symphonies 25 & 40/33CX 1457/SAX 2278
mozart symphonies 38 & 39/33CX 1486
mozart symphony 36/33CX 1786/SAX 2436
beethoven weihe des hauses overture/35329 (usa)

0616/27 july 1956/hmv session
philharmonia orchestra/anatole fistoulari
grieg last spring from elegiac melodies/ALP 1570

0617/1-3 august 1956/hmv sessions
royal philharmonic orchestra/robert irving
lecocq mlle angot; glazunov birthday offering/
CLP 1140/CSD 1252

0618/3 august 1956/hmv session
**london symphony orchestra/walter susskind/
soloists**
rossini scenes from otello/7EP 7111
recorded for the series "history of music in sound"

0619/25-31 august 1956/hmv sessions
bbc symphony orchestra/malcolm sargent/
*denis matthews
sibelius symphony 1/ALP 1542/ASD 260
sibelius symphony 5; pohjolas daughter/
ALP 1732/ASD 303
holst beni mora suite/BLP 1101/BSD 754
*rubbra piano concerto/CLP 1194

0620/5-6 september 1956/decca sessions for rca
london philharmonic orchestra/anatole fistoulari
gliere red poppy suite/LM 2133/RB 16049
khachaturian 3 dances from gayaneh/unpublished

0621/7-8 september 1956/decca sessions
london philharmonic orchestra/adrian boult
vaughan williams symphony 8/LXT 5314/SXL 2207/SDD 199

0622/12-14 september 1956/hmv sessions
philharmonia orchestra/eugene goossens/
yehudi menuhin
lalo symphonie espagnole/ALP 1571/ASD 290/
SXLP 30277/CFP 40364
philharmonia orchestra/walter susskind/
yehudi menuhin
bruch violin concerto 1/ALP 1669/ASD 534

0623/27 september-10 october 1956/columbia sessions
philharmonia orchestra/carlo maria giulini
stravinsky firebird suite; ravel mother goose suite/
33CX 1518/SAX 2279/XLP 30067/SXLP 30067
tchaikovsky symphony 2; mussorgsky night on bare
mountain/33CX 1523/SAX 2416
haydn symphony 94; boccherini symphonies
in d and c minor/33CX 1539

0624/11-13 october 1956/decca sessions
**london symphony orchestra/anatole fistoulari/
mischa elman**
bruch violin concerto 1/LW 5290
mendelssohn violin concerto/unpublished

0625/15 and 19 october 1956/decca sessions
london symphony orchestra/josef krips
schumann symphony 4/LXT 5347/SXL 2223/
ADD 157/SDD 157

0626/20-26 october 1956/decca sessions
**london symphony orchestra/pierino gamba/
alfredo campoli**
sarasate zigeunerweisen; wieniawski legende/LXT 5298
paganini violin concerto 1; saint-saens
violin concerto 3/LXT 5302

0627/29 october-1 november 1956/columbia sessions
philharmonia orchestra/otto klemperer
brahms symphony 2/33CX 1517/SAX 2362
brahms symphony 1/unpublished
brahms symphony 4/unpublished

0628/2-3 november 1956/hmv sessions
philharmonia orchestra/charles mackerras
verdi overtures/DLP 1185/SXLP 30019

0629/5-6 november 1956/columbia sessions
philharmonia orchestra/alceo galliera
brahms tragic overture/33CX 1487/SAX 2264/SXLP 30185
opera intermezzi/33CX 1545
bizet carmen suite 1/33CX 1663/SAX 2303/CFP 120

0630/12-13 november 1956/decca sessions
london philharmonic orchestra/adrian boult
vaughan williams partita/LXT 5314/SXL 2207/SDD 199

0631/19-24 november 1956/columbia sessions
philharmonia orchestra/paul hindemith/*louis cahuzac
hindemith konzertmusik; symphony for
concert band/33CX 1512
hindemith nobilissima visione; *clarinet concerto/33CX 1533
philharmonia orchestra/paul hindemith/*dennis brain
hindemith sinfonia serena; *horn concerto/33CX 1676

0632/4-7 december 1956/decca sessions
london philharmonic orchestra/adrian boult/
*kirsten flagstad
*arias by bach and handel/LXT 5316
holst marching song/unpublished

0633/5-6 december 1956/decca sessions
new symphony orchestra/anthony collins
orchestral works by sullivan and grainger/LW 5297

0634/10-22 december 1956/columbia sessions
philharmonia orchestra/herbert von karajan/
*heinrich schmidt/chorus/soloists
strauss der rosenkavalier/33CX 1492-1495/SAX 2269-2272
*smetana marenka's aria from the bartered bride/
SAX 5288/SXDW 3049
*wagner scenes from meistersinger/unpublished
prokofiev peter and the wolf/unpublished

0635/27 december 1956-1 january 1957/decca sessions
london symphony orchestra/ataulfo argenta/
*alfredo campoli
*tchaikovsky violin concerto/LXT 5313/SXL 2029/SPA 183
orchestral works on a spanish theme by rimsky-korsakov,
granados, chabrier and moszowski/
LXT 5333/SXL 2020/SDD 216

0636/3-4 january 1957/decca session
london philharmonic orchestra/ataulfo argenta/
julius katchen
liszt piano concerti 1 and 2/LXT 5330/SXL 2097/SPA 318

0637/7-9 january 1957/decca sessions
london symphony orchestra/pierino gamba
orchestral pieces by verdi, mancinelli, martucci,
mascagni and ponchielli/LXT 5325
black overture to a costume comedy/LW 5325/ACL 108

0638/9 january 1957/decca sessions for rca
new symphony orchestra/raymond agoult
overtures by adam, auber, herold and suppe/
LM 2134/LSC 2134
recordings completed in february 1957

0639/10 january 1957/decca sessions for rca
london philharmonic orchestra/adrian boult/
ania dorfman
schumann piano concerto/unpublished

0640/15-16 january 1957/decca sessions
london symphony orchestra/pierino gamba/
ruggiero ricci
bruch violin concerto 1; mendelssohn violin concerto/
LXT 5334/SXL 2006/SPA 88

0641/22-29 january 1957/columbia sessions
philharmonia orchestra/alceo galliera
opera intermezzi by wolf-ferrari, zandonai,
pick-mangielli and mascagni/33CX 1545
respighi pini di roma; ravel daphnis et chloe
second suite/33CX 1663/SAX 2303/CFP 120
strauss don juan; wagner siegfried idyll/33C 1060

0642/7-14 february 1957/columbia sessions
philharmonia orchestra/alceo galliera/
chorus/soloists
rossini il barbiere di siviglia/33CX 1507-1509/
SAX 2266-2268

0643/15-22 february 1957/hmv sessions
philharmonia orchestra/constantin silvestri
tchaikovsky symphony 5/ALP 1491/ASD 261
tchaikovsky symphony 6/ALP 1495/ASD 273
tchaikovsky symphony 4/ALP 1511/ASD 253

0644/27-28 february 1957/decca sessions
london symphony orchestra/peter maag/
royal opera chorus/soloists
mendelssohn sommernachtstraum incidental music/
LXT 5344/SXL 2060/SPA 451

0645/4 and 12-13 march 1957/hmv sessions
philharmonia orchestra/efrem kurtz
shostakovich symphony 1; prokofiev symphony 1/
ALP 1554/ASD 263

0646/6-7 march 1957/decca sessions for rca
london philharmonic orchestra/anatole fistoulari
ippolitov-ivanov caucasian sketches/
LM 2133/RB 16049

0647/14 march 1957/hmv sessions
philharmonia orchestra/anatole fistoulari
grieg symphonic dance 4/ALP 1570
borodin nocturne from string quartet/
ALP 1582/SXLP 30119
tchaikovsky swan lake waltz; glazunov concert waltz 1/
7EB 6028/RES 4255/SXLP 30119

0648/19-28 march 1957/hmv sessions
royal philharmonic orchestra/thomas beecham/
*beecham choral society/*ilse hollweg
*grieg peer gynt incidental music/ALP 1538/ASD 258
beethoven symphony 2/ALP 1596/ASD 287/HQS 1154
these were the completion of recordings started
in abbey road studios

0649/26 march 1957/columbia session
philharmonia orchestra/william walton
walton façade suites 1 and 2; Johannesburg
festival overture/33C 1054/HQM 1006 (overture)

0650/26-29 march 1957/columbia sessions
philharmonia orchestra/otto klemperer
brahms symphony 1/33CX 1504/SAX 2262
brahms tragic overture/33CX 1517/SAX 2362
brahms symphony 3; academic festival overture/
33 CX 1536/SAX 2351
brahms symphony 4/33CX 1591/SAX 2350

0651/2-5 april 1957/columbia sessions
philharmonia orchestra/paul kletzki/emmy loose
mahler symphony 4/33CX 1541/SAX 2348/
XLP 30054/SXLP 30054
recording completed in june 1957

0652/24-26 april 1957/decca sessions
**london philharmonic orchestra/adrian boult/
kirsten flagstad**
recital of sacred songs/LXT 5392/SXL 2049

0653/28 april 1957/columbia session
philharmonia orchestra/herbert von karajan/peter ustinov
prokofiev peter and the wolf/33CX 1559/SAX 2375

0654/30 april 1957/decca sessions for rca
london symphony orchestra/arthur bliss
bliss film music for things to come/LM 2257/LSC 2257/
SB 2026/SDD 255

0655/2-8 may 1957/decca sessions for rca
royal opera orchestra/hugo rignold
prokofiev cinderella suites 1 and 2/
LM 2135/RB 16048/VICS 1138

0656/7-8 may 1957/decca sessions
haydn orchestra/harry newstone/jennifer vyvyan
haydn scena di berenice & arias from cecilia mass/
LW 5334/SXL 2233

0657/9 may 1957/decca session for rca
london philharmonic orchestra/adrian boult
rimsky-korsakov russian easter festival overture/
LM 2185/RB 16147/SB 2035

0658/11-14 & 27-28 may 1957/columbia sessions
philharmonia orchestra/thomas schippers
prokofiev symphony 5/33CX 1561
tchaikovsky symphony 4/33CX 1609/MFP 2073

0659/14-16 may 1957/columbia sessions
philharmonia orchestra/leopold ludwig/birgit nilsson
arias by wagner and verdi/33CX 1522

0660/20-22 may 1957/hmv sessions
royal philharmonic orchestra/robert irving
prokofiev cinderella selection from the ballet/
CLP 1144/CSD 1256

0661/23-24 may 1957/decca sessions
london symphony orchestra/josef krips
schumann symphony 1/LXT 5347/SXL 2223/
ADD 157/SDD 157

0662/3-7 and 11-13 june 1957/decca sessions for rca
london symphony orchestra/pierre monteux/
*philippe entremont
tchaikovsky sleeping beauty selection from the ballet/
LM 2177/LSC 2177/RB 16063/SB 2013/VIC 1011/VICS 1011
rimsky-korsakov scheherazade/LM 2208/LSC 2208/
RB 16077/SB 2003/VIC 1013/VICS 1013/SPA 89
*tchaikovsky piano concerto 1/VEL 3078

0668/18-19 june 1957/hmv sessions
philharmonia orchestra/robert irving
arnold 4 scottish dances; britten matinees musicales;
soirees musicales/CLP 1172

0669/24-25 june and 1 july 1957/hmv sessions
london philharmonic orchestra/constantin silvestri
dvorak symphony 8/ALP 1537/ASD 470/CFP 40075

0670/26-29 june 1957/hmv sessions
philharmonia orchestra/constantin silvestri/
*christian ferras
*tchaikovsky and mendelssohn violin concerti/
ALP 1543/ASD 278/SXLP 30112
liszt les preludes/ALP 1648/SXLP 30447

0671/2-5 july 1957/columbia sessions
philharmonia orchestra/otto ackermann/chorus/
elisabeth schwarzkopf
arias from viennese operetta/33CX 1570/SAX 2283
arias from zigeunerbaron and nacht in venedig/unpublished
philharmonia orchestra/otto ackermann/otto edelmann
wagner arias for bass-baritone/33CX 1568

0672/16-17 july 1957/capitol sessions
philharmonia orchestra/william steinberg
strauss don juan; der roenkavalier suite/P 8423

0673/25-30 july 1957/columbia sessions
philharmonia orchestra/carlo maria giulini
franck symphony/33CX 1589/XLP 30055/SXLP 30055
falla el sombrero de 3 picos suite/33CX 1694/SAX 2311/
SXLP 30140/CFP 4512

0674/12 august 1957/hmv sessions
bbc symphony orchestra/malcolm sargent/bbc chorus
holst the planets/ALP 1600/ASD 269
recording completed in september 1957

0675/2-12 september 1957/columbia sessions
philharmonia orchestra/wolfgang sawallisch/soloists
strauss capriccio/33CX 1600-1602
tchaikovsky nutcracker suite/33CX 1623/SAX 2285/
CFP 40002
recording of capriccio completed in march 1958

0676/14 september 1957/hmv sessions
**philharmonia orchestra/eugene goossens/
yehudi menuhin**
saint-saens introduction and rondo capriccioso;
havanaise/ALP 1571/ASD 290/SXLP 30277/CFP 40364

0677/16-17 september 1957/columbia sessions
**philharmonia orchestra/carlo maria giulini/
janos starker**
saint-saens cello concerto 1; schumann
cello concerto/33CX 1579

0678/4-8 october 1957/columbia sessions
philharmonia orchestra/otto klemperer
beethoven symphony 6/33CX 1532/SAX 2260
beethoven symphony 2/33CX 1615/SAX 2331

0679/14-19 october 1957/decca sessions
new symphony orchestra/isidore godfrey/
d'oyly carte chorus/soloists
sullivan the mikado/LK 4251-4252/SKL 4006-4007

0680/21-31 october 1957/columbia sessions
philharmonia orchestra/otto klemperer
beethoven symphonies 1 & 8/33CX 1554/SAX 2318
beethoven coriolan and prometheus overtures/
33CX 1615/SAX 2331
beethoven symphony 4/33CX 1702/SAX 2354
philharmonia orchestra/otto klemperer/
philharmonia chorus/soloists
beethoven symphony 9; egmont overture and
klärchen-lieder/33CX 1574-1575/
SAX 2276-2277 (symphony only)
certain recordings in these sessions were
completed in november 1957

0681/1-3 november 1957/hmv sessions
royal philharmonic orchestra/eugene goossens/
abbey simon
chopin piano concerti 1 and 2/ALP 1580

0682/26-30 november 1957/decca sessions
new symphony orchestra/isidore godfrey/
d'oyly carte chorus/soloists
sullivan the pirates of penzance/
LK 4249-4250/SKL 4038-4039

0683/27-29 november 1957/decca sessions
london symphony orchestra/anatole fistoulari/
inge borkh
operatic arias by dvorak, gluck, debussy,
verdi and mascagni/LW 5335

0684/2-3 december 1957/columbia sessions
royal philharmonic orchestra/paul kletzki
tchaikovsky francesca da rimini; 1812 overture;
marche slave/33CX 1565

0685/5-6 december 1957/decca sessions for rca
new symphony orchestra/alexander gibson
witches brew: orchestral showpieces by arnold,
mussorgsky, saint-saens, humperdinck and liszt/
LM 2225/LSC 2225/RB 16156/SB 2020

0686/9-11 december 1957/decca sessions for rca
london symphony orchestra/jean martinon
shostakovich symphony 1; age of gold **suite/**
LM 2322/LSC 2322/RB 16170/SB 2051/
VIC 1184/VICS 1184

0687/16-20 december 1957/decca sessions
friedrich gulda
beethoven piano sonatas 11 and 12/LXT 5435
beethoven piano sonatas 15 and 16/LXT 5436
beethoven piano sonatas 17 and 18/LXT 5437
beethoven piano sonatas 13 and 14/ECS 720

0688/3-8 january 1958/columbia sessions
philharmonia orchestra/henry krips/
*charles mackerras
nussio folklore d'engadine; schönherr austrian
peasant dances/33SX 1157/SCX 3269
waltzes by ziehrer, gungl, ivanovici, lanner & lehar/
33SX 1169/SCX 3279/SXLP 30027/CFP 40213
*ballet music from verdi operas/XLP 30019/SXLP 30019
orchestra described for the krips recordings as
philharmonia promenade orchestra

0689/9-18 january 1958/columbia sessions
philharmonia orchestra/herbert von karajan
orchestral works by respighi, berlioz and liszt/
33CX 1548/SXLP 30450
orchestral works by berlioz-weber, liszt, berlioz,
sibelius & tchaikovsky/33CX 1571/SAX 2202
orchestral works by offenbach, rossini & gounod/
33CX 1588/SAX 2274
bizet l'arlesienne and carmen suites/
33CX 1608/SAX 2289/EMX 2028
strauss der rosenkavalier suite; johann strauss
sphärenklänge/unpublished

0690/4-8 february 1958/hmv sessions
philharmonia orchestra/*london philharmonic orchestra/constantin silvestri
*dvorak carnival overure/ALP 1537/ASD 470/CFP 40075
hindemith mathis der maler symphony; bartok divertimento for strings/ALP 1597
liszt tasso/ALP 1648/SXLP 30447

0691/10-19 february 1958/decca sessions
london symphony orchestra/oivin fjeldstad/ *kirsten flagstad
grieg selection from peer gynt/LXT 5441/SXL 2012/JB 141
*sibelius 14 orchestral songs/LXT 5444/SXL 2030/SDD 248
london symphony orchestra/oivin fjeldstad/ ruggiero ricci
sibelius violin concerto; tchaikovsky serenade melancholique; souvenir d'un lieu cher/ SXL 2077/SDD 276

0692/17-19 february 1958/decca sessions
london philharmonic orchestra/adrian boult/ peter katin
rachmaninov piano concerto 1; tchaikovsky concert fantasy/LXT 5447/SXL 2034/SPA 169

0693/21-28 february 1958/columbia sessions
philharmonia orchestra/wolfgang sawallisch
tchaikovsky swan lake suite/33CX 1623/SAX 2285/CFP 40002
weber oberon, euryanthe & freischütz overtures/
33CX 1652/SAX 2343/XLP 30038/SXLP 30038
wagner rhine journey & funeral music from
götterdämmerung/33CX 1655
dvorak symphony 9; carnival overture/
33CX 1677/SAX 2322/CFP 104

0694/march 1958/hmv sessions
**bbc symphony orchestra/malcolm sargent/
joan hammond/shura cherkassky**
an evening at the proms/ALP 1658/ASD 536

0695/17-28 march 1958/hmv sessions
royal philharmonic orchestra/thomas beecham
rimsky-korsakov scheherazade/ALP 1564/ASD 251

0696/9-14 april 1958/hmv sessions
royal philharmonic orchestra/rafael kubelik
janacek taras bulba; martinu fresques de
piero della francesca/ALP 1675
bartok concerto for orchestra/ALP 1744/ASD 312
dvorak scherzo capriccioso/ALP 1769/ASD 347
dvorak recording was completed in abbey road studios

0697/10-14 and 25 april 1958/hmv sessions
philharmonia orchestra/efrem kurtz/*yehudi menuhin
tchaikovsly selection from the nutcracker/ALP 1609/ASD 289
*tchaikovsky selection from swan lake/
ALP 1644/ASD 271/CFP 40296
swan lake recording completed later in abbey road studios

0698/15-23 april 1958/hmv sessions
**royal philharmonic orchestra/thomas beecham/
*beecham choral society/*alexander young**
tchaikovsky symphony 4: first movement/ALP 1667
*liszt a faust symphony; orpheus//ALP 1737-1738/
ASD 317-318/SXDW 3022
strauss ein heldenleben/ALP 1847/ASD 421/SXLP 30295
handel-beecham gods go a'begging/ALP 1912/ASD 480
*remaining movements of the tchaikovsky symphony
were recorded earlier in paris salle wagram*

0699/22-24 april 1958/columbia sessions
**philharmonia orchestra/walter susskind/*warwick
braithwaite/aase nordmo-loevberg**
operatic arias by wagner and *verdi/33CX 1651/
SAX 2353 and SEL 1670/ESL 6280

0700/2 and 8 may 1958/decca sessions
london symphony orchestra/kenneth alwyn/
*band of the grenadier guards
tchaikovsky capriccio italien; marche slave;
*1812 overture/SXL 2001/ADD 112/SDD 112/SPA 108

0701/6-7 may 1958/decca sessions
london philharmonic orchestra/adrian boult/
alfredo campoli
mendelssohn violin concerto; bruch scottish fantasy/
LXT 5453/SXL 2026/ADD 110/SDD 110

0702/6-7 may 1958/decca sessions for rca
london symphony orchestra/jean martinon
borodin symphony 2; rimsky-korsakov capriccio
espagnol; march from tsar sultan/
LM 2298/LSC 2298/RB 16233/SB 2105

0703/21-23 may 1958/decca sessions
london symphony orchestra/josef krips
schubert symphony 9/LXT 5471/SXL 2045/SPA 467
weber oberon overture/unpublished

0704/29 may-4 june 1958/columbia sessions
philharmonia orchestra/carlo maria giulini/
***janos starker**
schumann-mahler symphony 3/33CX 1662
*haydn cello concerto 2; boccherini cello
concerto in b flat/33CX 1665

0705/10-25 june 1958/decca sessions for rca
london symphony orchestra/pierre monteux/
***henryk szeryng**
*brahms violin concerto/LM 2281/LSC 2281/
RB 16168/SB 2049/VIC 1028/VICS 1028
sibelius symphony 2/LM 2342/LSC 2342/
RB 16186/SB 2070/SDD 234
elgar enigma variations/LM 2418/LSC 2418/RB 16237/
SB 2108/VIC 1107/VICS 1107/SPA 121

0706/18-21 june 1958/decca sessions for rca
royal opera orchestra/georg solti
overtures by verdi, rossini, offenbach and ponchielli/
LM 2313/LSC 2313/RB 16172/SB 2058

0707/4-7 july 1958/hmv sessions
**philharmonia orchestra/andre vandernoot/györgy
cziffra/oralia dominguez**
grieg piano concerto; liszt piano concerto 2/
ALP 1678/ASD 301
falla el amor brujo/ALP 1727/ASD 297

0708/10-11 july 1958/hmv sessions
philharmonia orchestra/walter susskind/joan hammond
operatic arias by tchaikovsky, smetana, dvorak, puccini, mascagni and giordano/ALP 1680/ASD 302/SXLP 30205
dvorak arias from rusalka/7ER 5118

0709/25-26 july 1958/hmv sessions
philharmonia orchestra/walter susskind/chistian ferras
bruch violin concerto 1; lalo symphonie espagnole/
ALP 1746/ASD 314/CFP 107

0710/28-29 july 1958/columbia sessions
philharmonia orchestra/wolfgang sawallisch
overtures by weber/33CX 1652/SAX 2343/
XLP 30038/SXLP 30038
overtures by wagner/33CX 1655

0711/13-15 august 1958/decca sessions
peter pears/benjamin britten (piano)
schubert die schöne müllerin/LXT 5574/SXL 2200
recording completed between april-october 1959

0712/29 august-4 september 1959/hmv sessions
philharmonia orchestra/paul kletzki/*hugh bean
brahms haydn variations; wagner siegfried idyll;
*traume/ALP 1696
rimsky-korsakov tsar siultan suite; glinka jota aragonesa;
tchaikovsky andante cantabile/ALP 1679/ASD 343
tchaikovsky capriccio italien/CFP 40083

0713/1-5 september 1958/columbia sessions
philharmonia orchestra/lovro von matacic
rimsky-korsakov scheherazade/33CX 1636/MFP 2013
mussorgsky night on bare mountain; rimsky-korsakov
russian easter overture; borodin prine igor overture,
polovtsian dances & march/33CX 1654/SAX 2327/
XLP 30070/SXLP 30070

0714/15-17 september 1958/decca sessions
**london symphony orchestra/pierino gamba/
julius katchen**
beethoven piano concerto 3; rondo in b flat/
LXT 5500/SXL 2106/SDD 226

0715/18-20 september 1958/decca sessions for rca
royal opera orchestra/jean morel
bizet l'arlesienne suite; chabrier espana; marche
joyeuse/LM 2327/LSC 2327/RB 16175/SB 2057

0716/29-30 september 1958/hmv sessions
**philharmonia orchestra/andre vandernoot/
györgy cziffra**
tchaikovsky piano concerto 1/ALP 1718/ASD 315
recording completed in april 1959

0717/7-8 october 1958/hmv sessions
robert masters chamber orchestra/yehudi menuhin
bach violin concerti BWV 1041 & BWV 1042/
ALP 1760/ASD 346

0718/14-15 october 1958/decca sessions for rca
london symphony orchestra/jean martinon
dvorak slavonic dances op 46 and op 72 no 7/
LM 2419/LSC 2419/RB 16246/SB 2115/
VIC 1054/VICS 1054

0719/20-31 october 1958/hmv sessions
royal philharmonic orchestra/thomas beecham
beethoven symphony 7/ALP 1748/ASD 311/SXLP 30286
handel-beecham amaryllis excerpts/ALP 1912/ASD 480
*beethoven recording completed later in
abbey road studios*

0720/22 and 28 october 1958/hmv sessions
royal philharmonic orchestra/douglas gamley
popular french overtures/XLP 20008/SMFP 6040

0721/24 october 1958/columbia session
philharmonia orchestra/alceo galliera
overtures by verdi/unpublished

0722/29 october 1958/hmv sessions
royal philharmonic orchestra/paul kletzki
schubert symphony 8; rosamunde overture and
ballet music/ALP 1725/ASD 296

0723/4-19 november 1958/columbia sessions
philharmonia orchestra/andre cluytens
berlioz symphonie fantastique/33CX 1673/CFP 168
ravel la valse; rimsky-korsakov capriccio espagnol;
borodin steppes of central asia; mussorgsky
night on bare mountain/33CX 1699/SAX 2355

0724/12 november 1958/columbia sessions
philharmonia orchestra/charles mackerras
meyerbeer-lambert les patineurs; ponchielli
dance of the hours from la gioconda/
33SX 1207/SCX 3291/MFP 2085

0725/20-21 november 1958/columbia sessions
philharmonia orchestra/heinz wallberg
tchaikovsky romeo and juliet; francesca da rimini;
marche slave/33CX 1674
wagner lohengrin preludes acts 1 and 3/unpublished

0726/24 november 1958/hmv session
philharmonia orchestra/andre vandernoot
ravel rapsodie espagnole; chabrier espana/
ALP 1727/ASD 297

0727/8-9 december 1958/decca sessions for rca
london symphony orchestra/pierre monteux
brahms haydn variations/LM 2418/LSC 2418/RB 16237/
SB 2108/VIC 1107/VICS 1107/SPA 121

0728/January 1959/decca sessions
new symphony orchestra/george szell/peter katin
chopin piano concerto 1/unpublished

0729/1-6 january 1959/columbia sessions
philharmonia orchestra/herbert von karajan
sibelius finlandia/33CX 1750/SAX 2392
ballet music from the operas/SAX 2294
tchaikovsky swan lake & sleeping beauty suites/
SAX 2306/SXLP 30200

183

0730/7 january 1959/hmv sessions
philharmonia orchestra/eugene goossens
weinberger polka and fugue from schwanda; smetana bartered bride overture, polka, furiant and dance of the tumblers; glinka jota aragonesa/
ALP 1785/ASD 366

0731/8 january 1959/hmv sessions
philharmonia orchestra/constantin silvestri
franck symphony/ALP 1831/ASD 408/CFP 40090
weber der freischütz overture/unpublished
recordings completed in march 1959

0732/10-13 january 1959/hmv sessions
philharmonia orchestra/igor markevitch
stravinsky sacre du printemps/
ALP 1745/ASD 313/CFP 129
recording completed in february 1959

0733/12 january 1959/decca session
london philharmonic orchestra/adrian boult/
julius katchen
dohnanyi variations on a nursery song/
LXT 5550/SXL 2176/SDD 428

0734/13-16 january 1959/decca sessions for rca
royal opera orchestra/ernest ansermet
ballet music by chopin, rossini-respighi, tchaikovsky, adam, delibes & schumann-glazunov/
LD 6065/LDS 6065

0735/21-24 january 1959/hmv sessions
royal philharmonic orchestra/rafael kubelik
brahms selection from hungarian dances/
ALP 1769/ASD 347
beethoven symphony 6/ALP 1771/ASD 349

0736/24-28 january 1959/decca sessions
london symphony orchestra/peter maag
mozart symphonies 32 & 38/LXT 5518/SXL 2135/
ADD 122/SDD 122
mozart german dances/BR 3082 & CEP 646/SEC 5056

0737/2-6 and 16 february 1959/columbia sessions
philharmonia orchestra/william walton/
***philharmonia chorus/*donald bell**
walton partita; *belshazzar's feast/
33CX 1679/SAX 2319

0738/5-6 february 1959/hmv sessions
royal philharmonic orchestra/*philharmonia orchestra/malcolm sargent
handel-elgar overure in d minor/ALP 1710/ASD 286
*grieg lyric suite/7ER 5161/RES 4264

0739/9-12 february 1959/decca sessions for rca
london symphony orchestra/alexander gibson
sibelius symphony 5; karelia suite/LM 2405/LSC 2405/
RB 16184/SB 2068/VIC 1016/VICS 1016/SPA 122

0740/12-13 february 1959/decca sessions for rca
royal opera orchestra/alexander gibson
gounod faust ballet music; funeral march of a
marionette; bizet carmen suite/
LM 2449/LSC 2449/VIC 1108/VICS 1108

0741/17-18 february 1959/hmv sessions
royal philharmonic orchestra/adrian boult/
yehudi menuhin
tchaikovsky violin concerto; serenade melancholique;
beethoven violin romances 1 and 2/unpublished

0742/27 february 1959/columbia session
philharmonia orchestra/tullio serafin
overtures by verdi/33CX 1684/SAX 2324

0743/10 and 13 march 1959/decca sessions
london philharmonic orchestra/kenneth alwyn
tchaikovsky swan lake suite; grieg peer gynt suite 1/
B 19057/S 29057 (usa)

0744/16-21 march 1959/columbia sessions
philharmonia orchestra/tullio serafin/
philharmonia chorus/soloists
donizetti lucia di lammermoor/
33CX 1723-1724/SAX 2316-2317

0745/31 march 1959/hmv sessions
philharmonia orchestra/constantin silvestri
overtures by humperdinck, mendelssohn,
rimsky-korsakov, borodin and glinka/
ALP 1749/ASD 338

0746/1 april 1959/hmv session
philharmonia orchestra/anatole fistoulari
prokofiev lieutenant kije excerpts/7ER 5145/
XLP 30119/SXLP 30119

0747/22-25 april 1959/hmv sessions
philharmonia orchestra/efrem kurtz/
michael flanders
prokofiev peter and the wolf/ALP 1728/ASD 299
philharmonia orchestra/efrem kurtz/
yehudi menuhin
tchaikovsky selection from sleeping beauty/
ALP 1790/ASD 371

0748/22-25 april 1959/columbia sessions
philharmonia orchestra/nicola rescigno/
elisabeth schwarzkopf
operatic arias by verdi & puccini/SAX 5286/SXDW 3049
operatic arias by verdi & puccini/unpublished

0749/27-28 april 1959/decca sessions
london symphony orchestra/pierre monteux/
royal opera chorus
ravel daphnis et chloe/LXT 5536/SXL 2164/
ADD 170/SDD 170/JB 69

0750/29 april 1959/decca session
peter pears/benjamin britten (piano)
recital of schubert lieder/BR 3066 & CEP 692/SEC 5084
recordings completed in september and october 1959

0751/1 may 1959/decca session
london philharmonic orchestra/adrian boult/
julius katchen
rachmaninov paganini rhapsody/LXT 5550/SXL 2176/
BR 8505/SWL 8505/SDD 428

0752/4 may 1959/decca sessions
new symphony orchestra/kenneth alwyn
overtures by rossini/B 19058/S 29058 (usa only)

0753/8 may 1959/decca sessions
new symphony orchestra/colin davis/peter katin
rachmaninov piano concerto 2/ACL 235/SPA 169

0754/11 may 1959/decca sessions
new symphony orchestra/edric cundell/peter katin
tchaikovsky piano concerto 1/SPA 168

0755/21-22 may 1959/hmv sessions
philharmonia orchestra/colin davis
mozart eine kleine nachtmusik; serenata notturna;
german dances and minuets/XLP 20029/SXLP 20019
mozart minuet from haffner serenade/unpublished

0756/25 may 1959/columbia sessions
philharmonia orchestra/charles mackerras
chopin-douglas les sylphides suite/33SX 1207/
SCX 3291/MFP 2085
brahms hungarian dances 5 & 6/33SX 1389/SCX 3427

0757/26-29 may 1959/columbia sessions
philharmonia orchestra/alceo galliera
dukas l'apprenti sorcier/33CX 1776/SAX 2419
overtures by rossini & verdi/unpublished

0758/2-10 june 1959/columbia sessions
philharmonia orchestra/carlo maria giulini
ravel alborada del gracioso; daphnis et chloe suite 2/
33CX 1694/SAX 2341/SXLP 30198
tchaikovsky symphony 6/33CX 1716/SAX 2368/SXLP 30208
rossini overtures/33CX 1726/SAX 2377/
SXLP 30094/CFP 40379

0759/15-19 june 1959/readers digest sessions
new symphony orchestra/alexander gibson
tchaikovsky symphony 6/RDM 7/RDS 7
orchestral works by chopin, dvorak, grieg & sibelius/
RDM 9/RDS 9
orchestra described for these sessions as
london festival orchestra

0760/16-17 june 1959/readers digest sessions
new symphony orchestra/rene leibowitz
stravinsky sacre du printemps; debussy
prelude a l'apres-midi/RDM 11/RDS 11
orchestra described for these sessions as
london festival orchestra

0761/22-23 june 1959/decca sessions
london symphony orchestra/oivin fjeldstad/
***clifford curzon**
*grieg piano concerto/LXT 5547/SXL 2173/JB 104
grieg sigurd jorsalfar suite/BR 3039/SPA 421/VIV 44

0762/25 june-2 july 1959/columbia sessions
philharmonia orchestra/otto ackermann/
*philharmonia chorus/*soloists
*johann strauss die fledermaus/33CX 1688-1689/
SAX 2336-2337
offenbach orfee aux enfers overture/unpublished
philharmonia orchestra/nicola rescigno
overtures and intermezzi by cherubini and
wolf-ferrari/unpublished

0763/july 1959/hmv sessions
bath festival orchestra/yehudi menuhin/
christian ferras
bach double violin concerto BWV1043/
ALP 1760/ASD 346

0764/20-24 july 1959/decca sessions
london symphony orchestra/josef krips/
artur rubinstein
mozart piano concerti 17, 20 & 23/unpublished

0765/28-29 july 1959/decca sessions
new symphony orchestra/robert sharples
orchestral works by ketelby/LK 4397/SKL 4077

0766/16-27 september 1959/columbia sessions
philharmonia orchestra/carlo maria giulini/
philharmonia chorus/soloists
mozart le nozze di figaro/33CX 1732-1735/SAX 2381-2384

0767/28-29 september 1959/decca sessions
london symphony orchestra/pierino gamba/
ruggiero ricci
works for violin & orchestra by saint-saens & sarasate/
LXT 5571/SXL 2197SDD 420

0768/2 october 1959/decca sessions
london philharmonic orchestra/colin davis/peter katin
grieg piano concerto; litolff scherzo/ACL 183/SPA 170

0769/15-20 october 1959/decca sessions for rca
london symphony orchestra/pierre monteux
dvorak symphony 7/LM 2489/LSC 2489/RB 16287/
SB 2155/VIC 1310/VICS 1310/SDD 260
beethoven symphony 4/VIC 1102/VICS 1102
beethoven leonore 3 overture/unpublished

0770/30 october 1959/decca sessions
peter pears/benjamin britten (piano)
folksong arrangements/CEP 711/SEC 5102/SDD 197

0771/21-24 november 1959/columbia sessions
philharmonia orchestra/carlo maria giulini
rossini la scala di seta overture/33CX 1726/SAX 2377/
SXLP 30094/CFP 40379

0772/24-26 november 1959/decca sessions
london symphony orchestra/peter maag/
barry tuckwell/gervase de peyer
mozart horn concerti 1 & 3; clarinet concerto/
LXT 5593/SXL 2238

0773/27 november 1959/decca sessions
royal opera orchestra/adrian boult/
***kenneth mckellar**
*arias by handel/LK 4380/SKL 4121
bach air from suite 3; sheep may safely graze/
CEP 736/SEC 5119
recordings completed in may 1960

0774/14-15 january 1960/columbia sessions
philharmonia orchestra/henry krips
works by johann strauss/33SX 1277/SCX 3346

0775/19-22 january 1960/decca sessions
london philharmonic orchestra/adrian boult/
***matyas seiber**
humphrey searle symphony 1; *seiber elegy/
LXT 5588/SXL 2232

0776/28 january 1960/decca session
royal opera orchestra/georg solti
gounod ballet music from faust/SXL 2280

0777/4 february 1960/world record club session
sinfonia of london/arthur bliss
works by bliss, handel and purcell/T 52/ST 52

0778/10-12 february 1960/decca sessions
london symphony orchestra/skitch henderson/
gary graffman/julius katchen/beatrice lillie
prokofiev peter & the wolf; saint-saens carnaval
des animaux/LXT 5577/SXL 2218

0779/19 february 1960/decca sessions
london philharmonic orchestra/adrian boult
stereo re-recording of orchestral accompaniments
to the recital of bach and handel arias by kathleen
ferrier (session 0430)/SXL 2234/SDD 286/SPA 311

0780/25-29 february 1960/columbia sssions
philharmonia orchestra/henry krips
waltzes by tchaikovsky, berlioz, gounod,
chabrier and delibes/33SX 1300/SCX 3362
tchaikovsy waltz from evgeny onegin/unpublished

0781/1-10 march 1960/columbia sessions
philharmonia orchestra/otto klemperer
wagner rienzi overture/33CX 1697/SAX 2347/SXLP 30436
wagner tristan prelude & liebestod; meistersinger overture; tanz der lehrbuben/33CX 1698/SAX 2348/SXLP 30525
strauss till eulenspiegel; don juan; schleiertanz from salome/33CX 1715/SAX 2367/SXLP 30298
wagner tannhäuser act 3 prelude; walkürenritt from die walküre/33CX 1820/SAX 2464/SXLP 30528

0782/21-22 march 1960/decca sessions
melos ensemble/matyas seiber/dorian singers/peter pears
seiber fragments from portrait of the artist as a young man/
LXT 5588/SXL 2232

0783/21-22 april 1960/decca sessions
london symphony orchestra/peter maag
mendelssohn symphony 3; hebrides overture/
LXT 5601/SXL 2246/ADD 145/SDD 145/SPA 503

0784/4-6 may 1960/hmv sessions
philharmonia orchestra/constantin silvestri
stravinsky symphony in three movements/
ALP 1819/ASD 401/CFP 40094

0785/11=19 may 1960/columbia sessions
philharmonia orchestra/otto klemperer/alan civil
mozart horn concerti 1-4/33CX 1760/SAX 2406/
CFP 41 44881

0786/26-27 may 1960/decca sessions
royal opera orchestra/georg solti .
offenbach-rosenthal gaite parisienne/
LXT 5642/SXL 2280

0787/27 may and 27 june 1960/columbia sessions
philharmonia orchestra/alceo galliera
rossini-respighi la boutique fantasque/
33CX 1776/SAX 2419

0788/30 may-3 june 1960/decca sessions
royal opera orchestra/argeo quadri/fernando corena
cimarosa il maestro di cappella; mozart concert arias/
LXT 5602/SXL 2247

0789/8-11 june 1960/decca sessions
**royal opera orchestra/alexander gibson/
teresa berganza**
operatic arias by handel, pergolesi, gluck,
paisiello and cherubini/LXT 5611/SXL 2251
lavilla lullaby/MET 201-203/SET 201-293

0790/12 july and 15-18 august 1960/decca sessions
royal opera orchestra/francesco molinari-pradelli/
royal opera chorus/joan sutherland
the art of the prima donna/LXT 5616-5617/SXL 2256-2257
arditi il bacio/unpublished

0791/12-22 july 1960/readers digest sessions
new symphony orchestra/alexander gibson/*adrian boult
orchestral works by tchaikovsky, suppe, johann strauss,
wagner, berlioz, paganini, grieg and smetana/
RDM 1001 and RDM 1005/RDS 5001 and RDS 5005
*orchestral works by liszt, mussorgsky, mendelssohn,
sullivan and elgar/RDM 1007/RDS 5007
*tchaikovsky swan lake & nutcracker suites/
RDM 1012/RDS 5012

0792/12-17 september 1960/capitol sessions
philharmonia orchestra/erich leinsdorf/*john browning
*ravel left hand concerto; prokofiev piano concerto 3/
P 8545/SP 8545
strauss till eulenspiegel; schleiertanz from salome;
die frau ohne schatten suite/P 8548/SP 8548
strauss der rosenkavalier suite/unpublished

0793/20-24 september 1960/columbia sessions
philharmonia orchestra/herbert von karajan
sibelius symphony 5/33CX 1750/SAX 2392/SXLP 30430
philharmonia promenade concert/33CX 1758/SAX 2404
ballet music from the operas/33CX 1774/SAX 2421

0794/27-29 september 1960/columbia sessions
philharmonia orchestra/otto klemperer
overtures by humperinck, weber & gluck/33CX 1770/SAX 2417
mozart entführung overture/33CX 1786/SAX 2436
cherubini anacreon overture/unpublished

0795/25 october 1960/columbia sessions
philharmonia orchestra/otto klemperer
beethoven symphony 7/33CX 1769/SAX 2415
recording completed in november & december 1960

0796/28 october 1960/columbia session
philharmonia orchestra/charles mackerras
dvorak slavonic dances 1, 3 & 10/33SX 1389/SCX 3427

0797/1-5 november 1960/columbia sessions
philharmonia orchestra/otto klemperer
bruckner symphony 7/33CX 1808-1809/SAX 2454-2455

0798/16-19 november 1960/columbia sessions
philharmonia orchestra/otto klemperer
schubert symphony 9/33CX 1754/SAX 2397

0799/22-26 november 1960/decca sessions
royal opera orchestra/benjamin britten/
royal opera chorus/soloists
britten spring symphony/LXT 5624/SXL 2264

0800/25-26 november 1960/columbia sessions
philharmonia orchestra/otto klemperer/philharmonia
and hampstead boys choirs/soloists
bach matthäus-passion/33CX 1799-1803/
SAX 2446-2450
recording completed between january-november 1961

0801/28 november-2 december 1960/hmv sessions
philharmonia orchestra/heinz wallberg
mendelssohn symphony 4/sommernachtstraum
overture, nocturne & scherzo/XLP 20037/SXLP 20037
bizet l'arlesienne suites 1 & 2; carmen suite 1/
XLP 20044/SXLP 20044

0802/30 november 1960/hmv sessions
royal philharmonic orchestra/george weldon
handel fireworks & water music suites/XLP 20033

0803/2 january 1961/columbia sessions
philharmonia orchestra/otto klemperer/
philharmonia chorus/soloists
brahms ein deutsches requiem/
33CX 1781-1782/SAX 2430-2431
recording completed between march-may 1961

0804/5-6 and 11 january 1961/decca sessions
london symphony orchestra/malcolm sargent/
ruggiero ricci
dvorak and tchaikovsky violin concerti/
LXT 5641/SXL 2279/ADD 126/SDD 126

0805/9-11 january 1961/decca sessions
new symphony orchestra/isidore godfrey/soloists
sullivan cox and box/LK 4402/SKL 4138

0806/13 january 1961/argo sessions
benjamin britten (piano)/soloists
britten canticles and other works/EAF 18/ZFA 18/
RG 277/ZRG 5277

0807/19-27 january 1961/columbia sessions
philharmonia orchestra/carlo maria giulini
dvorak symphony 9 and carnival overure/
33CX 1759/SAX 2405/SXLP 30163
brahms symphony 1/33CX 1773/SAX 2420
brahms haydn variations; schubert symphony 8/
33CX 1778/SAX 2424/SXLP 30278

0808/20-23 february 1961/readers digest sessions
new symphony orchestra/rene leibowitz
an anthology of popular orchestral music/
RDM 2001-2002/RDS 6001-6002

0809/15 march 1961/decca sessions
london philharmonic orchestra/adrian boult
holst the perfect fool suite; egdon heath/
LXT 6006/SXL 6006/JB 49

0810/15-20 march 1961/decca sessions
royal opera orchestra/robert sharples
sibelius karelia suite/unpublished test recording

0811/16-17 march 1961/oiseau lyre sessions
**english chamber orchestra/raymond leppard/
helen watts**
recital of handel arias/OL 50215/SOL 60046
**london symphony orchestra/george malcolm/
lso chorus/soloists**
choral works by britten/OL 50206/SOL 60037

0812/6-10 and 25 april 1961/columbia sessions
philharmonia orchestra/otto klemperer/
*elisabeth schwarzkopf
*mahler symphony 4/33CX 1793/SAX 2441
wagner siegfried idyll/33CX 1809/SAX 2455
recording of the wagner work completed in october 1961

0813/21 and 24 april 1961/decca sessions
london symphony orchestra/peter maag/
barry tuckwell
mozart horn concerti 2, 4 & anhang/
BR 3102/SWL 8011

0814/15-16 may 1961/decca sessions
london symphony orchestra/adrian boult/
lso chorus/soloists
handel messiah/MET 218-220/SET 218-220
recording completed in august 1961

0815/16-17 may 1961/oiseau lyre sessions
english chamber orchestra/raymond leppard/
helen watts
recital of handel cantatas/OL 50215/SOL 60046

0816/23-27 may 1961/decca sessions for rca
london symphony orchestra/pierre monteux
beethoven symphony 5; egmont overture/SPA 585
beethoven symphony 7/VIC 1061/VICS 1061/SPA 586

0817/20-21 june 1961/capitol sessions
philharmonia orchestra/robert irving
shostakovich age of gold suite; bartok miraculous mandarin suite/P 8576/SP 8576

0818/23 june-13 july 1961/hmv sessions
philharmonia orchestra/franco ferraris/franco corelli
recital of operatic arias/ALP 1978/ASD 529

0819/19-20 july 1961/decca sessions
mistislav rostropovich/benjamin britten (piano)
cello sonatas by britten and debussy; schumann stücke im volkston/LXT 5661/SXL 2298

0820/16-17 october 1961/columbia sessions
philharmonia orchestra/carlo maria giulini/
victoria de los angeles
falla el amor brujo/33CX 5265/SAX 5265/ SXLP 30140/CFP 4512
recording completed in april 1964

0821/18 october-2 december 1961/columbia sessions
philharmonia orchestra/otto klemperer/
*philharmonia chorus/*soloists
strauss tod und verklärung; metamorphosen/
33CX 1789/SAX 2437
tchaikovsky symphony 6/33CX 1812/SAX 2458
works by johann strauss, weill and klemperer/
33CX 1814/SAX 2460
wagner einzug der götter; waldweben; parsifal prelude;
siegfried's rhine journey/33CX 1820/SAX 2464
*mahler symphony 2/33CX 1829-1830/SAX 2473-2474
mahler recording completed in march 1962

0822/6-9 november 1961/decca sessions
peter pears/benjamin britten (piano)
haydn canzonettas; britten hölderlin fragments/
BR 8507/SWL 8507

0823/13-16 november 1961/columbia sessions
philharmonia orchestra/antonio tonini/
philharmonia chorus/maria callas
operatic scenes and arias by rossini, donizetti
and bellini/EL 749 4281
recordings completed in april 1962

0824/15-17 november 1961/hmv sessions
sadlers wells orchestra/colin davis/
sadlers wells chorus/soloists
stravinsky oedipus rex/ALP 1960/ASD 511

0825/4-9 december 1961/columbia sessions
philharmonia orchestra/otto klemperer/
philharmonia chorus
bach choruses from b minor mass/SBT 1138

0826/11-13 december 1961/decca sessions
london symphony orchestra/pierre monteux
debussy nuages et fetes; prelude a l'apres-midi;
ravel rapsodie espagnole; pavane pour une
infant defunte/LXT 5677/SXL 2312/SPA 425

0827/14-15 december 1961 and 4 march 1962/
bbc recording sessions
london symphony orchestra/pierre monteux
falla el sombrero de 3 picos/BBCL 40962
elgar enigma variations; chabrier fete polonaise;
berlioz marche hongroise/BBCL 41722

0828/15 december 1961/decca session
london symphony orchestra/benjamin britten
god save the queen arranged by britten/
45-71146/CEP 736/SEC 5119

0829/17-19 january 1962/columbia sessions
philharmonia orchestra/carlo maria giulini
dvorak symphony 8 and scherzo capriccioso/
33CX 1815/SAX 2461
recordings completed in april 1962

0830/25 january-3 february 1962/hmv sessions
royal opera orchestra/edward downes/amy shuard
operatic arias by verdi, mascagni, puccini and
giordano/XLP 20046/SXLP 20046
recordings completed in march 1962

0831/3-17 february 1962/columbia sessions
philharmonia orchestra/otto klemperer/
phiharmonia chorus/soloists
beethoven fidelio/33CX 1804-1806/SAX 2452-2453

0832/27 february-2 march 1962/decca sessions
royal opera orchestra/john lanchbery
herold-lanchbery la fille mal gardee/
LXT 5682/SXL 2313

0833/6-30 march 1962/columbia sessions
philharmonia orchestra/otto klemperer/
*philharmonia chorus/*christa ludwig
*brahms alto rhapsody; wagner wesendonck lieder/
33CX 1817/SAX 2462
mozart symphonies 38 & 39/33CX 1824/SAX 2468
mozart symphonies 40 & 41/33CX 1843/SAX 2486
stravinsky symphony in three movements/
33CX 1949/SAX 2588
some recordings in these sessions were
completed in may 1962

0834/9-13 april 1962/columbia sessions
philharmonia orchestra/antonio tonini/
philharmonia chorus/maria callas
operatic arias by verdi and weber/unpublished

0835/9-26 april 1962/columbia sessions
philharmonia orchestra/carlo maria giulini
*philharmonia chorus
*debussy la mer and trois nocturnes/
33CX 1818/SAX 2463/SXLP 30146
tchaikovsky romeo and juliet; francesca da
rimini/33CX 1840/SAX 2483
tchaikovsky symphony 5/unpublished (incomplete)

0836/10-14 april & 4 july 1962/world record club sessions
philharmonia orchestra/alexander gibson
overtures & intermezzi by rossini & verdi/T 250/ST 520

0837/25-27 april 1962/columbia sessions
philharmonia orchestra/antonio tonini/
elisabeth schwarzkopf
operatic arias by rossini, verdi & puccini/unpublished

0838/8-11 may 1962/hmv sessions
philharmonia orchestra/*sinfonia of london/
john barbirolli
vaughan williams symphony 5/ALP 1957/ASD 518
*elgar introduction and allegro; serenade for strings;
vaughan williams fantasia on greensleeves/
ALP 1970/ASD 521
elgar enigma variations/ALP 1998/ASD 548
recordings completed in august 1962;
ALP 1970/ASD 521 also contained vaughan
williams tallis fantasia, which was recorded
in london temple church

0839/30 may-1 june 1962/decca sessions
london symphony orchestra/george szell/
clifford curzon
brahms piano concerto 1/LXT 6023/SXL 6023/JB 102

0840/13-14 june 1962/hmv sessions
band of the grenadier guards
the big bands/CSD 1460

0841/19-29 june 1962/columbia sessions
philharmonia orchestra/lorin maazel
strauss also sprach zarathustra; till eulenspiegel/
33CX 1823/SAX 2467/SXLP 30133
mussorgsky-ravel pictures from an exhibition; debussy
prelude a l'apres-midi/33CX 1841/SAX 2484
recordins completed in august 1962

0842/22-23 june 1962/hmv sessions
philharmonia orchestra/paul kletzki/christian ferras/paul tortelier
brahms double concerto/ALP 1999/ASD 549/CFP 40081

0843/2-12 july 1962/hmv angel sessions
philharmonia orchestra/lovro von matacic/philharmonia chorus/soloists
lehar die lustige witwe/AN 101-102/SAN 101-102

0844/19 august 1962/world record club session
pro arte orchestra/george weldon
elgar pomp & circumstance marches 1 & 4/T 296/ST 296

0845/27-29 august 1962/hmv sessions
philharmonia orchestra/john barbirolli
elgar symphony 1/ALP 1989/ASD 540/SXLP 30268
elgar cockaigne overture/ALP 1998/ASD 548
elgar pomp and circumstance marches 1 and 4/
ALP 2292/ASD 2292

0846/10-18 september 1962/hmv angel sessions
philharmonia orchestra/karl böhm/
philharmonia chorus/soloists
mozart cosi fan tutte/AN 103-106/SAN 103-106

0847/4-12 october 1962/columbia sessions
philharmonia orchestra/carlo maria giulini
brahms symphony 2/33CX 1855/SAX 2498
brahms symphony 3; tragic overture/
33CX 1872/SAX 2516
britten young persons guide and 4 sea interludes/
33CX 1915/SAX 2555/SXLP 30240
recording of britten works completed in
november 1962

0848/22-23 october 1962/hmv sessions
philharmonia orchestra/colin davis/yehudi menuhin
berlioz harold en italie/ALP 1986/ASD 537/SXLP 30314

0849/26 october-2 november 1962/decca sessions
**london symphony orchestra/edward downes/
nicolai ghiaurov**
recital of operatic arias/LXT 6038/SXL 6038

0850/26 october-3 november 1962/decca sessions
**london symphony orchestra/richard bonynge/
ambrosian singers/joan sutherland**
command performance/MET 247-248/SET 247-248

0851/1 and 7-8 november 1962/decca sessions
london symphony orchestra/stanley black
film spectacular/LK 4525/SKL 4525
*orchestra described for this recording as
london festival orchestra*

0852/27-28 november 1962/hmv sessions
philharmonia orchestra/georges pretre
shostakovich symphony 12/ALP 2009/ASD 559/CFP 141
recording completed in march 1963

0853/13-14 december 1962/columbia sessions
philharmonia orchestra/carlo maria giulini
overtures by rossini/33CX 1919/SAX 2560/SXLP 30143

0854/15-21 december 1962/decca sessions
**london symphony orchestra/john pritchard/
teresa berganza**
recital of mozart arias/LXT 6045/SXL 6045/
ADD 176/SDD 176

0855/3-10 january 1963/decca sessions
**london symphony orchestra/benjamin britten/
lso chorus/bach choir/highgate school choir/soloists**
britten war requiem/MET 252-253/SET 252-253

0856/16 january-18 february 1963/columbia sessions
philharmonia orchestra/otto klemperer
tchaikovsky symphony 4/33CX 1851/SAX 2494
tchaikovsky symphony 5/33CX 1854/SAX 2497
schubert symphony 8/33CX 1870/SAX 2514
stravinsky pulcinella/33CX 1949/SAX 2588
stravinsky recording completed in may 1963

0857/22-26 february 1963/decca sessions
london symphony orchestra/istvan kertesz
dvorak symphony 8; scherzo capriccioso/
LXT 6044/SXL 6044
bartok hungarian sketches/unpublished

0858/13-16 march 1963/decca sessions for rca
london symphony orchestra/rene leibowitz/
leonard pennario
liszt piano concerti 1 and 2/LM 2690/LSC 2690/
RB 6568/SB 6568/VICS 1426

0859/1-2 april 1963/readers digest sessions
london philharmonic orchestra/john pritchard/
chorus/soloists
handel selection from messiah/RDS 470

0860/11 april 1963/columbia sessions
philharmonia orchestra/george weldon
orchestral works by dvorak, mendelssohn, verdi,
smetana & tchaikovsky/33SX 1570/SCX 3499

0861/22-24 april 1963/hmv sessions
philharmonia orchestra/jerzy semkow/boris christoff
operatic arias by verdi, borodin and gluck/
ALP 2025/ASD 574

0862/23-26 april 1963/columbia sessions
philharmonia orchestra/otto klemperer
berlioz symphonie fantastique/
33CX 1898/SAX 2537/EMX 2030

0863/7-10 may 1963/decca sessions
royal opera orchestra/edward downes/birgit nilsson
arias by beethoven, weber & wagner/LXT 6077/SXL 6077

0864/13-16 may 1963/columbia sessions
philharmonia orchestra/otto klemperer
schubert symphony 5/33CX 1870/SAX 2514

0865/18-21 may 1963/columbia sessions
philharmonia orchestra/george weldon
tchaikovsky 1812 overture/33SX 1570/SCX 3499/
SXLP 30127
wagner einzug der gäste from tannhäuser/
unpublished

0866/23-28 may 1963/decca sessions
**london symphony orchestra/benjamin britten/
*peter pears**
britten young persons guide; *serenade/
LXT 6110/SXL 6110

0867/21-25 and 28 may 1963/decca sessions for rca
**london symphony orchestra/malcolm sergeant/
erick friedman**
works for violin and orchestra by wieniawski,
chausson, saint-saens, sarasate and ravel/
LM 2689/LSC 2689

0868/27 may-1 june 1963/decca sessions
royal opera orchestra/edward downes/regine crespin
recital of Italian opera arias/LXT 6075/SXL 6075

0869/18-19 june 1963/hmv sessions
philharmonia orchestra/paul kletzki/yehudi menuhin
bloch violin concerto/ALP 2035/ASD 584/SXLP 30177

0870/20 june 1963/hmv sessions
philharmonia orchestra/anatole fistoulari
grieg holberg suite; tchaikovsky andante cantabile/
XLP 20058/SXLP 20058
recordings completed in july 1963

0871/20-21 june 1963/hmv sessions
philharmonia orchestra/pierino gamba
tchaikovsky romeo and Juliet; saint-saens danse
macabre; rimsky-korsakov capriccio espagnol/
CLP 1848/CSD 1592
recordings completed in july 1963

0872/25-29 june 1963/decca sessions
london symphony orchestra/richard bonynge/
lso chorus/joan sutherland
the art of bel canto/MET 268-269/SET 268-269

0873/26-27 june 1963/decca sessions
london symphony orchestra/stanley black
film spectacular II/LK 4657/PFS 4030
orchestra described for this recording as
london festival orchestra

0874/6-10 september 1963/decca sessions
new symphony orchestra/edward downes/
robert merrill
recital of italian opera arias/LXT 6083/SXL 6083

0875/13-14 september 1963/decca sessions
london symphony orchestra/stanley black
grofe grand canyon suite/LK 4584/PFS 4036
orchestra described for this recording as
london festival orchestra

0876/16-27 september 1963/hmv angel sessions
philharmonia orchestra/carlo maria giulini/
philharmonia chorus/soloists
verdi messa da requiem/AN 133-134/SAN 133-134
recording completed in april 1964

0877/14-21 october 1963/decca and *argo sessions
peter pears/benjamin britten (piano)
schubert winterreise; schumann dichterliebe/
MET 270-271/SET 270-271
*recital of songs by english composers/
RG 418/ZRG 5418

0878/28-30 october 1963/hmv sessions
**philharmonia orchestra/rafael frühbeck de burgos/
victoria de los angeles**
falla el sombrero de 3 picos/ALP 2059/ASD 608/
SXLP 30187
recording completed in december 1963

0879/30 october-8 november 1963/columbia sessions
philharmonia orchestra/otto klemperer
beethoven leonore overtures 1, 2 amd 3/
33CX 1902/SAX 2542/SXDW 3032
dvorak symphony 9/33CX 1914/SAX 2554
schubert symphony 4/unpublished (incomplete)

0880/5-11 december 1963/decca sessions
**london symphony orchestra/benjamin britten/
*peter pears**
mozart symphony 40; maurerische trauermusik; cosi
fan tutte overture; *concert arias/all unpublished

0881/10-17 and 31 december 1963/decca sessions
london symphony orchestra/georg solti
bartok music for strings percussion and celesta;
miraculous mandarin suite/LXT 6111/SXL 6111

0882/13-14 december 1963/decca sessions
london symphony orchestra/benjamin britten/
lso chorus/soloists
britten cantata misericordium/LXT 6175/SXL 6175

0883/17-18 january & 3-4 february 1964/decca sessions
london symphony orchestra/georg solti
mahler symphony 1/LXT 6113/SXL 6113

0884/10-11 february 1964/columbia sessions
philharmonia orchestra/otto klemperer
schumann symphony 1/unpublished

0885/14-15 february 1964/argo sessions
academy of st martin in the fields/neville marriner
handel concerti grossi op 3/RG 400/ZRG 5400
recording completed in march 1964

0886/17-19 february 1964/columbia sessions
philharmonia orchestra/otto klemperer/
christa ludwig
mahler orchesterlieder/ASD 2391/SXLP 27 00001

0887/24 february-19 march 1964/hmv angel sessions
philharmonia orchestra/otto klemperer/
philharmonia chorus/soloists
handel messiah/AN 146-148/SAN 146-148

0888/28 february & 2 march 1964/decca sessions
london symphony orchestra/istvan kertesz/*olga szönyi
kodaly dances of galanta; "hary janos/
LXT 6136/SXL 6136/JB 55

0889/3-4 march 1964/decca sessions
london symphony orchestra/george malcolm/
rosemarie voges
recital of oratorio arias/unpublished

0890/5-6 march 1964/decca sessions
london symphony orchestra/istvan kertesz
dvorak symphony 7/LXT 6115/SXL 6115/JB 116

0891/24 march-10 april 1964/hmv angel sessions
philharmonia orchestra/otto klemperer/
philharmonia chorus/soloists
mozart die zauberflöte/AN 137-139/SAN 137-139

0892/1-3 april 1964/columbia sessions
philharmonia orchestra/carlo maria giulini
overtures by rossini/33CX 1919/SAX 2560/SXLP 30143

0893/13-14 and 25-29 april 1964/decca sessions
london symphony orchestra/richard bonynge
immortal pas de deux/LXT 6137/SXL 6137
adam le diable a quatre/LXT 6188/SXL 6188

0894/20-21 april and 1-3 june 1964/hmv sessions
halle orchestra/john barbirolli
elgar symphony 2; falstaff/ALP 2061-2062/ASD 610-611
schubert symphony 9/ALP 2085/ASD 632
barbirolli tlks to ronald kinloch anderson/CDSJB 1999

0895/4-5 may 1964/decca sessions
royal opera orchestra/edward downes/
luciano pavarotti/*birgit nilsson
opera arias by verdi & puccini/CEP 5532/SEC 5532
*beethoven ah perfido/CEP 5533/SEC 5533

0896/7 may 1964/hmv session
band of the royal marines
grainger churchill march; their finest hour; bliss
call to arms; welcome to the queen/7EG 8866

0897/20-25 may 1964/readers digest sessions
royal philharmonic orchestra/rudolf kempe/
*rudolf firkusny
strauss don juan; respighi pini di roma/RD 4015
*beethoven piano concerto 5/RD 4060

0898/4-5 june 1964/decca sessions
london symphony orchestra/stanley black
tchaikovsky capriccio italien; rimsky-korsakov
capriccio espagnol/LK 4632/PFS 4055
orchestra described for this reording as
london festival orchestra

0899/16-18 july 1964/decca sessions
english chamber orchestra/benjamin britten/
mstislav rostropovich
britten cello symphony; haydn cello concerto in c/
LXT 6138/SXL 6138

0900/22-24 july 1964/hmv sessions
new philharmonia orchestra/georges pretre
tchaikovsky symphony 5/ALP 2089/ASD 636

0901/15-20 august 1964/decca sessions
royal opera orchestra/edward downes/sandra
warfield/james mccracken
recital of operatic duets/LXT 6144/SXL 6144

0902/21-25 august 1964/decca sessions
royal opera orchestra/edward downes/marilyn horne
recital of operatic arias/LXT 6149/SXL 6149

0903/1-2 september 1964/hmv sessions
london symphony orchestra/john barbirolli
tchaikovsky serenade for strings; arensky tchaikovsky variations/ALP 2099/ASD 646/SXLP 30239

0904/11-18 september 1964/decca sessions
new philharmonia orchestra/oliviero de fabritiis/ renata tebaldi
recital of italian opera arias/LXT 6152/SXL 6152

0905/22 september 1964/decca sessions
london symphony orchestra/leopold stokowski
rimsky-korsakov scheherazade/LK 4658/PFS 4062

0906/27 september 1964/hmv sessions
bbc symphony orchestra/antal dorati
koechlin bandar-log; messiaen chronochomie/ ALP 2092/ASD 639
recording completed in october 1964

0907/22-23 october 1964/hmv sessions
bath festival orchestra/yehudi menuhin/*michael tippett
britten frank bridge variations; *tippett corelli fantasy/
ALP 2090/ASD 637

0908/6-19 november 1964/columbia sessions
new philharmonia orchestra/otto klemperer
bruckner symphony 6/33CX 1943/SAX 2582/SXLP 30448

0909/14-15 december 1964/argo sessions
peter pears/viola tunnard (piano)
recital of songs by british composers/RG 439/ZRG 5439

0910/14-19 december 1964 and 5 january 1965/
decca sessions
london wind soloists
beethoven chamber works for wind/
LXT 6170/SXL 6170

0911/17-18 december 1964/decca sessions
new philharmonia orchestra/benjamin britten
britten sinfonia da requiem/LXT 6175/SXL 6175

0912/1-6 january 1965/decca sessions
london symphony orchestra/david zinman/
vladimir ashkenazy
chopin piano concerto 2; bach piano concerto BWV1052/
LXT 6174/SXL 6174

0913/22-23 january & 3 february 1965/columbia sessions
london symphony orchestra/david willcocks/westminster
abbey and bach choirs/soloists
vaughan williams hodie/33SX 1782/SCX 3570

0914/27-28 january 1965/hmv sessions
royal air force central band
music for ceremonial occasions/CLP 1892/CSD 1615
march in honour of a great man/7EG 8899

0915/5-6 and 24 february 1965/hmv sessions
new philharmonia orchestra/antal dorati/
yehudi menuhin
bartok violin concerto 1/ALP 2281/ASD 2281
bartok violin concerto 2/ALP 2323/ASD 2323

0916/8-9 february 1965/decca sessions
london symphony orchestra/sixteen ehrling/
***hans leygraf**
rosenberg marionettes overture; lidholm rites ballet
suite; *blomdahl chamber concerto/
LXT 6180/SXL 6180

0917/15, 20 & 26 february & 7 may1965/decca sessions
london symphony orchestra/georg solti
bartok concerto for orchestra; dance suite
LXT 6212/SXL 6212/JB 144

0918/17-20 february 1965/decca sessions
**london symphony orchestra/rafael frühbeck de burgos/
ion voicu**
mendelssohn violin concerto; bruch violin
concerto 1/LXT 6184/SXL 6184/SDD 443

0919/9-10 march 1965/decca sessions
rosemarie voges/geoffrey parsons (piano)
recital of folksongs/LXT 6216/SXL 6216

0920/27-30 april 1965/readers digest sessions
rca orchestra/charles gerhardt
gliere red poppy suite; rossini scala di seta
overture/RDS 6106

0921/10 and 27-31 may 1965/decca sessions
**new philharmonia orchestra/richard bonynge/
joan sutherland**
joy to the world: christmas carols/
LXT 6193/SXL 6193

0922/11-21 may 1965/readers digest sessions
royal philharmonic orchestra/malcolm sargent/
royal choral society/soloists
handel messiah/RDM 1084-1086/RDS 5084-5086

0923/14-15 may 1965/decca sessions
london symphony orchestra/rafael frühbeck de burgos
schumann symphony 3; mendelssohn
sommernachtstraum overture/
LXT 6213/SXL 6213/SDD 323

0924/17-18 may 1965/decca sessions
new philharmonia orchestra/rafael frühbeck de burgos/
***nati mistral**
granados goyescas intermezzo; ravel alborada
del gracioso; ravel pavane pour une infant defunte;
*falla el amor brujo suite/LXT 6287/SXL 6287

0925/24-25 may 1965/decca sessions
new philharmonia orchestra/stanley black
works by gershwin/LK 4769/PFS 4098
works by russian composers/LK 4781/PFS 4084

0926/26-30 july 1965/hmv sessions
derek collier/ernest lush (piano)
the voice of the violin/SXLP 20080

0927/9-13 august 1965/rca sessions
orchestra/carlo felice cillario/montserrat caballe
opera arias by bellini and donizetti/
LM 2862/LSC 2862/RB 6647/SB 6647

0928/19 and 24 august 1965/hmv sessions
london symphony orchestra/john barbirolli/
*jacqueline du pre
*elgar cello concerto/ALP 2106/ASD 655
delius walk to the paradise garden/
ALP 2305/ASD 2305/ESD 7092
delius irmelin prelude/unpublished

0929/10 september 1965/bbc recording session
new philharmonia orchestra/leopold stokowski
tchaikovsky sleeping beauty suite/BBCL 41152

0930/10-11 and 15 september 1965/decca sessions
new philharmonia orchestra/leopold stokowski
mussorgsky-stokowski pictures from an exhibition;
debussy cathedrale engloutie/LK 4766/PFS 4095
tchaikovsky swan lake & sleeping beauty suites/
LK 4807/PFS 4083/VIV 10

0931/30 september-13 october 1965/hmv angel sessions
new philharmonia orchestra/otto klemperer/
new philharmonia chorus/soloists
beethoven missa solemnis/AN 165-166/SAN 165-166

0932/15 october 1965/argo sessions
english chamber orchestra/imogen holst/purcell singers/soloists
holst savitri/NF 6/ZNF 6

0933/18-22 october & 1 november 1965/decca sessions
new philharmonia orchestra/carlo maria giulini
mozart symphonies 40 & 41/LXT 6225/SXL 6225/JB 8

0934/20-25 october 1965/decca sessions
london symphony orchestra/istvan kertesz
bruckner symphony 4/LXT 6227/SXL 6227/SDD 464

0935/25-29 october 1965/argo sessions
academy of st martin in the fields/neville marriner/
*bernadette greevy
mendelssohn string symphonies 9, 10 and 12/
RG 467/ZRG 5467
*arias from handel operas/RG 501/ZRG 5501
handel recordings completed in february 1966

0936/5 november 1965/rca sessions for readers digest
new philharmonia orchestra/charles gerhardt
works by british composers/RDS 6106/GL 25006

0937/9-12 november 1965/decca sessions
london symphony orchestra/istvan kertesz/
julius katchen
bartok piano concerto 3; ravel piano concerto in g/
LXT 6209/SXL 6209
london symphony orchestra/istvan kertesz/soloists
bartok bluebeard's castle/MET 311/SET 311

0938/24 november-15 december 1965/argo sessions
english chamber orchestra/imogen holst/
purcell singers/peter pears
holst partsongs & choruses/RG 495 and RG 497/
ZRG 5495 and ZRG 5497

0939/3-4 december 1965/decca sessions
dietrich fischer-dieskau/benjamin britten (piano)
britten songs & proverbs of william blake/SXL 6391

0940/6-10 december 1965/decca sessions
london symphony orchestra/istvan kertesz
dvorak symphony 6; carnival overture/LXT 6253/SXL 6253
dvorak symphony 5; my home overture/LXT 6273/SXL 6273

0941/10-11 december 1965/decca sessions
new philharmonia orchestra/charles munch
offenbach-rosenthal gaite parisienne/
LK 4767/PFS 4096/VIV 60

0942/13-18 december 1965/lyrita sessions
london philharmonic orchestra/adrian boult
orchestral works by john ireland/
RCS 31-32/SRCS 31-32

0943/28-30 december 1965/hmv sessions
**new philharmonia orchestra/adrian boult/
yehudi menuhin**
elgar violin concerto/ALP 2259/ASD 2259/
SXLP 29 00001

0944/3-4 january 1966/lyrita sessions
**city of birmingham symphony orchestra/
hugo rignold**
bliss meditation on a theme of john blow/
RCS 833/SRCS 833

0945/5-6 january 1966/oiseau lyre sessions
english chamber orchestra/raymond leppard
works by rameau and gretry/OL 297 and OL 300/
SOL 297 and SOL 300

0946/6-8 january 1966/decca and *argo sessions
english chamber orchestra/emanuel hurwitz/soloists
works by eighteenth century composers/
ADD 147/SDD 147
*holst terzetto/RG 497/ZRG 5497

0947/19 january and 25 february 1966/argo sessions
instrumentalists
chamber works by twentieth century composers/
RG 475/ZRG 5475

0948/21-25 january 1966/hmv sessions
**new philharmonia orchestra/otto klemperer/
yehudi menuhin**
beethoven violin concerto/ALP 2285/ASD 2285

0949/31 january-3 february 1966/decca sessions
london symphony orchestra/georg solti
russian orchestral music/LXT 6263/SXL 6263
brahms symphony 1/unpublished

0950/11-12 february 1966/decca sssions
**london symphony orchestra/istvan kertesz/
barry tuckwell**
horn concerti by richard and franz strauss/
LXT 6285/SXL 6285/JB 17

0951/11-16 february 1966/decca sessions
london symphony orchestra/claudio abbado
prokofiev suites from chout and romeo & juliet/
LXT 6286/SXL 6286/JB 56
recordings completed in october 1966

0952/9 march & 8-9 may 1966/decca sessions
royal philharmonic orchestra/antal dorati/
sean connery
britten young person's guide to the orchestra;
prokofiev peter & the wolf/
LK 4801/PFS 4104/VIV 40

0953/10-16 march 1966/decca sessions
new philharmonia orchestra/richard bonynge/
ambrosian singers/joan sutherland
love live forever/MET 349-350/SET 349-350
recordings completed in july 1966

0954/16-17 march 1966/lytita sessions
english chamber orchestra/imogen holst
works by gustav holst/RCS 34/SRCS 34

0955/21 march-2 april 1966/decca sessions
**london philharmonic orchestra/richard bonynge/
ambrosian singers/joan sutherland**
the songs of noel coward/LXT 6255/SXL 6255
opera scenes by graun & bononcini/
MET 351-352/SET 351-352
noel coward recordings completed in july 1966

0956/14-16 april 1966/argo sessions
**academy of st martin in the fields/neville marriner/
barry tuckwell** haydn horn concerti 1 & 2; overture
and german dances/RG 498/ZRG 5498

0957/18-27 april 1966/rca and *readers digest sessions
**royal philharmonic orchestra/rudolf kempe/
*shura cherkassky**
strauss eine alpensinfonie/LM 2923/LSC 2923/
RB 6696/SB 6696
*chopin piano concerto 2/RC 4414

0958/25-29 april 1966/rca sessions
london symphony orchestra/andre previn
rachmaninov symphony 2/LM 2899/LSC 2899/
RB 6685/SB 6685/LSB 4089

0959/6 may 1966/hmv session
london philharmonic orchestra/yehudi menuhin/
*yaltah and jeremy menuhin
mozart piano concerto K242/ALP 2280/ASD 2280/
CFP 40291

0960/12-13 may and 2 june 1966/decca sessions
vladimir ashkenazy
mozart piano concerti 8 & 9; rondo K386/
LXT 6259/SXL 6259

0962/20 may 1966/decca sessions
royal philharmonic orchestra/robert farnon
gershwin porgy and bess symphonic suite/
LK 4815/PFS 4109
orchestra described for this recording as
london festival orchestra

0963/21-27 may 1966/decca sessions
london symphony orchestra/georg solti/
lso chorus/*soloists
*mahler symphony 2/MET 325-326/SET 325-326
borodin polovtsian dances/LXT 6263/SXL 6263

0964/1-18 june and 6-9 july 1966/decca sessions
london symphony orchestra/richard bonynge/
ambrosian & highgate choirs/soloists
meyerbeer les huguenots/MET 327-330/SET 327-330

0965/21-22 june 1966/decca sessions
london symphony orchestra/leopold stokowski
wagner einzug der götter; walkürenritt; waldweben;
rheinfahrt & trauermarsch/LK 4851/PFS 4116/SPA 537

0966/29-30 june 1966/emi sessions
**english chamber orchestra/charles mackerras/
ambrosian singers/soloists**
handel messiah/RLS 693/SLS 774
recording completed in july and august 1966

0967/july 1966/emi sessions
**bath festival orchestra/yehudi menuhin/
janet baker**
bach cantatas 82 and 169/ALP 2302/ASD 2302

0968/1-2 july 1966/decca sessions
royal philharmonic orchestra/stanley black
spectacular dances for orchestra/
LK 4862/PFS 4118

0969/11 july 1966/decca session
**downside school orchestra/benjamin britten/
downside school choir**
britten psalm 150/LXT 6264/SXL 6264

0970/14-21 july 1966/emi sessions
new philharmonia orchestra/*london symphony orchestra/john barbirolli
elgar froissart overture; elegy for strings; sospori;
pomp and circumstance marches 2, 3 and 5/
ALP 2292/ASD 2292/SXLP 30456
*delius song of summer; irmelin prelude/
ALP 2305/ASD 2302/ESD 7092

0971/18-20 july 1966/lyrita sessions
new philharmonia orchestra/norman del mar
bax symphony 6/SRCS 35

0972/21-22 july 1966/emi sessions
new philharmonia orchestra/adrian boult/ ambrosian singers
holst the planets/ALP 2301/ASD 2301/SXLP 30456
recording completed in november 1966

0973/25-28 july 1966/emi sessions
halle orchestra/john barbirolli
sibelius symphony 2/ASD 2308
sibelius symphonies 5 & 7/ASD 2326

0974/24 august 1966/decca sessions
royal philharmonic orchestra/stanley black
tchaikovsky nutcracker suite; serenade for strings/
LK 4876/PFS 4126

0975/6-9 september 1966/argo sessions
academy of st martin in the fields/neville marriner/
*forbes robinson
rossini string sonatas 1, 3, 5 & 6/RG 506/ZRG 5506
*recital of handel arias/RG 604/ZRG 5604

0976/12 september 1966/decca sessions
new philharmonia orchestra/leopold stokowski
tchaikovsky symphony 5/LK 4882/PFS 4129/VIV 39

0977/16-17 september 1966/emi sessions
london symphony orchestra/alceo galliera/
elisabeth schwarzkopf
tchaikovsky letter scene from evgeny onegin/
SAX 5286/SXDW 3049

0978/19-20 september 1966/decca sessions
london symphony orchestra/leopold stokowski/
john alldis choir/soloists
handel selection from messiah/
LK 4840/PFS 4113/SPA 284

0979/28-29 september 1966/emi sessions
new philharmonia orchestra/antal dorati/
yehudi menuhin
bartok viola concerto/ASD 2323

0980/11-17 october 1966/decca sessions
london symphony orchestra/istvan kertesz
dvorak symphony 4; amid nature overture/
LXT 6257/SXL 6257/JB 113
dvorak symphony 3; husitska overture/
LXT 6290/SXL 6290/JB 112

0981/18-22 october 1966/emi sessions
new philharmonia orchestra/malcolm sergeant
walton symphony 1/ALP 2299/ASD 2299/SXLP 30138

0982/24-27 october 1966/argo sessions
elizabethan singers/roger norrington/soloists
choral works by schütz/RG 527/ZRG 6527

0983/8-11 november 1966/argo sessions
academy of st martin in the fields/neville marriner/
erna spoorenberg
recital of mozart arias/RG 524/ZRG 6524

0984/10-11 november 1966/decca sessions
jacques orchestra/myer fredman/ambrosian singers
works by rubbra and still/LXT 6281/SXL 6281

0985/16-17 november 1966/emi sessions
new philharmonia orchestra/rafael frühbeck de burgos
stravinsky fireworks/TWO 239/CFP 40348/ESD 7019
ravel bolero/ESD 7019

0986/16-18 november 1966/emi sessions
new philharmonia orchestra/wilhelm pitz/
new philharmonia chorus
choral works by brahms, wolf, mozart, beethoven
and van nuffel/ASD 2325

0987/21-22 november & 1-3 december 1966/
decca sessions
london symphony orchestra/istvan kertesz
dvorak symphony 1/LXT 6288/SXL 6288/JB 110
dvorak symphony 2/LXT 6289/SXL 6289/JB 111
dvorak symphony 9; othello overture/
LXT 6291/SXL 6291/JB 118

0988/25-26 november 1966/decca sessions
royal philharmonic orchestra/stanley black
sputniks for orchestra/LK 4899/PFS 4133

0989/6-9 december 1966/decca sessions
london philharmonic orchestra/*new philharmonia orchestra/antal dorati
waltzes by johann strauss/LK 4850/PFS 4117/VIV 2
*dvorak symphony 9/LK 4880/PFS 4128/JB 37

0990/19-20 december 1966/decca sessions
english chamber orchestra/benjamin britten/ *peter pears
britten frank bridge variations; *les illuminations/ LXT 6316/SXL 6316

0991/21-22 december 1966/argo sessions
purcell consort/grayston burgess/choir of all saints margaret street
mediaeval christmas carols/RG 526/ZRG 6526

0992/28-31 december 1966/emi sessions
halle orchestra/john barbirolli
sibelius symphony 1/ASD 2366
viennese night/TWO 180
berlioz carnaval romain overture/SJB 103

0993/4-5 january 1967/decca sessions
new philharmonia orchestra/charles munch
bizet carmen & l'arlesienne suites/
LK 4877/PFS 4127/SDD 492
respighi fontane di roma; pini di roma/
LK 4886/PFS 4131

0994/23-26 january 1967/decca sessions
tom krause/pentti koskimies (piano)
recital of songs by sibelius/LXT 6314/SXL 6314

0995/24-25 january 1967/argo sessions
john alldis choir/john alldis
choral works by bruckner, messiaen, schoenberg
and debussy/RG 523/ZRG 523
tippett the weeping babe/RG 535/ZRG 535

0996/8-9 february 1967/rca sessions
london symphony orchestra/andre previn
nielsen symphony 1; saul & david act 2 prelude/
LM 2961/LSC 2961/RB 6714/SB 6714/GL 42872

0997/15-24 february 1967/emi sessions
new philharmonia orchestra/otto klemperer
mahler symphony 9/SAX 5281-5282/SXDW 3021

0998/15-25 february 1967/emi sessions
**new philharmonia orchestra/franco ferraris/
franco corelli**
recital of operatic arias/unpublished

0999/1-3 march 1967/decca sessions
josef suk/julius katchen (piano)
brahms violin sonatas 1-3 and fae scherzo/
LXT 6321/SXL 6321

1000/9-15 march 1967/emi sessions
new philharmonia orchestra/otto klemperer
bruckner symphony 5/SAX 5288-5289
mozart serenade K388/SAX 5290/CFP 41 44881

1001/22 and 29 march 1967/argo sessions
london symphony orchestra/colin davis
tippett symphony 2/RG 535/ZRG 535

1002/28-31 march 1967/readers digest sessions
**royal philharmonic orchestra/charles gerhardt/
earl wild**
faure ballade/PMC 7141
liszt un sospiro/RDM 2326/RDS 6326
*orchestra described for this recording as
metropolitan symphony orchestra*
**new philharmonia orchestra/christoph
von dohnanyi/earl wild**
dohnanyi variations on a nursery song/RDS 9451
**new philharmonia orchestra/jascha horenstein/
erich gruenberg**
beethoven violin concerto/RDS 9908

1003/4-6 april 1967/argo sessions
bbc symphony orchestra/norman del mar
gerhard concerto for orchestra; rawsthorne
symphony 3/RG 553/ZRG 553

1004/13 april 1967/readers digest session
**royal philharmonic orchestra/rudolf kempe/
alan civil**
strauss horn concerto 1/RDS 9634

1005/17-21 april 1967/readers digest sessions
national philharmonic orchestra/charles gerhardt
orchestral and concertante works by korngold, bruch,
kabalevsky, weinberger and rachmaninov/
all unpublished
**london symphony orchestra/alfred wallenstein/
itzhak perlman**
tchaikovsky violin concerto/RDS 9383

1006/27 april 1967/argo session
tuckwell horn quartet
tippett for four horns/RG 535/ZRG 535

1007/28-29 april & 2-11 may 1967/decca sessions
london symphony orchestra/georg solti
mahler symphony 9/MET 360-361/SET 360-361

1008/12-15 may 1967/decca sessions
regine crespin/john wustman (piano)
recital of french & german song/LXT 6333/SXL 6333

1009/17-18 may 1967/emi sessions
london symphony orchestra/jascha horenstein
tchaikovsky symphony 6/ASD 2332/MFP 57017

1010/17-20 may 1967/hmv angel sessions
new philharmonia orchestra/rafael frühbeck de burgos/philharmonia chorus/soloists
mozart requiem/SAN 193/SXLP 30237

1011/25-31 may 1967/argo sessions
academy of st martin in the fields/neville marriner/ *barry tuckwell/*alan stringer
*haydn horn concerto; trumpet concerto; allemandes and marches/RG 543/ZRG 543
mozart divertimenti K136-138; serenata notturna/ RG 554/ZRG 554

1012/5-6 june 1967/decca sessions
vladimir ashkenazy
mussorgsky pictures from an exhibition/ LXT 6328/SXL 6328

1013/10 june 1967/emi session
new philharmonia orchestra/frederick prausnitz
schoenberg chamber symphony 2/ASD 2349

1014/13 june 1967/argo sessions
academy of st martin in the fields/
neville marriner
mendelssohn octet/RG 569/ZRG 569

1015/16-19 june 1967/decca sessions
london symphony orchestra/leopold stokowski
stravinsky firebird suite; tchaikovsky marche slave;
mussorgsky night on bare mountain/
LK 4927/PFS 4139

1016/20-23 june 1967/decca sessions
ion voicu/monique haas (piano)
violin sonatas by prokofiev, debussy and
milhaud/LXT 6351/SXL 6351

1017/26 june-14 july 1967/decca sessions
english chamber orchestra/richard bonynge
handel overtures/LXT 6360/SXL 6360
sinfonias by j.c. bach/LXT 6397/SXL 6397

1018/27-30 june 1967/decca sessions
london symphony orchestra/zubin mehta/
vladimir ashkenazy
brahms piano concerto 2/LXT 6309/SXL 6309

1019/july 1967/unidentified sessions
unidentified performers and works

1020/4-7 july 1967/decca sessions
vladimir ashkenazy
beethoven piano sonata 29/LXT 6335/SXL 6335
mozart piano sonatas 8 and 18; rondo K511/
LXT 6439/SXL 6439
mozart recordings completed in october 1967

1021/17-27 july 1967/decca sessions
royal opera orchestra/richard bonynge/
royal opera chorus/soloists
donizetti la fille du regiment/MET 372-373/
SET 372-373

1022/29 july and 4 august 1967/world
record club sessions
london philharmonic orchestra/adrian boult
marches on parade/T 750/ST 570/CFP 173

1023/14-15 august 1967/rca sessions
london symphony orchestra/andre previn
rachmaninov symphony 3; the rock/LM 2990/
LSC 2990/RB 6729/SB 6729/LSB 4090

1024/17-19 august & 25 september 1967/emi sessions
new philharmonia orchestra/john barbirolli
mahler symphony 6/ASD 2376-2377/CFP 41 44243
schoenberg pelleas und melisande/ASD 2459

1025/29-30 august 1967/rca sessions
english chamber orchestra/andre previn/soloists
mozart der schauspieldirektor/
LM 3000/LSC 3000/SB 6764

1026/4-6 september 1967/decca sessions
michael portal/julius katchen (piano)
brahms clarinet sonata/unpublished

1027/11-18 september 1967/decca sessions
bracha eden/alexander tamir
bartok sonata for 2 pianos & percussion; poulenc
sonata for 2 pianos/LXT 6357/SXL 6357

1028/14-16 september 1967/rca sessions
london symphony orchestra/andre previn/
ambrosian singers/heather harper
vaughan williams symphony 7/LSC 3066/
RB 6736/SB 6736/RL 43371

1029/4-11 october 1967/decca sessions
london symphony orchestra/istvan kertesz/
*clifford curzon
brahms serenade 1/LXT 6340/SXL 6340/JB 86
*mozart piano concerto 24/LXT 6354/SXL 6354
*mozart piano concerto 27/unpublished

1030/20-21 september 1967/decca sessions
london symphony orchestra/leopold stokowski/
lso chorus/soloists
beethoven symphony 9/PFS 4183/VIV 1

1031/1-2 november 1967/decca sessions
new philharmonia orchestra/rafael frühbeck de burgos
albeniz suite espanola/LXT 6355/SXL 6355

1032/13-17 november 1967/argo sessions
academy of st martin in the fields/neville marriner
stravinsky apollon musagete; pulcinella suite/
RG 575/ZRG 575

1033/22-27 november 1967/lyrita sessions
london philharmonic orchestra/adrian boult/
*eric parkin/*john carol case
*ireland piano concerto; *these things shall be/SRCS 36
works by moeran, bax and holst/SRCS 37

1034/1-6 december 1967/decca sessions
london symphony orchestra/istvan kertesz/
*clifford curzon
*mozart piano concerto 23/LXT 6354/SXL 6354
*mozart piano concerto 26/unpublished
brahms serenade 2/LXT 6368/SXL 6368/JB 87

1035/7-15 december 1967/decca sessions
london symphony orchestra/benjamin britten/
ambrosian singers/soloists
britten billy budd/MET 379-381/SET 379-381

1036/18 december 1967/rca session for
readers digest
national philharmonic orchestra/charles gerhardt
howard hanson symphony 2/GL 25021

1037/27-28 december 1967/emi sessions
new philharmonia orchestra/john barbirolli/
janet baker
ravel sheherazade/ASD 2444

1038/1-6 january 1968/decca sessions
london symphony orchestra/georg solti/ambrosian
and wandsworth choirs/helen watts
mahler symphony 3/MET 385-386/SET 385-386

1039/8-12 january 1968/decca sessions
london symphony orchestra/richard bonynge/
*ossian ellis
*gliere harp concerto/SXL 6406
burgmüller la peri/SXL 6407

1040/18-20 january 1968/emi sessions
london symphony orchestra/david willcocks/
bach choir/soloists
vaughan williams sancta civitas; benedictus/ASD 2422

1041/23-25 january 1968/decca sessions
*london symphony orchestra/*hans schmidt-isserstedt/
vladimir ashkenazy
prokofiev piano sonata 8; 2 pieces from romeo
and juliet/LXT 6346/SXL 6346
*mozart piano concerti 6 and 20/LXT 6353/SXL 6353

1042/26-29 january & 9-12 february 1968/decca sessions
royal opera orchestra/edward downes/gwyneth jones
recital of opera arias by verdi/SXL 6376

1043/5-16 february 1968/decca sessions
london symphony orchestra/claudio abbado/
*dino ciani
mendelssohn symphonies 3 & 4/
LXT 6363/SXL 6363/JB 103
hindemith symphonic metamorphoses;
janacek sinfonietta/SXL 6398
*janacek concertino/unpublished
*solo piano pieces by weber/unpublished

1044/14-16 february 1968/emi sessions
new philharmonia orchestra/adrian boult/
*margaret price
vaughan williams norfolk rhapsody 1/ASD 2375
vaughan williams in the fen country;
*symphony 3/ASD 2393

1045/22 february-july 1968/decca sessions
royal opera orchestra/edward downes/reginald
goodall/rafael kubelik/georg solti/william walton/
john williams (guitar)/soloists
opera excerpts by beethoven, berlioz, britten,
mozart, mussorgsky, puccini, strauss, tippett,
verdi, wagner and walton/MET 392-393/SET 392-393
these recordings were made for the covent garden
opera anniversary album

1046/28-29 february 1968/decca sessions
new philharmonia orchestra/rafael frühbeck de burgos/ ambrosian singers/soloists
mendelssohn sommernachtstraum incidental music/
SXL 6404/JB 72

1047/6-16 march 1968/emi sessions
new philharmonia orchestra/rafael frühbeck de burgos
respighi fontane di roma; pini di roma/
TWO 239/CFP 40348
chabrier espana; turina rapsodia sinfonica/ESD 7019
espla la pagare pinta; turina la nacion del torero/
unpublished

1048/18-20 march & 1-5 april 1968/rca sessions
london symphony orchestra/andre previn
rimsky-korsakov scheherazade; selection from
tsar sultan/LSC 3042/SB 6774/GL 42703
vaughan williams symphonies 6 & 8/LSC 3114/SB 6769
vaughan williams england of elizabeth suite/
LSC 3280/SB 6842/GL 42953

1049/22-23 march 1968/decca sessions
julius katchen
beethoven piano sonata 32; bagatelles op 126/
SXL 6373

1050/29-30 march 1968/argo sessions
academy of st martin in the fields/neville marriner
mozart symphonies 13, 14, 15 & 16/RG 594/ZRG 594

1051/april 1968/argo sessions
don smithers/simon preston (organ)
works for trumpet by baroque composers/ZRG 601

1052/9-10 april 1968/argo sessions
academy of st martin in the fields/neville mariner
tchaikovsky serenade for strings; souvenir
de florence/ZRG 584
recording completed in october 1968

1053/16-17 april 1968/decca sessions
janos starker/julius katchen (piano)
brahms cello sonata 2/SXL 6589

1054/18-20 april 1968/readers digest sessions
new philharmonia orchestra/massimo freccia
respighi fontane di roma; feste romane/RD 4068
orchestra/douglas gamley
balakirev islamay/unpublished

1055/23 april 1968/emi sessions
new philharmonia orchestra/carlo maria giulini
brahms symphony 4/SLS 5241
recording completed in july 1968

1056/29-30 april 1968/readers digest sessions
new philharmonia orchestra/jascha horenstein
tchaikovsky symphony 5/RDS 9364/GL 25007

1057/1-2 may 1968/decca sessions
london symphony orchestra/sixten ehrling
berwald symphonies in c & e flat/LXT 6374/SXL 6374

1058/8-9 may 1968/decca sessions
**london symphony orchestra/richard bonynge/
joan sutherland**
vocal works by gliere, gretchaninov & stravinsky/
SXL 6406

1059/10-14 may 1968/decca sessions
london symphony orchestra/istvan kertesz
dvorak wind serenade/LXT 6368/SXL 6368/JB 87
respighi pini di roma; fontane di roma;
gli uccelli/SXL 6401/JB 59

1060/14 may 1968/decca session
royal opera orchestra/henry lewis/marilyn horne
unidentified arias/unpublished

1061/15-18 may 1968/decca sessions
london symphony orchestra/istvan kertesz/wandsworth and edinburgh festival choirs/peter ustinov
kodaly hary janos/SET 399-400

1062/18 may 1968/decca sessions
london symphony orchestra/istvan kertesz/ edinburgh festival choir/soloists
mozart masonic works/SXL 6409
recordings completed in november 1968

1063/20-24 may 1968/decca sessions
thea king/julius katchen (piano)
brahms clarinet sonata/unpublished

1064/31 may-5 june 1968/decca sessions
israel philharmonic orchestra/zubin mehta
tchaikovsky symphony 5/SXL 6380
dvorak symphony 7/SXL 6381

1065/10-13 june 1968/decca sessions
werner krenn/georg fischer (piano)
mozart masonic arias/SXL 6409

1066/19-20 june 1968/decca sessions
new philharmonia orchestra/leopold stokowski
berlioz symphonie fantastique/PFS 4160/SDD 495
wagner rienzi overture/unpublished

1067/20-24 june 1968/decca sessions
new philharmonia orchestra/claudio abbado/
ambrosian singers/james king
brahms rinaldo; schicksalslied/SXL 6386

1068/1-9 july 1968/hmv angel sessions
new philharmonia orchestra/rafael frühbeck
de burgos/new philharmonia chorus/soloists
mendelssohn elijah/SAN 212-214

1069/19 july-2 august 1968/decca sessions
english chamber orchestra/richard bonynge/
***ambrosian singes/*soloists**
*mozart don giovanni/SET 412-415
concerti by salieri/SXL 6397

1070/5-6 august 1968/decca sessions
academy of st martin in the fields/neville marriner/
george malcolm
harpsichord concerti by haydn and j.c.bach/SXL 6385

1071/19-29 august 1968/decca sessions
bracha eden/alexander tamir
piano duets by stravinsky, brahms and dvorak/
SXL 6389 and SXL 6403

1072/3-5 september 1968/rca sessions
london symphony orchestra/andre previn/
itzhak perlman
lalo symphonie espagnole; ravel tzigane/
LSC 3073/SB 6800/GL 11329

1073/10-14 september 1968/decca sessions
bernadette greevy/paul hamburger (piano)
chain of lullabies; folksong arrangements/SXL 6411

1074/10-18 september 1968/emi sessions
london symphony orchestra/george szell/
elisabeth schwarzkopf
mozart concert arias; strauss orchesterlieder/
ASD 2493

1075/18-29 september 1968/emi sessions
new philharmonia orchestra/otto klemperer
mahler symphony 7/SLS 781/CFPD 41 44423

1076/23-26 september 1968/emi sessions
london philharmonic orchestra/adrian boult/
***london philharmonic choir/*soloists**
*vaughan williams symphony 1; the wasps suite/
SLS 780
vaughan williams symphony 8/ASD 2469
recording of symphony 8 completed in
december 1968 and march 1969

1077/7-11 october 1968/argo sessions
academy of st martin in the fields/neville marriner
works by donizetti and rossini/ZRG 603
works by baermann, strauss and wagner/ZRG 604

1078/15-16 october 1968/decca sessions
weller string quartet
beethoven string quartet 12; haydn string
quartet op 103/SXL 6423

1079/4-7 november 1968/argo sessions
noelle barker/robert sherlaw johnson (piano)/
*louis halsey singers
*partsongs by delius and elgar/ZRG 607
messiaen harawi/ZRG 608

1080/11-13 november 1968/decca sessions
edinburgh festival chorus/istvan kertesz/
werner krenn
mozart masonic choral works/SXL 6409

1081/18-22 november 1968/decca sessions
new philharmonia orchestra/ernest ansermet
stravinsky firebird performance & rehearsal/
SET 468

1082/26-29 november 1968/decca sessions
london ymphony orchestra/istvan kertesz/
julius katchen
works for piano and orchestra by ravel,
prokofiev and gershwin/SXL 6411

1083/9-14 december 1968/decca sessions
london symphony orchestra/istvan kertesz/
ambrosian singers/soloists
dvorak requiem mass/SET 416-417

1084/16-23 december 1968 & 7 february 1969/
emi sessions
london philharmonic orchestra/adrian boult/
london philharmonic choir/soloists
elgar the kingdom/SLS 939

1085/30-31 december 1968 & 11 january 1969/
decca sessions
new philharmonia orchestra/carlos paita
wagner meistersinger overture; fliegende holländer
overture; tristan prelude & liebestod/PFS 4158

1086/3-6 january 1969/argo sessions
bbc symphony orchestra/norman del mar/soloists
works by elizabeth lutyens & nicholas maw/ZRG 622

1087/7-8 january 1969/argo sessions
academy of st martin in the fields/neville marriner/
brenda lucas/john ogdon
piano concerti by mendelssohn/ZRG 605

1088/8-9 january 1969/argo sessions
marisa robles/delme string quartet
chamber works by ravel, debussy and bax

1089/13-16 january 1969/decca sessions
barry tuckwell/margaret kitchin (piano)
chamber works for horn and piano/unpublished

1090/16-22 january 1969/decca sessions
**london symphony orchestra/claudio abbado/
nicolai ghiaurov**
recital of verdi opera arias/SXL 6443/GRV 6

1091/23-25 january 1969/emi sessions
**new philharmonia orchestra/david willcocks/
bach choir/soloists**
vaughan williams five tudor portraits/ASD 2489

1092/3-5 february 1969/decca sessions
ivan davis
the art of the piano virtuoso/SXL 6415

1093/10-12 february 1969/decca sessions
royal philharmonic orchestra/eric rogers/chorus
music of ketelby/PFS 4170

1094/14 february 1969/decca sessions
**london symphony orchestra/erich leinsdorf/
chorus**
wagner tannhäuser overture & venusberg;
strauss der rosenkavalier suite/PFS 4187

1095/15 february-6 march 1969/decca sessions
**new philharmonia orchestra/anton guadagno/
*richard bonynge/renata tebaldi**
an operatic anthology/SET 439-440
*french opera overtures/SXL 6422

1096/20-28 february & 4-7 march 1969/
decca sessions
**english chamber orchestra/richard bonynge/
ambrosian singers/soloists**
handel messiah/SET 465-467

1097/10-11 march 1969/rca sessions
**london symphony orchestra/andre previn/
*james oliver buswell**
vaughan williams symphony 4; *concerto
accademico/LSC 3178/SB 6801

1098/1-25 april 1969/decca sessions
new philharmonia orchestra/richard bonynge/ ambrosian singers/soloists
meyerbeer les huguenots/SET 460-463

1099/17-18 april 1969/emi sessions
new philharmonia orchestra/rafael frühbeck de burgos/soloists
granados la maya y el ruisenor; villa-lobos bachianas brasilieras 5 & 7/unpublished

1100/23 april 1969/decca sessions
new philharmonia orchestra/george hurst/ *david ward
wagner rienzi overture; lohengrin preludes acts 1 & 3; *wotan's farewell & magic fire music from die walküre/PFS 4205

1101/28-30 april 1969/oiseau lyre sessions
melos ensemble/soloists
chamber works by brahms, schumann and schubert/SOL 314

1102/9-14 may 1969/argo sessions
heinrich schütz choir/roger norrington
choral works by berlioz/ZRG 635

1103/12-16 may 1969/decca sessions
london symphony orchestra/alexander gibson/
jean-rodolphe kars
delius piano concerto; debussy fantaisie/SXL 6435

1104/20-23 may 1969/decca sessions
london philharmonic orchestra/bernard herrmann
orchestral showpieces by liszt, sibelius, dukas
and saint-saens/PFS 4169

1105/27-30 may 1969/emi sessions
halle orchestra/john barbirolli/*evelyn rothwell
sibelius symphony 4/ASD 2494
purcell suite for strings; *schafe können
sicher weiden/ASD 2496
sibelius symphony 3/ASD 2648

1106/9-10 june 1969/argo sessions
monteverdi choir/john eliot gardiner
*academy of st martin in the fields/neville marriner
*concerti by pre-classical composes/ZRG 644
motets by monteverdi and gesualdo/ZRG 645

1107/16-17 june 1969/decca sessions
royal philharmonic orchestra/leopold stokowski/
*band of the grenadier guards/chorus
borodin polovtaian dances; stravinsky pastorale;
*tchaikovsky 1812 overture/PFS 4189

1108/27 june-23 july 1969/decca sessions
royal opera orchestra/georg solti/
royal opera chorus/soloists
gluck orfeo ed euridice/SET 443-444

1109/2 and 5 july 1969/decca sessions
london symphony orchestra/istvan kertesz
kodaly peacock variations/SXL 6497

1110/15-22 july 1969/decca sessions
royal philharmonic orchestra/henry lewis/
*marilyn horne
*wagner wesendonck-lieder; mahler
kindertotenlieder/SXL 6446
beethoven symphony 6/PFS 4188

1111/4-6 august 1969/emi sessions
halle orchestra/john barbirolli/*evelyn rothwell
sibelius rakastava; romance in c/ASD 2494
*marcello oboe concerto/ASF 2496
grieg lyric suite; sigurd jorsalfar suite/ASD 2773
sibelius scenes historiques/SXLP 30162

1112/27 september 1969/emi session
london symphony orchestra/john barbirolli
wagner meistersinger overture/ASD 2642

1113/1 october 1969/decca session
london symphony orchestra/richard bonynge
overtures by handel/SXL 6496
recordings completed in january and july 1970

1114/5 november 1969/emi sssions
london philharmonic orchestra/adrian boult/soloists
vaughan williams serenade to music/ASD 2538

1115/18-21 november 1969/emi sessions
london philharmonic orchestra/adrian boult/
london philharmonic choir/norma burrowes
vaughan williams symphony 7/ASD 2631/ED 29 12041

1116/24-25 november 1969/decca sessions
royal philharmonic orchestra/eric rogers
the music of leonard bernstein/PFS 4211

1117/1-5 december 1969/decca sessions
london symphony orchestra/richard bonynge
homage to pavlova/SET 523-524

1118/8-11 december 1969/decca sessions
pascal roge
piano works by liszt/SXL 6485

1119/18-23 december 1969/emi sessions
london philharmonic orchestra/adrian boult/
*london philharmonic choir/*peter katin
vaughan williams symphony 9; *fantasy on
the old hundredth/ASD 2581

1120/31 december 1969-1 january 1970/emi sessions
london symphony orchestra/alexander gibson
overtures by berlioz/SXLP 30128

1121/9-10 and 23 january 1970/decca sessions
english chamber prchestra/david atherton
works by welsh composers/SXL 6468

1122/12-21 january 1970/decca sessions
english chamber orchestra/richard bonynge/
ambrosian singers/soloists
donizetti l'elisir d'amore/SET 503-505
recording completed in july 1970

1123/26 january-4 february 1970/decca sessions
alicia de larrocha
piano music by spanish composers/SXL 6466
piano music by mendelssohn & grieg/SXL 6467

1124/6-21 february 1970/emi sessions
new philharmonia orchestra/otto klemperer
bruckner symphony 9/ASD 2719

1125/9-16 february 1970/rca sessions
london symphony orchestra/andre previn/
lso chorus/soloists
vaughan williams symphony 1/LSC 3170/SER 5585
vaughan williams tuba concerto/LSC 3281/SB 6861
recordings completed in may 1970

1126/12 and 25 february 1970/decca sessions
english chamber orchestra/benjamin britten/
peter pears
bach cantatas 55 and 189/unpublished

1127/18-21 february 1970/emi sessions
new philharmonia orchestra/david willcocks/
bach choir/soloists
herbert howells hymnus paradisi/ASD 2600

1128/2-3 march 1970/decca sessions
royal philharmonic orchestra/henry lewis
strauss don juan; till eulenspiegel/PFS 4215
works by aaron copland/unpublished

1129/25-26 march 1970/decca sessions
london symphony orchestra/andre previn/
vladimir ashkenazy
rachmaninov piano concerto 1/SXL 6554

1130/31 march-10 april 1970/emi sessions
london symphony orchestra/charles mackerras/
montserrat caballe
opera arias by puccini/ASD 2632/SXLP 30562
opera arias by donizetti, giordano, meyerbeer
and verdi/ASD 2723

1131/11-15 may 1970/argo sessions
academy of st martin in the fields/neville marriner/
*john wilbraham
*trumpet concerti by albrechtsberger, hummel
and leopold mozart/ZRG 669
dvorak serenade for strings; grieg holberg suite/
ZRG 670

1132/21-22 may 1970/emi sessions
halle orchestra/john barbirolli
sibelius symphony 6/ASD 2648
grieg norwegian dances/ASD 2773

1133/26-30 may 1970/decca sessions
royal philharmonic orchestra/henry lewis/
*ivan davis
*tchaikovsky piano concerto 1/PFS 4196
strauss also sprach zarathustra/PFS 4202
*rachmaninov piano concerto 2/PFS 4214

1134/1-3 june 1970/decca sessions
**london symphony orchestra/andre previn/
kyung wha chung**
tchaikovsky and sibelius violin concerti/SXL 6493

1135/5 june 1970/decca sessions
**royal philharmonic orchestra/henry lewis/
chorus/soloists**
bizet scenes from carmen/PFS 4204

1136/15 june 1970/decca sessions
new philharmonia orchestra/erich leinsdorf
stravinsky petrushka/PFS 4207/VIV 42

1137/16-17 june 1970/emi sessions
**london symphony orchestra/lorin maazel/
sviatoslav richter**
prokofiev piano concerto 5/ASD 2744

1138/22-26 june 1970/decca sessions
**london symphony orchestra/leopold
stokowski/*lso chorus**
*works by messiaen and ives/PFS 4203
debussy la mer; ravel daphnis et chloe second
suite; berlioz danse des sylphes from
damnation de faust/PFS 4220/JB 136

1139/29 june-2 july 1970/decca sessions
london symphony orchestra/istvan kertesz
dvorak symphonic variations; the golden spinning wheel/SXL 6510
dvorak the water goblin; the noonday witch/SXL 6543

1140/7-11 july 1970/decca sessions
english chamber orchestra/richard bonynge
eighteenth century overtures/SXL 6531

1141/15-17 july 1970/emi sessions
halle orchestra/john barbirolli/*ambrosian singers
delius brigg fair; *appalachia/ASD 2835
cd reissue of appalachia includes rehearsal sequence

1142/4-14 august 1970/emi sessions
london symphony orchestra/adrian boult
brahms symphony 3; tragic overture/ASD 2660
vaughan williams job/ASD 2673
elgar enigma variations; vaughan williams greensleeves fantasia; english folksong suite/ASD 2750

1143/17-28 august 1970/decca sessions
london philharmonic orchestra/lamberto gardelli/ambrosian singers/soloists
verdi macbeth/SET 510-512

1144/8-9 september 1970/decca sessions
london symphony orchestra/istvan kertesz/brighton festival & wandsworth choirs/lajos kozma
kodaly psalmus hungaricus/SXL 6497/JB 122

1145/15-17 september 1970/emi sessions
new philharmonia orchestra/adrian boult/*josef suk
beethoven coriolan overture; *violin concerto/
ASD 2667/CFP 41 44091

1146/27-30 september 1970/decca sessions
royal philharmonic orchestra/jacques loussier
bach brandenburg concerto 2/PFS 4253
recording completed in august 1971

1147/20-23 october 1970/decca sessions
london symphony orchestra/andre previn/ vladimir ashkenazy
rachmaninov piano concerto 2/SXL 6554
rachmaninov piano concerto 4/SXL 6556

1148/22 and 26-27 october 1970/decca sessions
london philharmonic orchestra/francois huybrechts
janacek taras bulba; lachian dances/SXL 6507

1149/5-20 november 1970/hmv angel sessions
london philharmonic orchestra/adrian boult/
london philharmonic choir/soloists
vaughan williams the pilgrim's progress/
SAN 297-299/SLS 959/SLS 143 5133
recording completed in january 1971

1150/25 november 1970/decca sessions
london philharmonic orchestra/bernard herrmann
works by impressionist composers/PFS 4224/SPA 570
recording completed in december 1970

1151/27 november 1970/decca sessions
london symphony orchestra/lawrence foster/
radu lupu
beethoven piano concerto 3/SXL 6053
recording completed in december 1970

1152/1-4 december 1970/decca sessions
english chamber orchestra/benjamin britten/
wandsworth school choir/soloists
britten owen wingrave/SET 501-502

1153/13-15 december 1970/oiseau lyre sessions
stuart burrows/john constable (piano)
song recital/SOL 323

1154/28-31 december 1970/decca sessions
london symphony orchestra/istvan kertesz/
lso chorus/soloists
rossini stabat mater/SXL 6534

1155/1-2 january 1971/argo sessions
robert tear/philip ledger (piano)
recital of songs by tchaikovsky/ZRG 707
recordings completed in december 1971

1156/2-4 january 1971/decca sessions
new philharmonia orchestra/leone magiera/
ambrosian singers/luciano pavarotti
operatic recital/SXL 6498

1157/6-9 january 1971/rca sessions
london symphony orchestra/andre previn/
*heather harper
vaughan williams symphony 9/LSC 3280/SB 6842
*vaughan williams symphony 3/LSC 3281/SB 6861

1158/8-9 january 1971/argo sessions
purcell consort of viols/grayston burgess
elizabeth on stage/ZRG 738

1159/11-14 january 1971/decca sessions
london symphony orchestra/david atherton/soloists
concerti by alan hoddinot & william mathias/SXL 6513

1160/8-19 january 1971/decca sessions
royal philharmonic orchestra/anatole fistoulari
tchaikovsky symphony 4/PFS 4225

1161/25 january-18 february 1971/hmv angel sessions
new philharmonia orchestra/otto klemperer/
john alldis choir/soloists
mozart cosi fan tutte/SAN 310-313/SLS 961

1162/26 february-2 march 1971/emi sessions
london philharmonic orchestra/adrian boult
vaughan williams symphony 2/ASD 2740

1163/15-20 march and 21 april 1971/
hmv angel sessions
london philharmonic orchestra/charles groves/
london philharmonic choir/soloists
delius a mass of life/SAN 300-301/SLS 958

1164/22-23 march 1971/decca sessions
london symphony orchestra/stanley black
orchestral works by dvorak & smetana/PFS 4245

1165/29-30 march 1971/decca sessions
london symphony orchestra/andre previn/
vladimir ashkenazy
rachmaninov piano concerto 3/SXL 6555

1166/1-8 april 1971/decca sessions
new philharmonia orchestra/anton guadagno/
ambrosian singers/renata tebaldi
recital of sacred arias/SXL 6524

1167/19-20 april 1971/decca sessions
royal philharmonic orchestra/erich leinsdorf
mahler symphony 1/PFS 4232

1168/26-27 april 1971/decca sessions
london philharmonic orchestra/lorin maazel/
vladimir ashkenazy
scriabin poem of fire; piano concerto/SXL 6527

1169/10-14 may 1971/argo sessions
academy of st martin in the fields/neville mariner
works by vaughan williams/ZRG 696
handel water music & fireworks music/ZRG 697

1170/19-21 may 1971/decca sessions
london symphony orchestra/richard bonynge
orchestral music from french opera/SXL 6541

1171/25-28 may 1971/rca sssions
london symphony orchestra/andre previn
vaughan williams symphony 5; the wasps overture/
LSC 3244/SB 6856

1172/14-26 june 1971/decca sessions
london symphony orchestra/richard bonynge/
ambrosian singers/soloists
verdi rigoletto/SET 542-544
recording completed in december 1971
and august 1972

1173/28 june-16 july 1971/decca sessions
royal opera orchestra/richard bonynge/
royal opera chorus/soloists
donizetti lucia di lammermoor/SET 528-530

1174/19-22 july 1971/emi sessions
academy of st martin in the fields/neville mariner
walton façade/ASD 2786
english string music/ASD 2831

1175/3-5 august 1971/decca sessions
london festival orchestra/robert sharples
overtures by suppe/PFS 4236

1176/2-3 september 1971/decca sessions
itzhak perlman/vladimir ashkenazy (piano)
beethoven violin sonatas 5 and 9/unpublished

1177/6-11 and 22 september 1971/
readers digest sessions
**national philharmonic orchestra/eric robinson/
douglas gamley/charles gerhardt**
eric robinson's world of music/RDS 6681-6690
recordings completed in october 1971

1178/17-18 september 1971/decca sessions
ivan davis
recital of chopin piano works/PFS 4262

1179/21-23 september 1971/argo sessions
thea musgrave
piano works by musgrave, bennett and williamson/ZRG 704

1180/4-6 october 1971/decca sessions
royal philharmonic orchestra/edward downes/ivan davis
liszt piano concerti 1 and 2/PFS 4252

1181/13 october 1971/decca sessions
vladimir ashkenazy
schumann kreisleriana/SXL 6642

1182/25-27 october 1971/argo sessions
purcell consort of viols/grayston burgess
works by vecchi/ZRG 709

1183/1-2 november 1971/emi sessions
london symphony orchestra/andre previn/
lso chorus/anna reynolds
prokofiev alexander nevsky/ASD 2800

1184/15-17 november 1971/emi sessions
london symphony orchestra/rafael frühbeck
de burgos/yehudi menuhin
mendelssohn violin concerti/ASD 2809

1185/16-18 november 1971/emi sessions
menuhin festival orchestra/yehudi menuhin
beethoven violin concerto; violin
romance 1/585 5622

1186/29-30 november 1971/decca sessions
**london symphony orchestra/andre previn/
vladimir ashkenazy**
rachmaninov paganini rhapsody/SXL 6556

1187/6-8 december 1971/decca sessions
london festival orchestra/stanley black
prokofiev symphony 1; march & scherzo from
love for 3 oranges/PFS 4244

1188/9-10 december 1971/decca sessions
**london festival brass ensemble/elgar howarth/
alan civil**
the magnificent sound of baroque brass/PFS 4290

1189/13 december 1971/argo sessions
academy of st martin in the fields/neville marriner
trumpet concerti by pre-classical composers/
unpublished

1190/14-16 december 1971/argo sessions
allegri string quartet
frank bridge string quartets 3 & 4/ZRG 714

1191/17-21 december 1971/emi sessions
london symphony orchestra/adrian boult/yehudi menuhin
bruch violin concerti 1 and 2/ASD 2832

1192/3 january 1972/decca session
london festival orchestra/stanley black/george raft
prokofiev peter and the wolf/PFS 4244

1193/4 january 1972/decca session
london symphony orchestra/bernard herrmann
ives symphony 2/PFS 4251

1194/6-7 january 1972/rca sessions
london symphony orchestra/andre previn
vaughan williams symphony 2/LSC 3282/SB 6860

1195/17-18 january 1972/kroll tv productions
london symphony orchestra/richard bonynge/
joan sutherland
opera arias filmed for vhs issue in usa only

1196/28 january-3 february 1972/decca sessions
london philharmonic orchestra/silvio varviso/
sherrill milnes
italian opera arias/SXL 6609

1197/8-10 february 1972/decca sessions
london sinfonietta/david atherton/jane manning
harrison birtwistle the fields of sorrow/HEAD 7

1198/12 february 1972/emi sessions
early music consort of london/david munrow
music for henry VIII/CSDA 9001

1199/16-21 february 1972/decca sessions
royal philharmonic orchestra/henry lewis/
ambrosian singers/marilyn horne
rossini scenes from le siege de corinth and
la donna del lago/SXL 6584

1200/21-25 february 1972/decca sessions
london philharmonic orchestra/georg solti
elgar symphony 1/SXL 6569

1201/14-28 february 1972/argo sessions
heinrich schütz choir/roger norrington/
felicity palmer
motets by mendelssohn/ZRG 716

1202/28 february 1972/decca sessions
itzhak perlman/vladimir ashkenazy (piano)
beethoven violin sonatas 5 and 9/unpublished

1203/2-14 march 1972/emi sessions
london philharmonic orchestra/adrian boult
brahms symphony 1/ASD 2871
brahms symphony 4; academic festival overture/ASD 2901

1204/9 march 1972/decca sessions
**new philharmonia orchestra/lorin maazel/
israela margalit**
chopin piano concerto 1/PFS 4311

1205/22-23 march 1972/decca sessions
london symphony orchestra/david atherton
works by alan hoddinott/SXL 6570

1206/28-30 march 1972/emi sessions
london philharmonic orchestra/adrian boult
schubert symphony 9/ASD 2856/SXLP 30538

1207/5 april 1972/decca session
**royal philharmonic orchestra/leone magiera/
luciano pavarotti**
puccini e lucevan le stelle from tosca/SXL 6649
opera arias by gounod & verdi/unpublished

1208/7-8 april 1972/decca sessions
vladimir ashkenazy
rachmaninov etudes tableaux; corelli variations/
SXL 6604
recordings completed in january 1973

1209/10-12 april 1972/decca sessions
wilbye consort/peter pears
madrigals by wilbye, gibbons & tomkins/SXL 6659
recordings completed in may 1973

1210/10-14 april 1972/decca sessions
**philip jones ensemble/john eliot gardiner/
monteverdi choir**
christmas in venice/SDD 363

1211/22 april 1972/decca sessions
**english chamber orchestra/daniel barenboim/
fou t'song/vladimir ashkenazy**
mozart concerti for 2 & 3 pianos/SXL 6716

1212/1-6 may 1972/emi sessions
london symphony orchestra/andre previn/
***ambrosian singers**
*tchaikovsky the nutcracker/SLS 834
tchaikovsky romeo and juliet; marche slave;
*1812 overture/ASD 2894

1213/9-12 may 1972/decca sessions
london philharmonic orchestra/rafael frühbeck
de burgos/alicia de larrocha
works for piano and orchestra by khachaturian
and franck/SXL 6599
faure fantaisie/SXL 6680

1214/15 and 20 may 1972/decca sessions
royal philharmonic orchestra/rudolf kempe/
kyung wha chung
bruch violin concerto 1; scottish fantasy/SXL 6573

1215/17-18 may 1972/argo sessions
bbc symphony orchestra/pierre boulez/
felicity palmer
messiaen poemes pour mi/ZRG 703

1216/3-7 june 1972/emi sessions
academy of st martin in the fields/neville marriner/ elly ameling
bach cantatas 202 and 209/ASD 2876
academy of st martin in the fields/neville marriner/ john wilbraham
recital of trumpet concerti/ASD 2938

1217/17 june 1972/decca session
london symphony orchestra/stanley black
khachaturian gayaneh suite/PFS 4349/VIV 54

1218/29 june-1 july 1972/decca sessions
vladimir ashkenazy
beethoven piano sonata 31/SXL 6630
chopin etudes op 10/SXL 6710
beethoven recording completed in october 1973

1219/3-6 july 1972/decca sessions
renata tebaldi/richard bonynge (piano)
recital of songs by italian composers/SXL 6579

1220/10-26 august 1972/decca sessions
new philharmonia orchestra/richard bonynge/
*joan sutherland
*recital of songs & ballads with orchestra/SXL 6619
delibes sylvia/SXL 6635-6636
*puccini vissi d'arte from tosca/D65 D3

1221/12-24 august 1972/decca sessions
london philharmonic orchestra/richard bonynge/
john alldis & wandsworth choirs/soloists
puccini turandot/SET 561-563

1222/14-17 and 25 august 1972/decca sessions
london symphony orchestra/richard bonynge
auber marco spada/SXL 6707

1223/6 september 1972/electrola session
new philharmonia orchestra/okko kamu/
ulf hoelscher
tchaikovsky serenade melancholique/SHZE 369

1224/22-23 september 1972/decca sessions
dartington string quartet
unidentified string quartets.unpublished

1225/27-29 september 1972/decca sessions
london symphony orchestra/andre previn/
kyung wha chung
violin concerti by walton & stravinsky/SXL 6601

1226/19-25 october 1972/decca sessions
royal opera orchestra/nello santi/
john alldis choir/maria chiara
opera arias by verdi/SXL 6605

1227/28 october 1972/argo sessions
allegri string quartet/orion piano trio
chamber works by alexander goehr/ZRG 748

1228/1-2 november 1972/argo sessions
ensemble/david munrow/christopher
hogwood (harpsichord)
the amorous flute/ZRG 746
recordings completed in february 1973

1229/6-7 november 1972/emi sessions
london bach players/paul steinitz/soloists
bach cantata 131; handel wedding cantata/
CSD 3741

1230/9-11 and 29 november 1972/oiseau lyre sessions
the music party/alan hacker (clarinet)
clarinet quintets by hummel & crusell/DSLO 501

1231/22-25 november 1972/emi sessions
london symphony orchestra/carlo maria giulini/
***lso chorus/*soloists**
beethoven symphonies 8 and *9/SLS 841

1232/29 november-1 december 1972/decca sessions
vladimir ashkenazy
schumann humoreske/SXL 6642
scriabin piano sonatas 3, 4, 5 & 9/SXL 6705
beethoven piano sonata 8/SXL 6706

1233/6-8 december 1972/kroll tv productions
london symphony orchestra/richard bonynge/
joan sutherland
opera arias filmed for vhs issue in usa only

1234/9 and 20-21 december 1972/decca sessions
kyung wha chung/unidentified pianist
violin sonatas by bach & saint-saens/unpublished

1235/2 january 1973/decca sessions
matrix/alan hacker/jane manning
harrison birtwistle death of orpheus/HEAD 7

1236/3-11 january 1973/emi sessions
london symphony orchestra/andre previn
rachmaninov symphony 2/ASD 2889
beethoven symphony 5; prometheus overture/
ASD 2960

1237/13-16 january 1973/decca sessions
london symphony orchestra/david atherton
orchestral works by william mathias/SXL 6607

1238/17-18 january 1973/decca sessions
new philharmonia orchestra/leopold stokowski
tchaikovsky capriccio italien/PFS 4333
beethoven symphony 7; egmont overture/PFS 4342

1239/19-20 january 1973/argo sssions
dartington string quartet
hugh wood string quartets 1 & 2/ZRG 750

1240/22-24 january 1973/decca sessions
alicia de larrocha
piano music by isaac albeniz/SXL 6586-6587

1241/30 january 1973/decca sessions
london symphony orchestra/andre previn/radu lupu
grieg piano concerto/SXL 6624

1242/6-9 february 1973/decca sessions
kingsway symphony orchestra/alan civil
bizet carmen for orchestra/PFS 4348

1243/12-13 february 1973/decca sessions
london sinfonietta/david atherton/
lso chorus/soloists
anthony milner roman spring/SXL 6699

1244/17 february 1973/decca sessions
london symphony orchestra/david atherton/
welsh national opera chorus
william mathias a carol sequence/SXL 6607

1245/21-23 february 1973/oiseau lyre sessions
london philharmonic orchestra/john pritchard/
stuart burrows
arias from mozart operas/DSLO 13
recording completed in june 1974

1246/28 february 1973/argo sessions
vesuvius ensemble
connolly triad III/ZRG 747

1247/12-17 march 1973/decca sessions
bracha eden/alexander tamir
ravel works for piano duo/SXL 6618

1248/13-15 march 1973/decca sessions
**royal philharmonic orchestra/andrew davis/
martin jones/barry tuckwell**
hoddinott piano concerto; horn concerto;
symphony 5/SXL 6606

1249/19-20 march 1973/argo sessions
april cantelo/paul hamburger (piano)
vocal works by hugh wood/ZRG 750

1250/2-5 april 1973/argo sessions
**philip jones wind ensemble/roger norrington/
heinrich schütz choir**
bruckner mass 2/ZRG 710

1251/16-18 april 1973/emi sessions
london philharmonic orchestra/adrian boult/
london philharmonic choir/soloists
vaughan williams dona nobis pacem; towards the unknown region/ASD 2962

1252/26-27 april 1973/kroll tv productions
london symphony orchestra/richard bonynge/
joan sutherland
opera arias filmed for vhs issue in usa only

1253/1 may 1973/decca sessions
london symphony orchestra/hans vonk/*liana vered
*rachmaninov paganini rhapsody/PFS 4327
glinka ruslan & lyudmila overture/SDDN 436-438

1254/2 and 5 may 1973/decca sessions
london philharmonic orchestra/walter weller
rachmaninov symphony 2/SXL 6623

1255/7-12 may 1973/decca sessions
new philharmonia orchestra/richard bonynge/
linden singers/soloists
massenet therese/SET 572

1256/14 may 1973/decca session
vladimir ashkenazy
beethoven piano sonata 21/SXL 6706

1257/15-31 may & 4 june 1973/decca sessions
london symphony orchestra/richard bonynge/
royal opera chorus/soloists
verdi rigoletto/SET 587-589
recording completed in july 1973

1258/21 may-6 june 1973/decca sessions
new philharmonia orchestra/richard bonynge/
renata tebaldi
eighteenth century arias/SXL 6629
new philharmonia orchestra/richard bonynge/
luciano pavarotti
puccini e lucevan le stele from tosca/SXL 6649
flotow ach so fromm from martha/unpublished

1259/25-26 may 1983/decca sessions
royal philharmonic orchestra/rudolf kempe/
brighton festival chorus/soloists
janacek glagolithic mass/SXL 6600

1260/28-29 may 1973/decca sessions
london sinfonietta/david atherton
harrison birwistle verses for ensemble/HEAD 7

1261/29 may 1973/decca sessions
london symphony orchestra/andre previn/radu lupu
schumann piano concerto/SXL 6624

1262/8-14 june 1973/emi sessions
london symphony orchestra/andre previn
prokofiev romeo and juliet/SLS 864

1263/18-28 june 1973/decca sessions
***london philharmonic orchestra/*lawrence foster/
alicia de larrocha**
piano works by bach and mozart/SXL 6669
*ravel the piano concerti/SXL 6680
piano works by manuel de falla/SXL 6683

1264/1-17 july 1973/decca sessions
**london philharmonic orchestra/georg solti/
royal opera chorus/soloists**
mozart cosi fan tutte/SET 575-578

1265/19-25 july 1975/emi sessions
**london symphony orchestra/julius rudel/ambrosian
and wandsworth choirs/soloists**
boito mefistofele/SLS 973
*previous sessions for this recording were
held in abbey road studios*

1266/10-15 august 1973/lyrita sessions
london philharmonic orchestra/*new philharmonia orchestra/adrian boult
*moeran symphony in g minor/SRCS 70
marches by british composers/SRCS 71
bridge suite for strings/SRCS 73
recordings completed in november 1973 and january 1974

1267/11-15 september 1973/decca sessions
royal opera orchestra/john matheson/ ambrosian singers/joseph rouleau
recital of opera arias/SXL 6637

1268/19-26 september 1973/emi sessions
london symphony orchestra/charles groves/ john alldis choir/soloists
delius koanga/SLS 974

1269/28-29 september 1973/emi sessions
london symphony orchestra/andre previn/ ambrosian singers
holst the planets/ASD 3002/EG 29 08501

1270/2-4 october 1973/decca sessions
itzhak perlman/vladimir ashkenazy (piano)
beethoven violin sonatas 2 & 9/SXL 6632
beethoven violin sonata 1/unpublished

1271/10-11 october 1973/emi sessions
london symphony orchestra/andre previn/
itzhak perlman
bartok violin concerto 2/ASD 3014
bartok violin rhapsody/unpublished

1272/13-17 october 1973/decca sessions
vladimir ashkenazy
beethoven piano sonata 26/SXL 6706
chopin etudes op 25/SXL 6710

1273/15 october 1973/decca sessions
london symphony orchestra/vladimir ashkenazy
mozart piano concerto 21/unpublished

1274/23 october-7 november 1973/
hmv angel sessions
london philharmonic orchestra/adrian boult/
london philharmonic choir/soloists
elgar the apostles/SAN 355-357/SLS 976

1275/12-14 november 1973/lyrita sessions
london sinfonietta/lennox berkeley
orchestral works by lennox berkeley/SRCS 74

1276/23 november 1973/electrola session
**london symphony orchestra/antal dorati/
nathan turning/martin berkofsky**
bruch concerto for two pianos/1C063 02493

1277/26 november 1973/emi sessions
london symphony orchestra/andre previn
britten sinfonia da requiem/ASD 3154

1278/28-30 november 1973/decca sessions
national philharmonic orchestra/bernard herrmann
film scores by bernard herrmann/PFS 4309

1279/10-11 december 1973/decca sessions
**london symphony orchestra/sergiu commisiona/
kyung wha chung**
lalo symphonie espagnole; chausson poeme/
unpublished

1280/15 december 1973/decca sessions
london philharmonic orchestra/erich leinsdorf
stravinsky le sacre du printemps/PFS 4307/VIV 31

1281/27-30 december 1973/emi sessions
english chamber orchestra/daniel barenboim/
scottish opera chorus/soloists
mozart don giovanni/SLS 978
haydn the 6 paris symphonies
don giovanni recording was started in edinburgh in
august 1973 and completed in may 1974; main
sessions for the haydn symphonies were held
later in abbey road studios

1282/7 january 1974/lyrita sessions
london philharmonic orchestra/nicholas braithwaite
orchestral works by cooke/SRCS 78

1283/7-8 january 1974/argo sessions
new philharmonia orchestra/norman del mar/
barry tuckwell
banks horn concerto; searle aubade/ZRG 726

1284/16 january 1974/decca sessions
barry tuckwell/vladimir ashkenazy (piano)
danzi horn sonata; saint-saens romance in e/SXL 6717

1285/21 january 1974/decca sessions
london sinfonietta/david atherton/
chorus/alfreda hodgson
milner salutatio angelica/SXL 6699

1286/28-29 january 1974/decca sessions
**london symphony orchestra/andre previn/
vladimir ashkenazy**
prokofiev piano concerto 1/SXL 6767
prokofiev piano concerto 3/SXL 6768

1287/4-11 february 1974/emi sessions
london philharmonic orchestra/adrian boult
orchestral miniatures by elgar/ASD 3050/CFP 4527

1288/6 february and 19 march 1974/decca sessions
london symphony orchestra/willi boskovsky
brahms selection from the hungarian dances;
dvorak selection from the slavonic dances/SXL 6696

1289/20-23 february 1974/rca sessions
**london philharmonic orchestra/jose serebrier/
john alldis choir**
ives symphony 4/ARL1-0587

1290/25-27 february 1974/lyrita sessions
**london philharmonic orchestra/leonard
dommett/malcolm williamson**
williamson piano concerto 3/SRCS 79

1291/5-9 march 1974/hmv angel sessions
london philharmonic orchestra/adrian boult/
london philharmonic choir/felicity palmer
holst a choral symphony/SAN 354/ED 29 03781

1292/11-12 march 1974/decca sessions
royal philharmonic orchestra/hans vonk
berlioz benvenuto cellini overture/PFS 4335
schubert symphony 9/unpublished

1293/21-25 march 1974/decca sessions
english chamber orchestra/uri segal/radu lupu
mozart piano concerti 12 and 21/SXL 6698

1294/27 march-4 april 1974/decca sessions
london philharmonic orchestra/*london
symphony orchestra/walter weller
*prokofiev symphonies 1 and 7/SXL 6702
rachmaninov symphony 3; the rock/SXL 6720/JB 93

1295/1-6 april 1974/decca sessions
national philharmonic orchestra/richard bonynge
tchaikovsky the nutcracker/SXL 6688-6689

1296/17 april 1974/lyrita sessions
london philharmonic orchestra/raymond leppard
bax symphony 7/SRCS 83

1297/26-30 april 1974/decca sessions
national philharmonic orchestra/richard bonynge/
*douglas gamley
ballet music by johann strauss/SXL 6701
*waltzes by waldteufel/SXL 6704

1298/27-29 april 1974/decca sessions
london symphony orchestra/francois
huybrechts/soloists
nielsen symphony 3/SXL 6695

1299/2-3 may 1974/decca sessions
london symphony orchestra/vladimir ashkenazy
prokofiev symphony 1/SXL 6768
mozart piano concerto 23/unpublished

1300/13-18 may 1974/decca sessions
alicia de larrocha
chopin complete preludes; berceuse/SXL 6733
spanish encores/SXL 6734

1301/20-23 may 1974/decca sessions
radu lupu
schubert piano sonata D894; scherzo D593/
SXL 6741

1302/28-30 may 1974/decca sessions
szymon goldberg/radu lupu (piano)
mozart complete violin sonatas/13BB 207-212
recordings completed in september 1974

1303/29 may-5 june 1974/decca sessions
itzhak perlman/vladimir ashkenazy (piano)
beethoven violin sonatas 4 & 5/SXL 6736
beethoven violin sonata 7/SXL 6791

1304/17-18 june 1974/hmv sessions
bournemouth symphony orchestra/paavo berglund
vaughan williams symphony 6/ASD 3127

1305/23 june-12 july 1974/decca sessions
royal opera orchestra/georg solti/
john alldis choir/soloists
tchaikovsky evgeny onegin/SET 596-598

1306/20-21 august 1974/argo sessions
london symphony orchestra/michael lankester/
sarah francis
crosse ariadne for oboe and orchestra/ZRG 842

1307/8-9 september 1974/decca sessions
new philharmonia orchestra/andrew davis/iiana vered
rachmaninov piano concerto 2/PFS 4327

1308/26-28 september 1974/decca sessions
elisabeth soederstroem/vladmimir ashkenazy (piano)
recital of songs by rachmaninov/SXL 6718

1309/30 september-2 october 1974/decca sessions
**london symphony orchestra/andre previn/
vladimir ashkenazy**
prokofiev piano concerto 2/SXL 6767
london symphony orchestra/vladimir ashkenazy
prokofiev autumnal sketches/SXL 6768

1310/3-4 october 1974/decca sessions
**london symphony orchestra/andre previn/
alicia de larrocha**
rachmaninov piano concerto 3/SXL 6746

1311/7-14 october 1974/decca sessions
london philharmonic orchestra/walter weller
dukas symphony in c; l'apprenti sorcier/SXL 6770

1312/9 october 1974/lyrita sessions
london philharmonic orchestra/adrian boult
orchestral works by finzi/SRCS 84
recordings completed in september 1975
and january 1977

1313/12-14 october 1974/decca sessions
london symphony orchestra/lawrence foster/
kyung wha chung
vieuxtemps violin concerto 5/SXL 6759

1314/22-24 october 1974/decca sessions
bracha eden/alexander tamir
works for piano duo by liszt/SXL 6708

1315/1-2 november 1974/decca sessions
london philharmonic orchestra/edo de waart/
radu lupu
brahms piano concerto 1/SXL 6728

1316/20-21 november 1974/decca sessions
london symphony orchestra/walter weller/
pascal roge
bartok piano concerto 1/SXL 6815
bartok piano concerto 2/SXL 6816
recordings completed in june 1975

1317/25-27 november 1974/emi sessions
london symphony orchestra/andre previn/
lso & clement danes choirs/soloists
orff carmina burana/ASD 3113/EG 29 10661

1318/2-3 december 1974/decca sessions
national philharmonic orchestra/willi boskovsky
orchestral music by grieg/SXL 6766

1319/6 december 1974/decca sessions
vladimir ashkenazy
beethoven piano sonata 3/SXL 6808
beethoven piano sonata 40/SXL 6809

1320/9 december 1974/decca sessions
london symphony orchestra/andre previn/
vladimir ashkenazy
prokofiev piano concerto 5/SXL 6769

1321/15-16 december 1974/emi sessions
london symphony orchestra/andre previn
andre previn's music night/ASD 3131
recordings completed in may 1975

1322/17 december 1974/decca session
unspecified soloist
piano works by chopin/unpublished

1323/19-20 december 1974/decca sessions
pascal roge/denise roge
works for piano duo by ravel/SXL 6715

1324/2-6 and 13 january 1975/lyrita sessions
eric parkin
piano works by john ireland/SRCS 87-89

1325/7-10 january 1975/decca sessions
national philharmonic orchestra/richard bonynge
ballet music by meyerbeer and massenet /SXL 6812
ballet music by massenet/SXL 6827

1326/15-17 january 1975/decca sessions
ivan davis
piano music by gottschalk/SXL 6725

1327/28-29 january 1975/decca sessions
gabrieli string quartet
schubert string quartets D 703 & D 887/SDD 512

1328/30 january 1975/decca sessions
**london symphony orchestra/andre previn/
kyung wha chung**
prokofiev violin concerto 2/SXL 6773

1329/11-12 february 1975/emi sessions
new philharmonia orchestra/riccardo muti
tchaikovsky symphony 1/ASD 3213

1330/14-15 february 1975/decca sessions
london philharmonic orchestra/georg solti
elgar symphony 2/SXL 6723

1331/10-11 march 1975/rca sessions
**london philharmonic orchestra/daniel barenboim/
artur rubinstein**
beethoven piano concerti 4 and 5/CRL5-1415

1332/13-17 march 1975/decca sessions
israel philharmonic orchestra/zubin mehta
bartok concerto for orchestra; hungarian sketches/SXL 6730

1333/17-20 march 1975/argo sessions
new philharmonia orchestra/david atherton/
welsh national opera chorus/soloists
works by alan hoddinott/ZRG 824

1334/22 march 1975/decca session
brighton festival chorus/laszlo heltay
gretchaninov the creed/SPA 400

1335/24-26 march 1975/decca sessions
london wind soloists
wind arrangements of beethoven fidelio and
mozart entführung/SDD 485

1336/25 march 1975/lyrita sessions
london philharmonic orchestra/john pritchard
rawsthorne symphony 1/SRCS 90
rawsthorne street corner overture/SRCS 95

1337/27 march 1975/decca sessions
royal philharmonic orchestra/ainslee cox
elgar serenade for strings; elegy for strings/
PFS 4338

1338/7-8 april 1975/rca sessions
london symphony orchestra/luciano berio/
bruno canino/antonio ballista
berio double piano concerto; nones/ARL1-1674

1339/9-11 april 1975/rca sessions
**london philharmonic orchestra/daniel barenboim/
artur rubinstein**
beethoven piano concerti 1, 2 & 3/CRL5-1415

1340/19-21 april 1975/decca sessions
**royal philharmonic orchestra/carlos paita/
london philharmonic choir/soloists**
verdi messa da requiem/OPFS 5-6

1341/24 april 1975/decca session
**gabrieli string quartet/vladimir ashkenazy/
keith puddy**
prokofiev overture on hebrew themes/15BB 218-220

1342/25 april 1975/decca sessions
**london symphony orchestra/andre previn/
vladimir ashkenazy**
prokofiev piano concerto 4/SXL 6769

1343/1-10 may 1975/hmv angel sessions
**london philharmonic orchestra/carlo maria giulini/
new philharmonia chorus/soloists**
beethoven missa solemnis/SAN 394-395/SLS 989

1344/18 may 1975/hmv angel sessions
new philharmonia orchestra/adrian boult/
london philharmonic choir/soloists
elgar the dream of gerontius/SAN 389-390/SLS 987
recording completed in july 1975

1345/19 may 1975/emi sessions
london symphony orchstra/andre previn
berlioz symphonie fantastique/ASD 3496/CFP 4401
recording completed later in abbey road studios

1346/20-21 may 1975/rca sessions
james galway/martha argerich (piano)
flute sonatas by franck & prokofiev/LRL1-5095

1347/22-24 may 1975/rca sessions
national philharmonic orchestra/charles gerhardt/
james galway
the man with the golden flute/LRL1-5094

1348/31 may 1975/decca sessions
london symphony orchestra/lawrance foster/
kyung wha chung
saint-saens violin concerto 3/SXL 6759

1349/3 june 1975/decca sessions
london sinfonietta/david atherton/aurele nicolet/
heinz holliger
ligeti double concerto/HEAD 12

1350/7-19 june 1975/decca sessions
national philharmonic orchestra/peter maag/
london opera chorus/soloists
verdi luisa miller/SET 606-608

1351/8 and 13 june 1975/decca sessions
royal philharmonic orchestra/rafael frühbeck
de burgos/alicia de larrocha
piano concerti by montsalvatge and surinach/
SXL 6757

1352/20-25 june 1975/decca sessions
alicia de larrocha
liszt piano sonata; schumann fantasy in c/SXL 6756

1353/2-15 july 1975/decca sessions
national philharmonic orchestra/richard bonynge/
john alldis choir/soloists
massenet cendrillon/SET 612-614
leoni l'oracolo/D34 D2

1354/16-17 july 1975/decca sessions
huguette tourangeau/richard bonynge (piano)
recital of songs by massenet/SXL 6765

1355/4-8 august 1975/decca sessions
national philharmonic orchestra/richard bonynge
tchaikovsky swan lake/D37 D3

1356/11-13 august 1975/decca sessions
radu lupu
schubert piano sonatas D557 & D959/SXL 6771

1357/18-19 august 1975/decca sessions
elisabeth soederstroem/vladimir ashkenazy (piano)
recital of songs by rachmaninov/SXL 6772
recordings completed in february 1976

1358/20 august 1975/decca session
vladimir ashkenazy
piano works by rachmaninov
*this was the completion of main sessions
held earlier in all saints church petersham*

1359/20-23 august 1975/decca sessions
itzhak perlman/vladimir ashkenazy (piano)
beethoven violin sonatas 1, 3 & 8/
SXL 6789-6790

1360/12-13 september 1975/decca sessions
**london symphony orchestra/kazimierz kord/
iiana vered**
tchaikovsky piano concerto 1/PFS 4362/VIV 16

1361/1-2 october 1975/emi sessions
new philharmonia orchestra/riccardo muti
mendelssohn symphony 3; meeresstille overture/
ASD 3184

1362/10 october 1975/decca sessions
**london symphony orchestra/andre previn/
kyung wha chung**
prokofiev violin concerto 1/SXL 6773

1363/12-14 october 1975/emi sessions
**london symphony orchestra/andre previn/
*lso chorus/*soloists**
rachmaninov vocalise; *the bells/ASD 3284
the isle of the dead/ASD 3259

1364/16 october 1975/manticore session
london philharmonic orchestra/john mayer
emerson bolero/unpublished

1365/20-22 october 1975/decca sessions
london sinfonietta/david atherton
ligeti melodies; chamber concerto/HEAD 12

1366/27-29 october 1975/decca sessions
pascal roge
brahms handel variations/SXL 6786

1367/5-6 november 1975/decca sessions
national philharmonic orchestra/bernard herrmann
british film scores/PFS 4363

1368/11-13 november 1975/decca sessions
london philharmonic orchestra/walter weller
prokofiev symphony 6/SXL 6777

1369/18 november 1975/lyrita sessions
new philharmonia orchestra/nicholas braithwaite/ john mccabe
moeran rhapsody 3/SRCS 91

1370/18-19 november 1975/lyrita sessions
london philharmonic orchestra/nicholas braithwaite
orchestral works by frank bridge/SRCS 91 & SRCS 104

1371/19 november 1975/decca session
vladimir ashkenazy
schubert ländler D366/SXL 6739
chopin berceuse/SXL 6810

1372/20-26 november 1975/decca sessions
itzhak perlman/vladimir ashkenazy (piano)
beethoven violin sonata 6/SXL 6790
beethoven violin sonata 10/SXL 6791

1373/22-24 november 1975/decca sessions
brighton festival chorus/laszlo heltay/soloists
kodaly missa brevis; pange lingua/SXL 6803
recordings completed in february-march 1976

1374/28-29 november 1975/decca sessions
new philharmonia orchestra/elgar howarth
works by xenakis/HEAD 13

1375/16-19 december 1975/decca sessions
alicia de larrocha
granados goyescas/SXL 6785
recording completed later in west hampstead studios

1376/21-22 december 1975/decca sessions
aldeburgh festival strings/steuart bedford/
london opera chorus/soloists
purcell dido and aeneas/SET 615
recording completed in september & december 1977

1377/5-6 january 1976/decca sessions
alicia de larrocha
piano works by haydn and mozart/SXL 6784

1378/11 january 1976/lyrita sessions
london philharmonic orchestra/john pritchard
rawsthorne symphonic studies/SRCS 90
chagrin helter skelter overture/SRCS 95

1379/27-29 january 1976/emi sessions
new philharmonia orchestra/riccardo muti
mozart symphonies 25 & 29/ASD 3326
verdi attila overture/ASD 3366

1380/2-3 february 1976/decca sessions
royal philharmonic orchestra/antal dorati/
brighton festival chorus/soloists
orff carmina burana/PFS 4368/JB 78

1381/5-6 february 1976/vox turnabout sessions
royal philharmonic orchestra/antal dorati/
*ilse von alpenheim
franck symphony; *variations symphoniques/TV 34663

1382/9-10 february 1976/decca sessions
london symphony orchestra/walter weller
prokofiev symphony 5/SXL 6787

1383/11-13 february 1976/decca sessions
london philharmonic orchestra/georg solti/
kyung wha chung
bartok violin concerto 2/SXL 6802

1384/15-17 february 1976/decca sessions
royal opera orchestra/lamberto gardelli/soloists
wolf-ferrari il segreto di susanna/SET 617

1385/27 february 1976/decca sssion
london philharmonic orchestra/georg solti
elgar cockaigne overture/SXL 6795

1386/3-6 march 1976/deutsche grammophon sessions
royal philharmonic orchestra/antal dorati
beethoven symphonies 6 & 8/2721 199

1387/8-10 march 1976/decca sessions
london symphony orchestra/georg solti/
john alldis choir/soloists
stravinsky oedipus rex/SET 616

1388/16-18 march 1976/decca sessions
bracha eden/alexander tamir
schubert works for piano duo/SXL 6794

1389/4 april 1976/lyrita sessions
new philharmonia orchestra/vernon handley
rubbra symphony 2/SRCS 96
harty fair day from irish symphony/SRCS 99

1390/8-9 april 1976/rca sessions
london symphony orchestra/loris tjeknavorian
tchaikovsky symphony 6/LRL1-5129

1391/13-14 april 1976/decca sessions
new philharmonia orchestra/kazimierz kord
sibelius finlandia; valse triste; swan of tuonela;
karelia suite/PFS 4378/SPA 549

1392/20-24 april 1976/decca sessions
vladimir ashkenazy
piano works by chopin/SXL 6801
beethoven piano sonata 2/SXL 6808
beethoven piano sonata 28/SXL 6809
beethoven piano sonata 17/SXL 6871

1393/28-29 april 1976/lyrita sessions
royal philharmonic orchestra/vernon handley/
*erich gruenberg
david morgan contrasts; *violin concerto/SRCS 97
bax irish landscape/SRCS 99

1394/2-3 may 1976/emi sessions
new philharmonia orchestra/riccardo muti
dvorak symphony 9/ASD 3285/EG 29 02751

1395/8-12 may 1976/deutsche grammophon sessions
royal philharmonic orchestra/antal dorati
beethoven symphony 5/2721 199

1396/14 may 1976/decca session
london symphony orchestra/vladimir ashkenazy
schumann introduction & allegro appasionao/
SXL 6861

1397/20-21 may 1976/decca sessions
gabrieli string quartet
tchaikovsky string quartet 1/SDD 524-525

1398/7-12 june 1976/decca sessions
london symphony orchestra/walter weller/
pascal roge
bartok piano rhapsody/SXL 6815
bartok piano concerto 3/SXL 6816

1399/10-16 june 1976/decca sessions
national philharmonic orchestra/gianandrea
gavazzeni/london opera chorus/soloists
mascagni cavalleria rusticana/D83 D3

1400/29 june-5 july 1976/emi sessions
london philharmonic orchestra/eugen jochum
brahms symphonies 2 and 4/SLS 5093

1401/5-21 july 1976/hmv angel sessions
new philharmonia orchestra/riccardo muti/
ambrosian singers/soloists
verdi macbeth/SAN 402-404/SLS 992

1402/6 july 1976/emi sessions
london symphony orchestra/andre previn
mozart piano concerto 20/ASD 3337

1403/26-31 july 1976/decca sessions
radu lupu
piano works by brahms/SXL 6831
recordings completed in december 1977

1404/3-6 august 1976/lyrita sessions
london philharmonic orchestra/nicholas braithwaite/*eric parkin
lennox berkeley symphony 2/SRCS 94
*hurlstone piano concerto; variations on a swedish air/SRCS 100

1405/10-19 august 1976/emi sessions
english chamber orchestra/daniel barenboim/ john alldis choir/soloists
mozart le nozze di figaro/SLS 995

1406/23-27 august 1976/lyrita sessions
london symphony orchestra/nicholas braithwaite/ malcolm binns
rawsthorne piano concerti 1 & 2/SRCS 101
stanford piano concerto 2/SRCS 102

1407/25 august 1976/lyrita sessions
new philharmonia orchestra/vernon handley
alan bush yorick overture/SRCS 95
rubbra festival overture/SRCS 96

1408/6-23 september 1976/decca sessions
national philharmonic orchestra/richard bonynge/
*london opera chorus/*soloists
massenet scenes dramatiques/SXL 6827
*opera scenes by bellini, donizetti and verdi/SXL 6828
*verdi il trovatore/D82 D3
il trovatore recording completed in march 1977

1409/22 september 1976/decca session
gabrieli string quartet
tchaikovsky string quartet 2/SDD 524-525
recording completed in december 1976

1410/28 september 1976/lyrita sessions
london symphony orchestra/vernon handley/
john georgiadis
moeran violin concerto/SRCS 105

1411/1-4 october 1976/decca sessions
vladimir ashkenazy
piano works by chopin/SXL 6801 & SXL 6810

1412/1-9 october 1976/emi sessions
london symphony orchestra/*london philharmonic orchestra/eugen jochum
beethoven symphony 3/ASD 3376/EMX 2016
beethoven leonore 3 overture/ASD 3627/EMX 2017
*brahms symphonies 1 & 3; *tragic overture;
*academic festival overture/SLS 5093

1413/6-27 october 1976/emi sessions
london philharmonic orchestra/mstislav rostropovich/*galina vishnevskaya
tchaikovsky complete symphonies including manfred/SLS 5099
*songs and arias by mussorgsky, rimsky-korsakov and tchaikovsky/ASD 3436

1414/10 october 1976/emi session
london philharmonic orchestra/adrian boult
marches by elgar and walton/ASD 3388
recordings completed in january 1977

1415/22-23 october 1976/emi sessions
new philharmonia orchestra/riccardo muti/
new philharmonia chorus/soloists
vivaldi magnificat RV611/ASD 3418
recording completed in november 1976

1416/2-3 november 1976/argo sessions
philip jones brass ensemble
fanfares for brass/ZRG 870

1417/4-10 november 1976/lyrita sessions
new philharmonia orchestra/vernon handley/
***adrian boult/guildford choir/soloists**
finzi in terra pax/SRCS 93
hadley the trees so high/SRCS 106
*music by eric coates/SRCS 107
eric coates recordings completed in december 1976

1418/11-15 november 1976/decca sessions
royal philharmonic orchestra/carlos paita
mahler symphony 1/PFS 4402

1419/16-17 and 30 november-1 december 1976/
rca sessions
i solisti di zagreb/james galway
vivaldi le 4 stagioni/RL 25034
bach flute concerti & suite 3/RL 25119

1420/8-9 december 1976/emi sessions
london symphony orchestra/andre previn/
***finchley childrens choir/*soloists**
rachmaninov womens dance from aleko/ASD 3369
*mendelssohn sommernachtstraum
incidental music/ASD 3377

1421/11-21 december 1976/decca sessions
royal philharmonic orchestra/antal dorati/
*brighton festival chorus/*soloists
rossini-respighi la boutique fantasque/
PFS 4407/JB 79
*haydn die schöpfung/D50 D2

1422/4-6 january 1977/classics for pleasure sessions
london philharmonic orchestra/vernon handley/
*norman del mar
vaughan williams symphony 2/CFP 40286
*strauss also sprach zarathustra; schleiertanz
from salome/CFP 40289

1423/14-16 january 1977/decca sessions
london philharmonic orchestra/bernard haitink
shostakovich symphony 10/SXL 6838

1424/20 january 1977/decca sessions
royal philharmonic orchestra/charles dutoit/
kyung wha chung
works for violin and orchestra by chausson
and saint-saens/SXL 6851
saint-saens recording completed in april 1977

1425/22-24 january 1977/decca sessions
royal philharmonic orchestra/hans vonk
mozart symphony 41; figaro overture; eine kleine nachtmusik/PFS 4425
stravinsky firebird/PFSS 1

1426/26-27 january 1977/emi sessions
london philharmonic orchestra/charles groves/ lso chorus
choral works by gustav holst/ASD 3435
recordings completed in march 1977

1427/31 january 1977/vox turnabout sessions
royal philharmonic orchestra/antal dorati
dvorak symphony 9/TV 34702

1428/february 1977/oiseau lyre sessions
alan hacker/richard burnett (fortepiano)
hymn to the sun/DSLO 17

1429/3 february 1977/rca sessions
national philharmonic orchestra/charles gerhardt
orchestral works by ravel, faure & satie/RL 25094

1430/4-7 february 1977/decca sessions
**new philharmonia orchestra/vladimir ashkenazy/
boris belkin**
tchaikovsky violin concerto/SXL 6854

1431/7 and 18 february 1977/decca sessions
**london philharmonic orchestra/georg solti/
*kyung wha chung**
*elgar violin concerto/SXL 6842
elgar pomp and circumstance marches 1-5
and national anthem/SXL 6848
recordings completed in april 1977

1432/16-21 february 1977/decca sessions
**london symphony orchestra/lamberto gardelli/
sylvia sass**
opera arias by verdi & puccini/SXL 6841

1433/19-25 february 1977/rca sessions
**national philharmonic orchestra/
loris tjeknavorian**
borodin symphonies 1-3 and other
orchestral works/RL 25098

1434/28 february-1 march 1977/emi sessions
london symphony orchestra/eugen jochum
beethoven egmont overture/ASD 3376/EMX 2016
beethoven symphony 5/ASD 3484/EMX 2018

1435/2-4 march 1977/decca sessions
london philharmonic orchestra/georg solti/
london philharmonic choir/benjamin luxon
walton belshazzars feast; coronation te deum/
SET 618

1436/17-21 march 1977/decca sessions
national philharmonic orchestra/richard bonynge
tchaikovsky sleeping beauty/D78 D3

1437/21-29 march 1977/lyrita sessions
english chamber orchestra/norman del mar
ballet music by constant lambert/SRCS 110
works by contemporary british composers/
SRCS 111
recordings completed in may 1977

1438/24 march 1977/decca sessions
london philharmonic orchestra/walter weller
prokofiev symphony 3; scythian suite/SXL 6852

1439/29 march-3 april 1977/decca sessions
national philharmonic orchestra/franco patane/
london opera chorus/soloists
leoncavallo I pagliacci/D83 D3

1440/4-6 april 1977/decca sessions
london philharmonic orchestra/georg solti
liszt tone poems/SXL 6867
recordings completed in june 1977

1441/13-14 april 1977/decca sessions
new philharmonia orchestra/vladimir ashkenazy/
*boris belkin
tchaikovsky manfred/SXL 6853
*tchaikovsky valse scherzo/SXL 6854

1442/16-24 april 1977/decca sessions
new philharmonia orchestra/pierino gamba/
luciano pavarotti
recital of songs and arias/SXL 7013/SPA 488

1443/29 april 1977/decca session
royal philharmonic orchestra/charles dutoit/
kyung wha chung
saint-saens havanaise/SXL 6851
ravel tzigane/unpublished

1444/9-12 may 1977/decca sessions
kyung wha chung/radu lupu (piano)
violin sonatas by debussy and franck/SXL 6944

1445/13-17 may 1977/rca sessions
london philharmonic orchestra/loris tjeknavorian
stravinsky le sacre du printemps/RL 25130
tchaikovsky symphony 5/RL 25221
debussy printemps/unpublished

1446/16-17 may 1977/argo sessions
philip jones brass ensemble
easy winners/ZRG 895
recordings completed in june 1977

1447/20-23 may 1977/decca sessions
pascal roge
piano works by debussy/SXL 6858

1448/24-27 may 1977/argo sessions
academy of st martin in the fields/neville marriner/*asmif chorus/*soloists
*mozart requiem/ZRG 876
string music by scandinavian composers/
ZRG 877

1449/1-2 june 1977/decca sessions
**london symphony orchestra/uri segal/
vladimir ashkenazy**
schumann piano concerto; introduction and allegro in d/SXL 6861

1450/3-4 june 1977/decca sessions
vladimir ashkenazy
piano works by scriabin/SXL 6868

1451/8-12 june 1977/decca sessions
alicia de larrocha
piano works by bach and mozart/SXL 6865

1452/13-21 june 1977/decca sessions
**royal philharmonic orchestra/antal dorati/
brighton festival chorus/soloists**
haydn die jahreszeiten/D88 D3

1453/24-25 june 1977/emi sessions
london symphony orchestra/eugen jochum
beethoven symphony 4/ASD 3627/EMX 2017
beethoven coriolan overture/
SLS 5178/EMX 2020

1454/10-21 july 1977/emi sessions
philharmonia orchestra/riccardo muti/
ambrosian singers/soloists
verdi nabucco/SLS 5132/EX 29 07833
recording completed in february 1978

1455/21-27 july 1977/emi sessions
philharmonia orchestra/riccardo muti/
ambrosian singers/irina arkhipova
prokofiev ivan the terrible/SLS 5110
philharmonia orchestra/giuseppe patane/
elena obraztsova
recital of operatic arias/ASD 3459
prokofiev recording completed september 1977

1456/2-3 august 1977/emi sessions
london philharmonic orchestra/
mstislav rostropovich
tchaikovsky romeo and juliet/ASD 3567/
EMX 41 20621

1457/30-31 august 1977/decca sessions
philharmonia orchestra/anatole fistoulari/
ilana vered
brahms piano concerto 2/PFS 4428

1458/3 september 1977/decca sessions
royal philharmonic orchestra/miklos rosza
rosza the music of quo vadis/PFS 4430

1459/7-10 september 1977/decca sessions
vladimir ashkenazy
beethoven piano sonata 18/SXL 6871
chopin rondo in c/SXL 6911

1460/21-23 september 1977/emi sessions
**london philharmonic orchestra/klaus tennstedt/
horacio gutierrez**
piano concerti by grieg & schumann/ASD 3521

1461/30 september-7 october 1977/emi sessions
london symphony orchestra/eugen jochum
beethoven fidelio overture/ASD 3484/EMX 2018
beethoven symphony 6/ASD 3583/EMX 2019
beethoven symphony 7/SLS 5178/EMX 2020

1462/3-4 october 1977/oiseau lyre sessions
jorge bolet
chopin arrangements by godovsky/DSLO 26

1463/12-16 october 1977/ensayo sessions
english chamber orchestra/antoni ros marba/
*jose carreras
*arias from spanish zarzuelas/ZL 506
el madrid de chueca/ZL 507

1464/18-21 october 1977/decca sessions
bracha eden/alexander tamir
mozart works for piano duo/SDD 548-SDD 550
recordings completed in april 1978

1465/24-26 october 1977/argo sessions
philip jones brass ensemble
mussorgsky pictures from an exhibition/ZRG 885
premru divertimento/unpublished

1466/2-8 november 1977/decca sessions
london philharmonic orchestra/walter weller
prokofiev symphony 4/SXL 6908
prokofiev love of 3 oranges suite/SXL 6945
recordings completed may 1978 and may 1979

1467/4-6 november 1977/argo sessions
london chamber choir/laszlo heltay/soloists
rossini petite messe solennelle/ZRG 893-894

1468/14-17 november 1977/emi sessions
philharmonia orchestra/rafael frühbeck de burgos/philharmonia chorus/soloists
haydn die schöpfung/SLS 5125

1469/21-22 november 1977/lodia sessions
london symphony orchestra/carlos paita
berlioz symphonie fantastique/LOD 777

1470/24-26 november 1977/classics for pleasure sessions
london philharmonic orchestra/walter susskind
orchestral works by kodaly/CFP 40292
dvorak symphony 8; scherzo capriccioso/CFP 40303

1470/27 november-6 december 1977/decca sessions
london philharmonic orchestra/georg solti/soloists
strauss ariadne auf naxos/D10 D3

1471/12-16 december 1977/decca sessions
philharmonia orchestra/vladimir ashkenazy
mozart piano concerti 17 and 21/SXL 6881
tchaikovsky symphony 5/SXL 6884

1472/14-17 december 1977/decca sessions
pascal roge
brahms fantasies op 116/SXL 6786

1473/18-22 december 1977/decca sessions
**london philharmonic orchestra/georg solti/
alicia de larrocha**
mozart piano concerti 25 and 27/SXL 6887

1474/29-30 december 1977/decca sessions
radu lupu
beethoven piano sonatas 19 & 20/SXL 6886

1475/4-5 january 1978/decca sssions
london sinfonietta/elgar howarth/soloists
ferneyhough transit/HEAD 18

1476/10-19 january 1978/philips sessions
**academy of st martin in the fields/neville
marriner/*janet baker**
bach the four orchestral suites/6769 012
*arie amorose/9500 557

1477/10-11 february 1978/decca sessions
**london philharmonic orchestra/georg solti/
vladimir ashkenazy**
bartok piano concerto 3/SXL 6937

1478/14-15 february 1978/decca sessions
london philharmonic orchestra/georg solti/
london philharmonic choir
holst the planets/SET 628

1479/17-20 february 1978/emi sessions
philharmonia orchestra/riccardo muti/
ambrosian singers/soloists
verdi messa da requiem/SLS 5185
recording completed in june 1978

1480/27 february-1 march 1978/emi sssions
london symphony orchestra/eugen jochum/
lso chorus/soloists
beethoven symphony 9/SLS 5178/EMX 2040
recording completed in october 1978

1481/12 march 1978/rca session
unidentified performers & works/unpublished

1482/20-21 march 1978/decca sessions
london philharmonic orchestra/bernard haitink
shostakovich symphony 15/SXL 6906

1483/23 march 1978/decca sessions
london symphony orchestra/stanley black
ballet suites by khachaturian/PFS 4434

1484/29 march 1978/rca sessions
**national philharmonic orchestra/charles gerhardt/
james galway**
a song for annie/KRL1-0294
recording completed later in walthamstow town hall

1485/31 march-1 april 1978/decca sessions
royal philharmonic orchestra/kazimierz kord
tchaikovsky symphony 6/SXL 6894

1486/12-15 april 1978/decca sessions
szymon goldberg/radu lupu (piano)
schubert works for violin and piano/D195 D2

1487/16-17 april 1978/argo sessions
**academy of st martin in the fields/laszlo heltay/
london chamber choir/soloists**
choral works by respighi/ZRG 904
*orchestra described for these sessions as
argo chamber orchestra*

1488/24 april 1978/decca sessions
**philharmonia orchestra/vladimir ashkenazy/
boris belkin**
sibelius violin concerto/SXL 6953

1489/2-7 may 1978/decca sessions
**national philharmonic orchestra/richard bonynge/
douglas gamley/joan sutherland**
mozart opera and concert arias/SXL 6911
scenes from wagner operas/SXL 6930
recordings completed in november-december 1978

1490/8 and 19 may 1978/decca sessions
royal philharmonic orchestra/walter weller
grieg peer gynt incidental music/SXL 6901

1491/12 and 30 may-4 june 1978/emi sessions
**london philharmonic orchestra/adrian boult/
geoffrey mitchell choir**
holst the planets/ASD 3649
*certain parts of the recording were made at
abbey road studios*

1492/13-14 may 1979/decca sessions
london philharmonic orchestra/walter weller
prokofiev russian festival overture/SXL 6908
prokofiev symphony 2/SXL 6945

1493/21-25 may 1978/rca sessions
london symphony orchestra/claudio abbado
verdi overtures/ARL1-3345/RL 31378
rossini overtures/ARL1-3634/RL 31379

1494/5-6 june 1978/emi sessions
philharmonia orchestra/rafael frühbeck
de burgos/vasso devetzi
mozart piano concerti 20 and 24/unpublished

1495/16-19 june 1978/decca sessions
national philharmonic orchestra/kurt adler
german opera overtures/SXL 6909

1496/20-21 june 1978/decca sessions
philharmonia orchestra/vladimir ashkenazy
mozart piano concerto 19/SXL 6947
mozart piano concerto 23/SXL 6982

1497/28-29 june 1978/emi sessions
london symphony orchestra/andre previn/
lso & st clement danes choirs/soloists
britten spring symphony/ASD 3650/EG 29 10471

1498/1-11 july 1978/emi sessions
philharmonia orchestra/riccardo muti
schumann hermann und dorothea overture/ASD 3648
schumann die braut von messina overture/ASD 3696
tchaikovsky symphony 5/ASD 3717
rossini semiramide overture/ASD 3903

1499/13-14 july 1978/emi sessions
london symphony orchestra/andre previn
mendelssohn symphony 4/ASD 3763
ravel daphnis et chloe second suite; pavane pour une infant defunte/ASD 3912

1500/2-4 august 1978/lyrita sessions
london symphony orchestra/nicholas braithwaite/*david atherton
alan bush symphony 1/SRCS 115
*maconchy serenata concertante/SRCS 116

1501/2-5 august 1978/lyrita sessions
**london philharmonic orchestra/
nicholas braithwaite**
orchestral works by bridge, grainger, warlock and berners/SRCS 99, SRCS 104, SRCS 114 & SRCS 120

1502/7-8 august 1978/decca sessions
philharmonia orchestra/vladimir ashkenazy
tchaikovsky symphony 4/SXL 6919

1503/10-15 august 1978/decca sessions
philharmonia orchestra/simon rattle
maxwell davies symphony 1/HEAD 21

1504/12-13 august 1978/decca sessions
london symphony orchestra/david atherton
panufnik symphonies 5 and 6/HEAD 22

1505/15 august 1978/argo session
philharmonia orchestra/david atherton
berners aubade/ZRG 907

1506/17-18 august 1978/rca sessions
london early music group/james tyler/paul elliott
la mantovana/RL 25119

1507/26-28 august 1978/decca sessions
national philharmonic orchestra/richard bonynge
lehar die lustige witwe (abridged version)/SET 629
this was the completion of sessions started in walthamstow town hall

1508/5-8 and 26 september-1 october 1978/
decca sessions
**thames chamber orchestra/david willcocks/
bach choir/soloists**
bach matthäus-passion/D139 D4

1509/9-13 september 1978/decca sessions
**national philharmonic orchestra/riccardo chailly/
ambrosian singers/soloists**
rossini william tell/D219 D4
recording completed in january and august 1979

1510/16-17 september 1978/emi sessions
**philharmonia orchestra/carlo maria giulini/
philharmonia chorus/soloists**
mozart requiem/ASD 3723

1511/4-6 and 30 october-8 november 1978/
decca sessions
**london philharmonic orchestra/georg solti/
london opera chorus/soloists**
mozart don giovanni/D162 D4

1512/11-13 october 1978/emi sessions
london symphony orchestra/eugen jochum
beethoven symphony 1/SLS 5178/EMX 2015
beethoven symphony 8/SLS 5178

345

1513/16 october 1978/decca sessions
philharmonia orchestra/vladimir ashkenazy/boris belkin
sibelius works for violin and orchestra/SXL 6953

1514/18-23 october 1978/rca sessions
philharmonia orchestra/eduardo mata/james galway
orchestral works by rodrigo/RL 25193

1515/14 november 1978/decca session
**royal philharmonic orchestra/charles dutoit/
kyung wha chung**
ravel tzigane/SXL 6851

1516/15-16 november 1978/decca sessions
london philharmonic orchestra/jesus lopez cobos
respighi ancient airs & dances suites 1-3/SXL 6846

1517/21-29 november 1978/decca sessions
**national philharmonic orchestra/richard
bonynge/*london opera chorus/soloists**
ballet music by massenet/SXL 6932
*puccini suor angelica/SET 627

1518/2-6 december 1978/decca sessions
**london philharmonic orchestra/jesus lopez cobos/
pilar lorengar**
recital of operatic arias/SXL 6923

1519/7-9 december 1978/oiseau lyre sessions
jorge bolet
piano works by liszt/DSLO 41

1520/16-17 december 1978/argo sessions
**royal college of music orchestra and chorus/
richard blackford**
blackford sir gawain and the green knight/ZRG 908

1521/18-20 december 1978/decca sessions
royal philharmonic orchestra/per dreier/peter pears
works by nordheim/HEAD 23
peter pears/osian ellis (harpsichord)
folksong arrangements/unpublished

1522/21-22 december 1978/argo sessions
london sinfonietta/david atherton/chorus/soloists
choral works by schubert/ZRG 916
recordings completed in january 1979

1523/8-9 january 1979/argo sessions
london sinfonietta/david atherton/tommy reilly
works for harmonium & orchestra/ZRG 905

1524/15-16 january 1979/decca sessions
philharmonia orchestra/vladimir ashkenazy
rachmaninov symphonic dances/SXL 6926

1525/17-18 january 1979/decca sessions
london philharmonic orchestra/bernard haitink
shostakovich symphony 4/SXL 6927

1526/22 and 28 january 1979/lyrita sessions
philharmonia orchestra/nicholas braithwaite
balfe gallop from the bohemian girl/SRCS 99
bantock oedipus coloneus overture/SRCS 123

1527/23-26 january 1979/lyrita sessions
philharmonia orchestra/vilem tausky/soloists
william alwyn miss julie/SRCS 121-123

1528/29-30 january 1979/decca sessions
radu lupu
schubert piano sonatas D157 & D845/SXL 6931

1529/1-3 march 1979/emi sessions
london philharmonic orchestra/
mstislav rostropovich
dvorak symphony 9/ASD 3786/EMX 41 20511
dvorak symphony 7/ASD 3869

1530/6 march 1979/decca sessions
national philharmonic orchestra/giancarlo chiaramello/luciano pavarotti
recital of neapolitan songs/SXL 6870

1531/12-13 march 1979/philips sessions
philharmonia orchestra/antonio de almeida
ballet music from donizetti operas/9500 673

1532/16-21 march 1979/decca sessions
london philharmonic orchestra/georg solti/ soloists/*vladimir ashkenazy
bartok bluebeard's castle/SET 630
*bartok piano concerto 2/SXL 6932

1533/9-10 april 1979/argo sessions
english chamber orchestra/george malcolm/ william bennett
mozart flute concerti K313 & K314/ZRG 910

1534/17-18 april 1979/decca sessions
royal philharmonic orchestra/walter weller/ mayumi fujikawa
mozart violin concerti 3 and 5/SXL 6939

1535/25-27 april 1979/lyrita sessions
philharmonia orchestra/edward downes
george lloyd symphony 5/SRCS 124

1536/8-13 may 1979/decca sessions
national philharmonic orchestra/kurt adler/
leona mitchell
recital of opera arias/SXL 6942

1537/16-18 may 1979/decca sessions
philharmonia orchestra/vladimir ashkenazy
tchaikovsky symphony 6/SXL 6941
mozart piano concerto 24/SXL 6947
mozart piano concerto 16/SXL 7010
tchaikovsky recording completed in march 1980

1538/21-24 may 1979/decca sessions
gabrieli string quartet
mozart string quartets K465 & K499/SDD 561

1539/30 may-4 july 1979/emi sessions
philharmonia orchestra/riccardo muti/
ambrosian singers/soloists
leoncavallo I pagliacci/SLS 5187
bellini i puritani/SLS 5201

1540/26 june-6 july 1979/emi sessions
london symphony orchestra/andre previn/
*lso chorus/*dimiter petkov
vaughan williams tallis fantasy/ASD 3857
*shostakovich symphony 13/ASD 3911
ravel bolero/ASD 3912

1541/12-14 july 1979/decca sessions
philharmonia orchestra/charles dutoit/pascal roge
saint-saens piano concerto 4/SXDL 7008
saint-saens piano concerto 1/D244 D3

1542/28 august-6 september 1979/decca sessions
national philharmonic orchestra/richard bonynge/
london opera chorus/soloists
massenet le roi de lahore/D210 D3

1543/13-14 september 1979/decca sessions
london sinfonietta/david zinman/alicia de larrocha
piano concerti by bach and mozart/SXL 6952

1544/27-31 october 1979/emi sessions
london philharmonic orchestra/klaus
tennstedt/london philharmonic &
southend choirs/ortrun wenkel
mahler symphony 3/SLS 5195

1545/2-10 november 1979/decca sessions
national philharmonic orchestra/richard bonynge/
london opera chorus/soloists
verdi la traviata/D212 D3

1546/10-11 november 1979/decca sessions
philharmonia orchestra/vladimir ashkenazy
sibelius symphony 2/SXDL 7513

1547/12-14 november 1979/decca sessions
london philharmonic orchestra/bernard haitink
shostakovich symphony 7; age of gold suite/
D213 D2

1548/15-23 november 1979/decca sessions
gabrieli string quartet
beethoven string quartets 7, 8 & 9/D314 D2

1549/27-28 november 1979/oiseau lyre sessions
national philharmonic orchestra/robin
stapleton/stuart burrows
operetta favourites/DSLO 16

1550/4-6 december 1979/decca sessions
london philharmonic orchestra/georg solti
elgar in the south; falstaff/SXL 6963

1551/14-21 december 1979/decca sessions
royal philharmonic orchestra/antal dorati/
brighton festival chorus/soloists
haydn il ritorno di tobia/D216 D4

1552/2-10 january 1980/decca sessions
national philharmonic orchestra/richard bonynge/
london opera chorus/soloists
bellini la sonnambula/D210 D3

1553/12-13 january 1980/decca sessions
philip jones brass ensemble/david willcocks/
bach choir
family christmas carols/SXDL 7514

1554/15-16 january 1980/decca sessions
london philharmonic orchestra/bernard haitink
shostakovich symphonies 1 & 9/SXDL 7515

1555/17-19 january 1980/decca sessions
martti talvela/ralf gothoni (piano)
songs by rachmaninov & mussorgsky/SXL 6974

1556/6-8 february 1980/argo sessions
**academy of st martin in the fields/iona brown/
marisa robles**
harp concerti by boieldieu, dittersdorf
and handel/ZRG 930

1557/9-10 february 1980/decca sessions
**royal philharmonic orchestra/walter weller/
mayumi fujikawa**
mozart violin concerti 4 & 7/D239 D4

1558/12-13 february 1980/argo sessions
academy of st martin in the fields/neville marriner
vaughan williams greensleeves fantasy;
english folksong suite/ZRG 931

1559/14-15 february 1980/emi sessions
academy of st martin in the fields/neville marriner
music for strings/ASD 3943

1560/26 february 1980/decca sessions
vladimir ashkenazy
beethoven piano sonata 12/SXL 6929
chopin rondo op 5/SXL 6981
chopin piano sonata 2/SXL 6996

1561/29 february-2 march 1980/decca sessions
jorge bolet
piano variations by brahms and reger/SXL 6969

1562/3-4 march 1980/oiseau lyre sessions
esterhazy string quartet/wim ten have (viola)
mozart string quintet K515/DSLO 61

1563/5-8 march 1980/lyrita sessions
**london philharmonic orchestra/david willcocks/
bach choir/teresa cahill**
vaughan williams song of light; parry ode
to the nativity/SRCS 125
london philharmonic orchestra/nicholas braithwaite
holst suite de ballet/SRCS 120
stanford irish rhapsody/SRCS 123
orchestral works by leigh/SRCS 126

1564/10-11 march 1980/ettore stratta productions
london symphony orchestra/ettore stratta
music for the galaxies/35876 (usa only)

1565/17-24 march 1980/decca sessions
**philharmonia orchestra/vladimir ashkenazy/
*elisabeth soederstroem**
mozart rondo K382/SXL 6982
sibelius symphony 4; finlandia; *luonnotar/SXDL 7517
mozart piano concerti 23 & 27/SXDL 7530

1566/19-20 march 1980/decca sessions
pascal roge
liszt italie from annees de pelerinage/SXL 6968

1567/22 march 1980/decca sessions
london sinfonietta/charles dutoit/pascal roge
saint-saens carnaval des animaux/414 4601

1568/31 march-8 april 1980/decca sessions
national philharmonic orchestra/richard bonynge
ballet music by johann strauss/D225 D2

1569/1 april 1980/lyrita sessions
philharmonia orchestra/norman del mar
rubbra symphony 6/SRCS 127

1570/3 april 1980/deutsche grammophon sessions
london symphony orchestra/claudio abbado/ gidon kremer
vivaldi le 4 stagioni/2531 287
completion for previous sessions in st johns smith square

1571/13 april 1980/decca sessions
london philharmonic orchestra/charles dutoit/ pascal roge
saint-saens piano concerto 3/D244 D3

1572/17-18 april 1980/argo sessions
royal philharmonic orchestra/richard hickox/
*lso chorus/*john shirley-quirk
delius appalachia; *sea drift/ZRG 934

1573/2-8 may 1980/emi sessions
london philharmonic orchestra/
mstislav rostropovich
dvorak symphony 8; scherzo capriccioso/ASD 4058
dvorak symphony 6/37716 (usa only)
dvorak carnival overture/unpublished

1574/28-30 may 1980/rca sessions
london symphony orchestra/claudio abbado/
lso chorus/zehava gal
choral and orchestral works by mussorgsky/
ARL1-3988

1575/12-14 june 1980/decca sessions
philharmonia orchestra/charles dutoit
orchestral works by saint-saens/SXL 6975

1576/26 june 1980/decca session
pascal roge
piano works by debussy/unpublished

1577/28 june-2 july 1980/ricordi sessions
london sinfonietta/riccardo chailly/soloists
vocal works by stravinsky/411 1141

1578/5-18 july 1980/emi sessions
philharmonia orchestra/riccardo muti/
*ambrosian singers/*soloists
*verdi la traviata/SLS 5240
rossini il barbiere di siviglia overture/ASD 3903
*opera choruses by verdi/ASD 3979
verdi ballet music from I vespri siciliani/ASD 4015
*cherubini requiem in c minor/ASD 4071

1579/24-25 july 1980/decca sessions
fitzwilliam string quartet
borodin string quartet 2/SXL 6983
tchaikovsky string quartet 2/unpublished

1580/29 july-11 august 1980/emi sessions
philharmonia orchestra/james levine/
ambrosian singers/soloists
puccini tosca/SLS 5213

1581/29-31 august 1980/decca sessions
royal philharmonic orchestra/*london sinfonietta/charles dutoit/*david zinman/ alicia de larrocha
rachmaninov piano concerto 2; schumann piano concerto/SXL 6978
*haydn piano concerto in d/unpublished

1582/1-5 september 1980/decca and oiseau lyre sessions
academy of ancient music/christopher hogwood
mozart the early symphonies/D167 D3 & D175 D3
gluck ballet music from orfeo ed euridice; vivaldi concerto RV 537/DSLO 594

1583/5 september 1980/lyrita session
philharmonia orchestra/norman del mar
rubbra symphony 8/SRCS 127

1584/16 september & 3-4 october 1980/ decca sessions
royal philharmonic orchestra/walter weller/ mayumi fujikawa
mozart violin concerti 1, 2 & 6; adagio and rondos/D239 D4

1585/20-28 october 1980/decca sessions
*philharmonia orchestra/vladimir ashkenazy
chopin piano sonata 2 and other pieces/
SXL 6981-6962
*sibelius symphony 5/SXDL 7541
*mozart piano concerto 12/SXDL 7556

1586/3-5 november 1980/argo sessions
**philip jones brass ensemble/elgar howarth/
paul crossley**
concert music by hindemith/ZRDL 1000
recordings completed in january 1981

1587/10-14 november 1980/oiseau lyre sssions
esterhazy string quartet/wim ten have (viola)
mozart string quintet K516/DSLO 510
mozart string quinter K406/unpublished

1588/22-27 november 1980/decca sessions
**london sinfonietta/david atherton/
choir/soloists**
tippett king priam/D246 D3

1589/8-13 december 1980/decca sessions
vladimir ashkenazy
beethoven piano sonatas 8 & 29/D258 D12

1590/15-17 december 1980/rca sessions
london symphony orchestra/eduardo mata/
*lso & st pauls choirs/*soloists
*orff carmina burana/ATC1-3925/RL 13925
orchestral music of carlos chavez/MRS 024 (mexico)

1591/15-18 december 1980/rca sessions
national philharmonic orchestra/ralph mace/
malcolm messiter
an oboe fantasia/RL 25367

1592/29-30 december 1980/emi sessions
philharmonia orchestra/simon rattle/
ambrosian singers
holst the planets/ASD 4047/EMX 2106

1593/7-9 january 1981/decca sessions
musikverein quartet/andre previn (piano)
mozart piano quartets K478 & K493/SXL 6989

1594/9-11 january 1981/decca sessions
national philharmonic orchestra/riccardo chailly
rossini overtures/SXDL 7534

1595/18-20 january 1981/argo sessions
philip jones brass ensemble
focus on the philip jones brass ensemble/ZRDL 1001

1596/21 january 1981/emi session
philharmonia orchestra/riccardo muti/
philharmonia chorus/soloists
mozart mass K427/unpublished (incomplete)

1597/25-28 january 1981/decca sessions
london philharmonic orchestra/bernard haitink
shostakovich symphonies 2 & 3/SXDL 7535

1598/30 january 1981/decca sessions
london philharmonic orchestra/kyrill kondrashin/
boris belkin
prokofiev violin concerto 1/SXDL 7579

1599/4-6 february 1981/emi sessions
philharmonia orchestra/kurt sanderling/
philharmonia chorus/soloists
beethoven symphony 9 final movement; fidelio, egmont and prometheus overtures/SLS 5239
movements 1-3 of the symphony were recorded in abbey road studios

1600/24-28 march 1981/decca sessions
philharmonia orchestra/vladimir ashkenazy
beethoven symphony 5; leonore 3 overture/
SXDL 7540
sibelius en saga/SXDL 7541
moxart piano concerto 13/SXDL 7556
beethoven andante favori/D258 D12

1601/25-30 march 1981/decca sessions
london philharmonic orchestra/georg solti
haydn symphonies 96 & 101/SXDL 7544

1602/2-3 april 1981/deutsche grammophon sessions
london symphony orchestra/claudio abbado
strauss tod und verklärung; till eulenspiegel/
2532 099

1603/8-9 april 1981/decca sessions
london philharmonic orchestra/georg solti/
vladimir ashkenazy
bartok piano concerto 1/410 1081

1604/13-18 april 1981/decca sessions
academy of ancient music/christopher
hogwood/soloists
handel la resurrezione/D256 D3

1605/4-11 may 1981/decca sessions
national philharmonic orchestra/richard bonynge/
***london voices/soloists**
ballet music by rossini-respighi & rossini-btitten/
SXDL 7539
gay the beggar's opera/D252 D2

1606/14-16 may 1981/emi sessions
london philharmonic orchestra/klaus tennstedt/
london philharmonic choir/soloists
mahler symphony 2/SLS 5243

1607/29 may-8 june 1981/decca sessions
london philharmonic orchestra/georg solti/
london opera chorus/soloists
mozart le nozze di figaro/D267 D4
recording completed in december 1981

1608/15 june 1981/rca sessions
london symphony orchestra/wolfgang sawallisch/uto ughi
beethoven violin concerto/RL 31590

1609/25 june-10 july 1981/emi sessions
philharmonia orchestra/riccardo muti/
***ambrosian singers/*soloists**
*gluck orfeo ed euridice/SLS 5255
tchaikovsky manfred/ASD 4169

1610/27 july 1981/decca sessions
radu lupu
piano works by brahms/SXDL 7561

1611/14-15 sepember 1981/oiseau lyre sessions
academy of ancient music/christopher hogwood/soloists
violin concerti by bach/DSDL 702

1612/12-14 october 1981/decca sessions
philip jones brass ensemble/elgar howarth
works by handel/SXDL 7564

1613/23-24 october 1981/argo sessions
city of london sinfonia/richard hickox/ lso chorus/woburn singers/soloists
geoffrey burgon requiem/ZRDL 1007

1614/4-8 november 1981/deutsche grammophon sessions
london symphony orchestra/claudio abbado/*rudolf serkin
*mozart piano concerti 12 & 20/2532 053
mussorgsky pictures & ravel bolero/2532 057
*mozart piano concerti 9 & 17/2532 060

1615/16-20 november 1981/decca sessions
academy of ancient music/christopher hogwood
mozart symphonies/D167 D3 and D172 D4

1616/24-27 november 1981/decca sessions
jorge bolet
schubert-liszt transcriptions/SXDL 7569

1617/10-11 december 1981/decca sessions
london sinfonietta/riccardo chailly
walton façade/421 7192 (cd only)

1618/14-16 december 1981/decca sessions
london philharmonic orchestra/georg solti
haydn symphonies 102 & 103/SXDL 7570

1619/17 december 1981/decca session
english chamber orchestra/vladimir ashkenazy
schoenberg verklärte nacht/410 1111

1620/20-23 december 1981/decca sessions
fitzwilliam string quartet/christopher van kampen (cello)
schubert string quintet D956/SXDL 7571

1621/4-9 january 1982/oiseau lyre sessions
mediaeval ensemble of london
works by machaut/DSDL 704

1622/15-16 january 1982/argo sessions
london symphony orchestra/richard hickox/
lso & westminster choirs/soloists
durufle requiem/ZRDL 1009

1623/22-29 january 1982/decca sessions
philip jones brass ensemble
festive music for christmas/SXDL 7576

1624/30 january 1982/decca sessions
london philharmonic orchestra/
rudolf barshai/boris belkin
prokofiev violin concerto 2/SXDL 7579

1625/9-12 february 1982/decca sessions
philharmonia orchestra/vladimir ashkenazy
beethoven symphony 6/SXDL 7578
mozart piano concerto 25/411 8101

1626/17-19 february 1982/decca sessions
jorge bolet
piano works by liszt/SXDL 7596

1627/25-26 february 1982/decca sessions
academy of ancient music/christopher hogwood
mozart symphonies/D172 D4 and D173 D3

1628/15-17 march 1982/decca sessions
philip jones brass ensemble
music of the gabrielis/SXDL 7581

1629/19-20 march 1982/deutsche grammophon
**london symphony orchestra/claudio abbado/
rudolf serkin**
mozart piano concerto 27/unpublished

1630/23 march 1982/emi sessions
**london philharmonic orchestra/zubin mehta/
ravi shankar**
shankar sitar concerto 2/ASD 4314

1631/24-25 march 1982/decca sessions
philharmonia orchestra/vladimir ashkenazy
sibelius symphony 7; tapiola/SXDL 7580

1632/30 march-4 april 1982/decca sessions
**welsh national opera orchestra/richard
bonynge/wno chorus/soloists**
verdi I masnadieri/D273 D3

1633/5-7 april 1982/decca sessions
national philharmonic orchestra/richard bonynge
ballet music by chopin-douglas and
ambroise thomas/SXDL 7583

1634/13-15 april 1982/decca sessions
andras schiff
bach keyboard works BWV 802, BWV 903
and BWV 988/D275 D2

1635/13-17 april 1982/decca sessions
vladimir ashkenazy/vovka ashkenazy
piano works by chopin, ravel and scriabin/
SXDL 7584, SXDL 7593 and 410 2551

1636/5-7 may 1982/emi sessions
london philharmonic orchestra/klaus tennstedt/lucia popp
mahler symphony 4/ASD 4344

1637/10-11 may 1982/decca sessions
royal philharmonic orchestra/walter weller
brahms complete hungarian dances/
SXDL 7585

1638/25 may-12 june 1982/decca sessions
national philharmonic orchestra/georg solti/
london opera chorus/soloists
verdi un ballo In maschera/410 2101
recording completed in may 1983

1639/14-19 june 1982/decca sessions
vladimir ashkenazy/*elisabeth soederstroem
piano works by chopin/SXDL 7593 & 410 1221
*recitalof songs by tchaikovsky/SXDL 7606
mussorgsky pictures from an exhibition/SXDL 7624

1640/25-26 june 1982/emi sessions
philharmonia orchestra/riccardo muti/
gidon kremer
violin concerti by sibelius and schumann/
ASD 143 5191

1641/28 june-11 july 1982/emi sessions
philharmonia orchestra/riccardo muti/
*ambrosian singers/*soloists
*donizetti don pasquale/SLS 143 4363
mozart symphony 24/ASD 143 5281

1642/14-22 july 1982/decca sessions
national philharmonic orchestra/
riccardo chailly
verdi overtures/SXDL 7595

1643/26-27 july 1982/argo sessions
academy of st martin in the fields/iona brown
mozart violin concerti 1 and 5/ZRDL 1014

1644/6-7 august 1982/rca sessions
**london symphony orchestra/georges pretre/
uto ughi**
mendelssohn violin concerto; bruch
violin concerto 1/RD 70111

1645/16-19 august 1982/decca sessions
**english chamber orchestra/jeffrey tate/
kiri te kanawa**
canteloube chants d'auvergne 1-3/SXDL 7604

1646/9 september 1982/decca sessions
vladimir ashkenazy/instrumentalists
bartok works for pianos and percussion/
410 1081

1647/14-22 september 1982/decca sessions
***london symphony orchestra/*ivan fischer/
jorge bolet**
*rachmaninov piano concerto 3/SXDL 7609
piano works by liszt/SXDL 7596, SXDL 7622
and 410 1611

1648/22 september 1982/decca session
vladimir ashkenazy
piano works by chopin/410 1221

1649/26-30 september 1982/decca sessions
philharmonia orchestra/vladimir ashkenazy/
*lynn harrell
mozart piano concerto 15/SXL 7010
*dvorak cello concerto; bruch kol nidrei/SXDL 7608
mussorgsky pictures from an exhibition/410 1211
mussorgsky recording completed in february 1983

1650/2-3 october 1982/decca sessions
lynn harrell
bach cello suites 1 and 3/414 1651

1651/7-9 october 1982/oiseau lyre sessions
academy of ancient music/christopher hogwood/
christopher coin
haydn cello concerti in c and d/DSDL 711

1652/11-12 october 1982/decca sessions
philip jones brass ensemble
saint-saens carnaval des animaux/410 1251

1653/22-24 october 1982/deutsche grammophon
london symphony orchestra/claudio abbado/
*rudolf serkin
*mozart piano concerti 21 and 27/2532 095
bartok miraculous mandarin/410 5981
bartok recording completed later in
walthamstow town hall

1654/8 november 1982/decca session
english chamber orchestra/vladimir ashkenazy
wagner siegfried idyll/410 1111

1655/16-17 november 1982/emi sessions
philharmonia orchestra/simon rattle
janacek sinfonietta; taras bulba/ASD 143 5221

1656/22 november-2 december 1982/oiseau lyre
academy of ancient music/christopher hogwood
vivaldi the concerti op 8/D279 D2

1657/26-27 november 1982/decca sessions
philharmonia orchestra/charles mackerras
sullivan pineapple poll; di ballo overture/
SXDL 7619

1658/3-4 december 1982/decca sessions
jorge bolet
liszt italie from annees de pelerinage/410 1611

1659/11-14 december 1982/decca sessions
fitzwilliam string quartet
beethoven string quartet op 132/411 6431

1660/11-12 and 23 january 1983/decca sessions
vladimir ashkenazy
piano works by russian composers/SXDL 7624
piano works by chopin/410 1231 and 410 2581

1661/17 january 1983/deutsche grammophon
**london symphony orchestra/claudio abbado/
schlomo mintz**
bartok two portraits/410 5981
recording completed later in walthamtow town hall

1662/31 january 1983/decca session
royal philharmonic orchestra/antal dorati
dvorak complete slavonic dances; american suite/
411 7151
recordings completed later in walthamstow town hall

1663/1-2 february 1983/decca sessions
philip jones brass ensemble
music for brass by french composers/410 1251

1664/9-10 february 1983/decca sessions
philharmonia orchestra/vladimir ashkenazy/
*london opera chorus
*borodin polovtsian dances from prince igor/410 1211
beethoven egmont overture/411 9411
mozart piano concerto 20/414 3371

1665/1-2 march 1983/decca sessions
lynn harrell
bach cello suite 2/414 1631

1666/3 and 13 march 1983/decca sessions
royal opera orchestra/john lanchbery
herold-lanchbery la fille mal gardee ballet/410 1901

1667/8-11 march 1983/decca sessions
jorge bolet
liszt suisse from annees de pelerinage/
410 1601

1668/16-17 march 1983/philips sessions
philharmonia orchestra/neville marriner/
ambrosian singers/soloists
mendelssohn sommernachtstraum
incidental music/411 1061

1669/6-18 april 1983/decca sessions
welsh national opera orchestra/richard bonynge/
*wno chorus/*soloists
*ambroise thomas hamlet/410 1841
massenet ballet music from le cid/410 1891

1670/19-20 april 1983/decca sessions
marc raubenheimer
piano works by schumann/414 0351
recordings completed in june 1983

1671/28 april-9 may 1983/emi sessions
london philharmonic orchestra/klaus tennstedt
mahler symphony 6/SLS 143 5743

1672/16-18 may 1983/decca sessions
pascal roge
piano works by satie/410 2201

1673/16-21 may 1983/deutsche grammophon
london symphony orchestra/claudio abbado/
rudolf serkin
mozart piano concerto 27/2532 070
mozart piano concerti 19 & 25/410 9891

1674/17 may 1983/decca sessions
philharmonia orchestra/vladimir ashkenazy
sibelius symphony 3/414 2671

1675/23 may & 11-13 june 1983/decca sessions
vladimir ashkenazy
piano works by chopin/410 1231 & 410 2531
piano works by ravel/410 2551

1676/24-25 june 1983/deutsche grammophon
philharmonia orchestra/giuseppe sinopoli
schubert symphony 8; mendelssohn symphony 4/
410 8621

1677/27-28 june 1983/decca sessions
philip jones brass ensemble/elgar howarth
marches by sousa/410 2901

1678/2-3 july 1983/cbs sessions
english chamber orchestra/murray perahia
mozart early piano concerto arrangements/39222

1679/2-3 august 1983/rca sessions
philharmonia orchestra/wolfgang sawallisch/uto ughi
brahms violin concerto/RD 70072

1680/8 august 1983/film soundtrack recording
london symphony orchestra/michel legrand
never say never again
recording completed later in olympia studios barnes

1681/16-18 august 1983/philips ensayo sessions
english chamber orchestra/enrique garcia asensio/ jose carreras
you belong to my heart/411 4221

1682/2-3 september 1983/decca sessions
london symphony orchestra/ivan fischer/boris belkin
brahms violin concerto/411 6771

1683/10-14 september 1983/decca sessions
vladimir ashkenazy
scriabin piano sonata 8/414 3531

1684/12-25 september 1983/decca sessions
andras schiff
bach partitas & inventions/411 7321 & 411 9741

1685/15-18 september 1983/decca sessions
lynn harrell
bach cello suites 4 and 5/414 1631

1686/16-17 september 1983/decca sssions
fitzwilliam string quartet/vladimir ashkenazy
shostakovich piano quintet/411 9401

1687/19-23 september 1983/oiseau lyre sessions
academy of ancient music/christopher hogwood/
*academy chorus/*soloists
*mozart requiem/411 7121
haydn symphony 94/411 8321
haydn symphony 100/414 3301

1688/26-28 september 1983/decca sessions
english chamber orchestra/jeffrey tate/
kiri te kanawa
canteloube chants d'auvergne/411 7301

1689/3-12 october 1983/oiseau lyre sessions
academy of ancient music/christopher hogwood
mozart serenades K239 & K286; eine kleine nachtmusik/411 7201
handel concerti HWV 332-334/411 7212

1690/19-22 october 1983/decca sessions
jorge bolet
piano works by liszt/411 8031

1691/25-31 october 1983/decca session
philharmonia orchestra/vladimir ashkenazy
mozart piano concerto 26/411 8101
beethoven symphony 7; coriolan overture/
411 8411
piano works by chopin/411 8961

1692/21-26 november 1983/oiseau lyre sessions
**academy of ancient music/christopher hogwood/
*westminster cathedral choir/*emma kirkby**
*mozart choral works/411 8321
haydn symphony 104/411 8331
purcell scenes from a fool's preferment/414 1731
beethoven symphony 1/414 3381

1693/27 november-10 december 1983/
decca sessions
london philharmonic orchestra/georg solti
haydn symphonies 94 and 100/411 8972

1694/30 november-3 december 1983/
deutsche grammophon sessions
london symphony orchestra/claudio abbado/soloists
pergolesi stabat mater/415 1031

1695/7 december 1983/decca sessions
national philharmonic orchestra/richard bonynge/*nigel kennedy
ballet music by berlioz, weber, lecocq and *massenet/410 1891 and 411 8981

1696/10-12 december 1983/decca sessions
fitzwilliam string quartet
beethoven string quartet op 130; grosse fuge/411 9431

1697/14-23 december 1983/philips sessions
philharmonia orchestra/claudio scimone/ ambrosian singers/soloists
rossini maometto secondo/412 1481

1698/28 december 1983-5 january 1984/
deutsche grammophon sessions
philharmonia orchestra/giuseppe sinopoli/ royal opera chorus/soloists
puccini manon lescaut/413 8931

APPENDIX A: INDEX OF CONDUCTORS

number in the first column is the session at which the conductor first worked in kingsway hall; list also includes instrumentalists who directed from the podium

0951	**claudio abbado**/1933-2014
0461	**otto ackermann**/1909-1960
1495	**kurt adler**/1907-1977
0638	**raymond agoult**/1911-1992
0995	**john alldis**/1929-2010
1531	**antonio de almeida**/1928-1997
0700	**kenneth alwyn**/1925
0375	**franz andre**/1903-1990
0199	**ernest ansermet**/1883-1969
0635	**ataulfo argenta**/1913-1958
0570	**malcolm arnold**/1921-2006
1681	**enrique garcia asensio**/1937
1273	**vladimir ashkenazy**/1937
1121	**david atherton**/1944
0375	**franco autori**/1903-1990
0373	**samuel barber**/1910-1981
0018	**john barbirolli**/1899-1970
1211	**daniel barenboim**/1942
1624	**rudolf barshai**/1924-2010
1376	**steuart bedford**/1939
0098	**thomas beecham**/1879-1961
0128	**sidney beer**/1899-1971
0224	**eduard van beinum**/1901-1961
0043	**vincenzo bellezza**/1888-1964
1304	**paavo berglund**/1929-2012
1338	**luciano berio**/1925-2003
1275	**lennox berkeley**/1903-1989

index of conductors/continued

0350	anthony bernard/1891-1963
0851	stanley black/1913-2002
1520	richard blackford/1954
0371	richard blareau/1910-1979
0477	harry blech/1910-1999
0073	leo blech/1871-1958
0496	arthur bliss/1891-1975
0335	ernest bloch/1880-1959
0846	karl böhm/1894-1981
0604	paul bonneau/1918-1998
0850	richard bonynge/1930
1288	willi boskovsky/1909-1991
1215	pierre boulez/1925-2016
0010	adrian boult/1889-1983
1556	iona brown/1941-2004
0991	grayston burgess/1932
1282	nicholas braithwaite/1939
0093	warwick braithwaite/1896-1971
0521	benjamin britten/1913-1976
0095	adolf busch/1891-1952
0256	salvador camerata/1913-2005
0162	basil cameron/1884-1975
0465	guido cantelli/1920-1956
0289	sergiu celibidache/1912-1996
1509	riccardo chailly/1953
1530	giancarlo chiaramello/1939
0927	carlo felice cillario/1915-2007
1242	alan civil/1929-1989
0432	andre cluytens/1905-1967

index of conductors/continued

0006 albert coates/1882-1953
0130 eric coates/1886-1957
0036 lawrance collingwood/1887-1982
0166 anthony collins/1893-1963
1279 sergiu commissiona/1928-2005
0050 piero coppola/1888-1971
1337 ainslee cox/1936-1988
0754 edric cundell/1893-1961
0580 glauco curiel
1248 andrew davis/1944
0753 colin davis/1927-2013
0971 norman del mar/1919-1994
0239 roger desormiere/1898-1963
0365 issay dobrowen/1891-1953
1290 leonard dommett/1928-2006
0090 antal dorati/1906-1988
0830 edward downes/1924-2009
1521 per dreier/1929-1997
1424 charles dutoit/1936
0916 sixten ehrling/1918-2005
0017 edward elgar/1857-1934
0263 george enescu/1881-1955
0276 alberto erede/1909-2001
0904 oliviero de fabritiis/1902-1982
0337 robert farnon/1917-2005
0552 dino fedri
0818 franco ferraris
1647 ivan fischer/1951
0129 anatole fistoulari/1907-1995

index of conductors/continued

0208	gregor fitelberg/1879-1953
0691	oivin fjeldstad/1903-1983
1151	lawrence foster/1941
1054	massimo freccia/1906-2004
0984	myer fredman/1932-2014
	louis de froment/1921-1994
0878	rafael frühbeck de burgos/1933-2014
0285	wilhelm furtwängler/1886-1954
0237	alceo galliera/1910-1996
1419	james galway/1939
0569	pierino gamba/1936
0720	douglas gamley/1924-1998
1143	lamberto gardelli/1915-1998
1106	john eliot gardiner/1943
1399	gianandrea gavazzeni/1909-1996
0366	peter gellhorn/1912-2004
0920	charles gerhardt/1927-1999
0685	alexander gibson/1926-1995
0344	don gillis/1912-1978
0623	carlo maria giulini/1914-2005
0112	isidore godfrey/1900-1977
0086	walter goehr/1905-1960
0189	reginald goodall/1901-1990
0041	eugene goossens/1893-1962
0220	charles groves/1915-1992
1095	anton guadagno/1925-2002
0454	vittorio gui/1885-1975

index of conductors/continued

1235	**alan hacker/1938-2012**
1423	**bernard haitink/1929**
0109	**charles hambourg**
1393	**vernon handley/1930-2008**
0230	**julius harrison/1885-1963**
0061	**robert heger/1886-1978**
1334	**laszlo heltay**
0031	**victor hely hutchinson/1901-1947**
0778	**skitch henderson/1918-2005**
1104	**bernard herrmann/1911-1975**
1572	**richard hickox/1948-2008**
0631	**paul hindemith/1895-1963**
1582	**christopher hogwood/1941-2014**
0931	**imogen holst/1907-1984**
1009	**jascha horenstein/1898-1973**
1374	**elgar howarth/1935**
1100	**george hurst/1926-2012**
0946	**emanuel hurwitz/1919-2006**
1148	**francois huybrechts**
0240	**ernest irving/1878-1953**
0408	**robert irving/1913-1995**
0195	**reginald jacques/1894-1969**
1400	**eugen jochum/1902-1987**
0174	**enrique jorda/1911-1996**
1223	**okko kamu/1946**
0338	**herbert von karajan/1908-1989**
0610	**rudolf kempe/1910-1976**
0857	**istvan kertesz/1929-1973**
0536	**aram khachaturian/1903-1978**
0248	**royalton kisch/1920-1995**

index of conductors/continued

0284	erich kleiber/1890-1956
0530	otto klemperer/1885-1973
0294	paul kletzki/1900-1973
0283	hans knappertsbusch/1888-1965
1598	kyril kondrashin/1914-1981
1360	kasimierz kord/1930
0265	clemens krauss/1893-1954
0585	henry krips/1912-1987
0270	josef krips/1902-1974
0428	rafael kubelik/1914-1996
0088	efrem kurtz/1900-1995
0097	constant lambert/1905-1951
0832	john lanchbery/1923-2003
1306	michael lankester
1680	michel legrand/1932
0760	rene leibowitz/1913-1972
0216	erich leinsdorf/1912-1993
0811	raymond leppard/1927
1580	james levine/1943
1060	henry lewis/1932-1996
1146	jacques loussier/1934
0659	leopold ludwig/1908-1979
0541	peter maag/1919-2001
0841	lorin maazel/1930-2014
1591	ralph mace
0609	charles mackerras/1925-2010

index of conductors/continued

1156	**leone magiera**/1934
0811	**george malcolm**/1917-1997
0339	**nicolai malko**/1883-1961
0194	**annunzio mantovani**/1905-1980
0367	**igor markevitch**/1912-1983
0885	**neville marriner**/1924-2016
0234	**jean martinon**/1910-1976
1590	**eduardo mata**/1942-1995
0527	**lovro von matacic**/1899-1985
1267	**john matheson**/1928-2009
0197	**muir mathieson**/1911-1975
0324	**hans may**/1886-1958
1018	**zubin mehta**/1936
0717	**yehudi menuhin**/1916-1999
0172	**maurice miles**/1908-1985
0790	**francesco molinari-pradelli**/1911-1996
0662	**pierre monteux**/1875-1964
0715	**jean morel**/1903-1975
0251	**charles munch**/1891-1968
1198	**david munrow**/1942-1976
1329	**riccardo muti**/1941
0132	**boyd neel**/1905-1981
0656	**harry newstone**/1921-2006
0076	**einar nilson**/1907-1996
0982	**roger norrington**/1934
0134	**victor olof**/1898-1974
1085	**carlos paita**/1932-2015
1439	**franco patane**/1908-1968
1678	**murray perahia**/1947

index of conductors/continued

0986	**wilhelm pitz/1897-1973**
0277	**gaston poulet/1892-1974**
1013	**frederick prausnitz/1920-2004**
0852	**georges pretre/1924-2017**
0958	**andre previn/1929**
0424	**john pritchard/1921-1989**
0788	**argeo quadri/1911-2004**
0145	**karl rankl/1898-1968**
1503	**simon rattle/1955**
0525	**alan rawsthorne/1905-1971**
0152	**clarence raybould/1886-1972**
0113	**wynn reeves**
0748	**nicola rescigno/1916-2008**
0445	**fritz rieger/1910-1978**
0655	**hugo rignold/1905-1976**
0374	**james robertson/1912-1991**
1177	**eric robinson/1908-1974**
0144	**stanford robinson/1904-1984**
1093	**eric rogers/1921-1981**
0028	**landon ronald/1873-1938**
1463	**antoni ros marba/1937**
1413	**mstislav rostropovich/1927-2007**
1458	**miklos rosza/1907-1995**
1265	**julius rudel/1921-2014**
0211	**victor de sabata/1892-1967**
1599	**kurt sanderling/1912-2011**

index of conductors/continued

1226	nello santi/1931
0029	malcolm sargent/1895-1967
0516	wolfgang sawallisch/1923-2013
0658	thomas schippers/1930-1977
0634	heinrich schmidt
0456	hans schmidt-isserstedt/1900-1973
0406	wilhelm schüchter/1911-1974
0286	carl schuricht/1880-1967
0413	rudolf schwarz/1905-1994
1697	claudio scimone/1934-2016
0312	george scott-wood
1293	uri segal/1944
0775	matyas seiber/1905-1960
0861	jerzy semkow/1926-2014
0742	tullio serafin/1878-1968
1289	jose serebrier/1938
0375	tibor serly/1901-1978
0765	robert sharples/1913-1987
0643	constantin silvestri/1913-1969
1676	giuseppe sinopoli/1946-2001
0330	georg solti/1912-1997
1549	robin stapleton
0672	william steinberg/1899-1978
1229	paul steinitz/1909-1988
0065	max steinmann
0252	fritz stiedry/1883-1968
0390	leopold stokowski/1882-1977
1564	ettore stratta/1936-2015
0319	oscar straus/1870-1954

index of conductors/concluded

0195	**walter susskind**/1913-1980
0096	**george szell**/1897-1970
1645	**jeffrey tate**/1943-2017
0410	**vilem tausky**/1910-2004
1460	**klaus tennstedt**/1926-1998
0305	**mansel thomas**/1909-1986
0907	**michael tippett**/1905-1998
1390	**loris tjeknavorian**/1937
0823	**antonio tonini**
0015	**geoffrey toye**/1889-1942
0140	**heinz unger**/1895-1965
0707	**andre vandernoot**/1927-1991
1196	**silvio varviso**/1924-2006
1253	**hans vonk**/1942-2004
1315	**edo de waart**/1941
0725	**heinz wallberg**/1923-2004
0333	**bruno walter**/1876-1962
0455	**william walton**/1902-1983
0118	**felix weingartner**/1863-1942
0215	**george weldon**/1908-1963
1254	**walter weller**/1939-2015
0913	**david willcocks**/1919-2015
0254	**carlo zecchi**/1903-1984
0912	**david zinman**/1936

APPENDIX B: GUIDE TO MAIN RECORD PREFIXES OCCURRING IN THIS DISCOGRAPHY

78 RPM RECORDS

His Master's Voice
DB series (12-inch)
C series (12-inch)
B series (10-inch)
DA series (10-inch)
D series (12-inch)
E series (10-inch)

Columbia
DX series (12-inch)
DB series (10-inch)
LX series (12-inch)
LB series (10-inch)

Decca
K/AK series (12-inch)
F series (10-inch)
X/AX series (12-inch)
M series (10-onch)

AK and AX prefixes were applied to sets of discs issued in auto coupling

45 RPM EXTENDED PLAY RECORDS

His Master's Voice
7EB series (7-inch)
7EP series (7-inch)
RES series (7-inch)
7EG series (7-inch)
7ER series (7- inch)

Columbia
SED series (7-inch)
SEL series (7-inch)
SEG series (7-inch)
ESL series (7-inch)

Decca
45-71000 series (7-inch)
SEC series (7-inch)
CEP series (7-inch)

guide to record prefixes/continued

33 RPM LONG PLAY RECORDS

His Master's Voice
ALP series (12-inch) ASD series (12-inch)
BLP series (10-inch) BSD series (10-inch)
CLP series (12-inch) CSD series (12-inch)
DLP series (10-inch)

ASD, BSD and CSD series were stereophonic versions

HMV Concert Classics
XLP series (12-inch) SXLP series (12-inch)

SXLP series was stereophonic version

HMV Encore
ENC series (12-inch)

HMV Angel
AN series (12-inch) SAN series (12-inch)

SAN series was stereophonic version

Columbia
33CX series (12-inch) SAX series (12-inch)
33C series (10-inch)   SBO series (10-inch)
33SX series (12-inch) SCX series (12-inch)

SAX, SBO and SCX series were stereophonic versions

Parlophone
PMC series (12-inch) PMD series (10-inch)

Music for Pleasure/Classics for Pleasure
MFP series (12-inch)   CFP series (12-inch)
SMFP series (12-inch) CFPD series (12-inch)

World Records
T series (12-inch)   ST series (12-inch)
SH series (12-inch)

guide to record prefixes/continued

EMI (amalgamation of HMV and Columbia)

ASD series (12-inch)
SLS series (12-inch)
RLS series (12-inch)
ED series (12-inch)
EL series (12-inch)
EMX series (12-inch)
ESD series (12-inch)
EX series (12-inch)
HLM series (12-inch)
HQM series (12-inch)
HQS series (12-inch)
SXDW series (12-inch)
TWO series (12-inch)

SLS, RLS and EX series were multiple sets of records

Decca

LXT series (12-inch)
SXL series (12-inch)
SXDL series (12-inch)
MET series (12-inch)
SET series (12-inch)
LK series (12-inch)
PFS series (12-inch)
OPFS series (12-inch)
D000 D0 series (12-inch)
LM series (10-inch)
LW series (10-inch)
LX series (10-inch)
BR series (10-inch)
SWL series (10-inch)
SPA series (12-inch)
JB series (12-inch)
VIV series (12-inch)[i]
HEAD series (12-inch)

D000 DO series were multiple sets of records; MET/SET and OPFS series also included multiple sets

Decca Ace of Clubs

ACL series (12-inch)

Decca Eclipse

ECM series (12-inch)
ECS series (12-inch)

Decca Ace of Diamonds

ADD series (12-inch)
SDD series (12-inch)

Argo

RG series (12-inch)
ZRG series (12-inch)
ZRDL series (12-inch)
NF series (12-inch)
ZNF series (12-inch)

guide to record prefixes/continued

Oiseau Lyre
OL series (12-inch) SOL series (12-inch)
DSDL series (12-inch)

Lyrita
RCS series (12-inch) SRCS series (12-inch)

RCA
LM series (12-inch) LSC series (12-inch)
LSB series (12-inch) LD series (12-inch)
LDS series (12-inch) RB series (12-inch)
SB series (12-inch) VIC series (12-inch)
VICS series (12-inch) GL series (12-inch)
RD series (12-inch) RL series (12-inch)
ARL1-0000 series (12-inch) ATC1-0000 series (12-inch)
LRL1-0000 series (12-inch) CRL5-0000 series (12-inch)

LD, LDS and CRL5-0000 series were multiple sets

Capitol
P series (12-inch) SP series (12-inch)

Readers Digest
RD series (12-inch) RDM series (12-inch)
RDS series (12-inch)

Vox Turnabout
TV series (12-inch) TVS series (12-inch)

Ensayo
ZL series (12-inch)

Lodia
LOD series (12-inch)

guide to record prefixes/concluded

Electrola
1C063 00000 series (12-inch)
SHZE series (12-inch)

EMI Italiana
3C053 00000 series (12-inch)

Philips
6500 000 series (12-inch)   9500 000 series (12-inch)
6769 000 series (12-inch)
6769 000 series were multiple sets of records

Deutsche Grammophon
2530 000 series (12-inch)   2531 000 series (12-inch)
2532 000 series (12-inch)   2721 000 series (12-inch)
2721 000 series were multiple sets of records

Polygram (amalgamation of Decca, Philips and Deutsche Grammophon)
410 0000 series (12-inch)   411 0000 series (12-inch)
412 0000 series (12-inch)   413 0000 series (12-inch)
414 0000 series (12-inch)
all series included both single and multiple sets of records

Books published by Travis & Emery Music Bookshop:

Anon.: Hymnarium Sarisburiense, cum Rubricis et Notis Musicis.
Anon.: Säcularfeier des Geburtstages von Ludwig van Beethoven
Agricola, Johann Friedrich from Tosi: Anleitung zur Singkunst.
Allen, Percy: The Stage Life of Mrs. Stirling: With ... C19th Theatre
Bach, C.P.E.: edited W. Emery: Nekrolog or Obituary Notice of J.S. Bach.
Bateson, Naomi Judith: Alcock of Salisbury
Bathe, William: A Briefe Introduction to the Skill of Song
Berlioz, Hector: Autobiography of Hector Berlioz, (2 vols.)
Buckley, Robert John: Sir Edward Elgar
Burney, Charles: The Present State of Music in France and Italy
Burney, Charles: The Present State of Music in Germany, The Netherlands ...
Burney, Charles: Account of an Infant Musician
Burney, Charles: An Account of the Musical Performances ... Handel
Burney, Karl: Nachricht von Georg Friedrich Handel's Lebensumstanden.
Burns, Robert: The Caledonian Musical Museum .. Best Scotch Songs. (1810)
Cobbett, W.W.: Cobbett's Cyclopedic Survey of Chamber Music. (2 vols.)
Corrette, Michel: Le Maitre de Clavecin
Cox, John Edmund: Musical Recollections of the Last Half Century. (2 vols.)
Crimp, Bryan: Dear Mr. Rosenthal ... Dear Mr. Gaisberg ...
Crimp, Bryan: Solo: The Biography of Solomon
Crotch, William: Substance of Several Courses of Lectures on Music
d'Indy, Vincent: Beethoven: Biographie Critique
d'Indy, Vincent: Beethoven: A Critical Biography
d'Indy, Vincent: Cesar Franck (in English)
d'Indy, Vincent: César Franck (in French)
Dianna, B.A.: Benjamin Britten's Holy Theatre
Dolge, Alfred: Pianos and Their Makers. A Comprehensive History
Fischhof, Joseph: Versuch einer Geschichte des Clavierbaues. (Faksimile 1853).
Fuller-Maitland, J.A.: The Music of Parry and Stanford
Geminiani, Francesco: The Art of Playing the Violin.
Häuser: Musikalisches Lexikon. 2 vols in one.
Hawkins, John: A General History of the Science & Practice of Music (5 vols.)
Holmes, Edward: A Ramble among the Musicians of Germany
Hopkins, Antony: The Concertgoer's Companion - Bach to Haydn.
Hopkins, Antony: The Concertgoer's Companion – Holst to Webern.
Hopkins, Antony: Music All Around Me
Hopkins, Antony: Sounds of Music / Sounds of the Orchestra
Hopkins, Antony: The Nine Symphonies of Beethoven
Hopkins, Antony: Understanding Music

Books published by Travis & Emery Music Bookshop:

Hopkins, Edward & Rimboult, Edward: The Organ. Its History & Construction.
Hunt, John: - see separate list of discographies at the end of these titles
Iliffe, Frederick: The Forty-Eight Preludes and Fugues of John Sebastian Bach
Isaacs, Lewis: Hänsel and Gretel. A Guide to Humperdinck's Opera.
Isaacs, Lewis: Königskinder (Royal Children). Guide to Humperdinck's Opera.
Kastner: Manuel Général de Musique Militaire
Kenney, Charles Lamb: A Memoir of Michael William Balfe
Klein, Hermann: Thirty years of musical Life in London, 1870-1900
Lacassagne, M. l'Abbé Joseph : Traité Général des élémens du Chant
Lascelles (née Catley), Anne: The Life of Miss Anne Catley.
McCormack, John: John McCormack: His Own Life Story.
Mainwaring, John: Memoirs of the Life of the Late George Frederic Handel
Malcolm, Alexander: A Treaty of Music: Speculative, Practical and Historical
Manshardt, Thomas: Aspects of Cortot
Marx, Adolph Bernhard: Die Kunst des Gesanges, Theoretisch-Practisch
May, Florence: The Life of Brahms
May, Florence: The Girlhood Of Clara Schumann: Clara Wieck And Her Time.
Mellers, Wilfrid: Angels of the Night: Popular Female Singers of Our Time
Mellers, Wilfrid: Bach and the Dance of God
Mellers, Wilfrid: Beethoven and the Voice of God
Mellers, Wilfrid: Caliban Reborn - Renewal in Twentieth Century Music
Mellers, Wilfrid: Darker Shade of Pale, A Backdrop to Bob Dylan
Mellers, Wilfrid: François Couperin and the French Classical Tradition
Mellers, Wilfrid: Harmonious Meeting
Mellers, Wilfrid: Le Jardin Retrouvé, The Music of Frederic Mompou
Mellers, Wilfrid: Music and Society, England and the European Tradition
Mellers, Wilfrid: Music in a New Found Land: ... ... American Music
Mellers, Wilfrid: Romanticism and the Twentieth Century (from 1800)
Mellers, Wilfrid: The Masks of Orpheus: …… the Story of European Music.
Mellers, Wilfrid: The Sonata Principle (from c. 1750)
Mellers, Wilfrid: Vaughan Williams and the Vision of Albion
Newmarch, Rosa: Henry J. Wood
Newmarch, Rosa: Jean Sibelius
Newmarch, Rosa: Mary Wakefield, a Memoir
Newmarch, Rosa: The Concert-Goer's Library
Newmarch, Rosa: The Music of Czechoslovakia
Newmarch, Rosa: The Russian Opera.
Nicholas, Jeremy: Godowsky, the Pianists' Pianist
Niecks, Frederick: The Life of Chopin. (2 vols.)

Books published by Travis & Emery Music Bookshop:

Panchianio, Cattuffio: Rutzvanscad Il Giovine
Pearce, Charles: Sims Reeves, Fifty Years of Music in England.
Pepusch, John Christopher: A Treatise on Harmony ...
Pettitt, Stephen: Philharmonia Orchestra: A Record of Achievement, 1948-1985
Pettitt, Stephen (ed. Hunt): Philharmonia Orchestra: Discography 1945-1987
Playford, John: An Introduction to the Skill of Musick.
Porte, John: Sir Charles Villiers Stanford.
Quantz, Johann: Versuch einer Anweisung die Flöte traversiere zu spielen.
Rameau, Jean-Philippe: Code de Musique Pratique, ou Methodes.
Rameau, Jean-Philippe: Erreurs sur La Musique dans l'Encyclopédie
Rastall, Richard: The Notation of Western Music.
Rimbault, Edward: The Pianoforte, Its Origins, Progress, and Construction.
Rousseau, Jean Jacques: Dictionnaire de Musique
Rubinstein, Anton : Guide to the proper use of the Pianoforte Pedals.
Sainsbury, John S.: Dictionary of Musicians. (1825). (2 vols.)
Schumann, Clara & Brahms, Johannes: Letters 1853-1896. (2 vols.)
Scott-Sutherland: Arnold Bax
Serré de Rieux, Jean de : Les dons des Enfans de Latone
Simpson, Christopher: A Compendium of Practical Musick in Five Parts
Smyth, Ethel: Impressions That Remained. (2 vols.)
Spohr, Louis: Autobiography
Spohr, Louis: Grand Violin School
Tans'ur, William: A New Musical Grammar; or The Harmonical Spectator
Terry, Charles Sanford: Bach's Chorals – Parts 1, 2 and 3.
Terry, Charles Sanford: John Christian Bach
Terry, Charles Sanford: J.S. Bach's Original Hymn-Tunes - Congregational Use.
Terry, Charles Sanford: Four-Part Chorals of J.S. Bach. (German & English)
Terry, Charles Sanford: Joh. Seb. Bach, Cantata Texts, Sacred and Secular.
Terry, Charles Sanford: The Origins of the Family of Bach Musicians.
Tosi, Pierfrancesco: Opinioni de' Cantori Antichi, e Moderni
Tosi, Pierfrancesco: Observations on the Florid Song.
Tovey, Donald Francis: A Musician Talks, The Integrity of Music
Tovey, Donald Francis: A Musician Talks, Musical Textures
Tovey, Donald Francis: A Companion to "The Art of the Fugue" J.S. Bach
Tovey, Donald Francis: A Companion to Beethoven's Pianoforte Sonatas
Tovey, Donald Francis: Beethoven
Tovey, Donald Francis: Essays in Musical Analysis. (6 vols.).
Tovey, Donald Francis: The integrity of music
Tovey, Donald Francis: Musical Textures

Books published by Travis & Emery Music Bookshop:

Tovey, Donald Francis: Some English Symphonists
Tovey, Donald Francis: The Main Stream of Music.
Van der Straeten, Edmund: History of the Violoncello, The Viol da Gamba ...
Van der Straeten, Edmund: History of the Violin, Its Ancestors... (2 vols.)
Walther, J. G. [Waltern]: Musicalisches Lexikon [Musikalisches Lexicon]
Wagner, Richard: Beethoven (Leipzig 1870)
Wagner, Richard: Lebens-Bericht (Leipzig 1884)
Wagner, Richard: The Musaic of the Future (Translated by E. Dannreuther).
Wyndham, Henry Saxe: The Annals of Covent Garden Theatre. (2 vols.)
Zwirn, Gerald: Stranded Stories From The Operas

Music published by Travis & Emery Music Bookshop:

Bach, Johann Sebastian: Sacred Songs for SCTB, arranged by Franz Wullner.
Bax, Arnold: Symphony #5, Arranged for Piano Four Hands by Walter Emery
Beranger, Pierre Jean de: Musique Des Chansons de Beranger: Airs Notes ...
Bizet, Georges: Djamileh. Vocal Score.
Donizetti, Gaetano: Betly. Dramma Giocoso in Due Atti. Vocal Score.
Frescobaldi, Girolamo: D'Arie Musicali per Cantarsi. Primo & Secondo Libro.
Handel, Purcell, Boyce, Greene ... Calliope or English Harmony: Volume First.
Hopkins, Antony: Sonatine
Purcell, Henry et al: Harmonia Sacra ... The First Book, (1726)
Purcell, Henry et al: Harmonia Sacra ... Book II (1726)
Sullivan, Arthur Seymour: Ivanhoe. Vocal score.
Sullivan, Arthur Seymour: The Rose of Persia. Vocal Score.
Weckerlin, Jean-Baptiste: Chansons Populaires du Pays de France

Other Books, not on Music:

Anon: A Collection of Testimonies Concerning Several Ministers of the Gospel Amongst People called Quakers, Deceased. [Facsimile of 1760 edn.].
Sandeman-Allen, Arthur: Bee-keeping with Twenty hives.

Available from: Travis & Emery at 17 Cecil Court, London, UK.
(+44) (0) 20 7 240 2129. email on sales@travis-and-emery.com .

Discographies by John Hunt.

3 Italian Conductors and 7 Viennese Sopranos: 10 Discographies: Arturo Toscanini, Guido Cantelli, Carlo Maria Giulini, Elisabeth Schwarzkopf, Irmgard Seefried, Elisabeth Gruemmer, Sena Jurinac, Hilde Gueden, Lisa Della Casa, Rita Streich.

A Gallic Trio: 3 Discographies: Charles Muench, Paul Paray, Pierre Monteux.

A Notable Quartet: 4 Discographies: Gundula Janowitz, Christa Ludwig, Nicolai Gedda, Dietrich Fischer-Dieskau.

American Classics: The Discographies of Leonard Bernstein & Eugene Ormand

Antal Dorati 1906-1988: Discography and Concert Register.

Austro-Hungarian Pianists, Discographies of Lili Kraus, Friedrich Gulda, Ingrid Haebler

Back From The Shadows: 4 Discographies: Willem Mengelberg, Dimitri Mitropoulos, Hermann Abendroth, Eduard Van Beinum.

Carlo Maria Giulini: Discography and Concert Register.

Columbia 33CX Label Discography.

Concert Hall Discography: Concert Hall Society and Concert Hall Record Club

Conductors On The Yellow Label: 8 Discographies: Fritz Lehmann, Ferdinand Leitner, Ferenc Fricsay, Eugen Jochum, Leopold Ludwig, Artur Rother, Franz Konwitschny, Igor Markevitch.

Dirigenten der DDR: Conductors of the German Democratic Republic

Fremd bin ich eingezogen - a critical discography of the piano music of Franz Schubert

From Adam to Webern: the Recordings of von Karajan.

Frosh: Discography of the Richard Strauss Opera Die Frau ohne Schatten

Giants of the Keyboard: 6 Discographies: Wilhelm Kempff, Walter Gieseking, Edwin Fischer, Clara Haskil, Wilhelm Backhaus, Artur Schnabel.

Gramophone Stalwarts: 3 Separate Discographies: Bruno Walter, Erich Leinsdorf, Georg Solti.

Great Violinists: 3 Discographies: David Oistrakh, Wolfgang Schneiderhan, Arthur Grumiaux.

Hans Knappertsbusch: Kna: Concert Register and Discography of Hans Knappertsbusch, 1888-1965. Second Edition.

Her Master's Voice: Concert Register and Discography of Dame Elisabeth Schwarzkopf [Third Edition].

Hungarians in Exile: 3 Discographies: Fritz Reiner, Antal Dorati, George Szell.

Kingsway: Classical Music's Premier Recording Venue.

Leopold Stokowski (1882-1977): Discography and Concert Register

Leopold Stokowski: Discography and Concert Listing.

Leopold Stokowski: Second Edition of the Discography.

Makers of the Philharmonia: 11 Discographies Alceo Galliera, Walter Susskind, Paul Kletzki, Nicolai Malko, Issay Dobrowen, Lovro Von Matacic, Efrem Kurtz, Otto Ackermann, Anatole Fistoulari, George Weldon, Robert Irving.

Metropolitan Sopranos: 4 Discographies: Rosa Ponselle, Eleanor Steber, Zinka Milanov, Leontyne Price.

Mezzo and Contraltos: 5 Discographies: Janet Baker, Margarete Klose, Kathleen Ferrier, Giulietta Simionato, Elisabeth Hoengen.

Mid-Century Conductors and More Viennese Singers: 10 Discographies: Karl Boehm, Victor De Sabata, Hans Knappertsbusch, Tullio Serafin, Clemens Krauss, Anton Dermota, Leonie Rysanek, Eberhard Waechter, Maria Reining, Erich Kunz.

More 20th Century Conductors: 7 Discographies: Eugen Jochum, Ferenc Fricsay, Carl Schuricht, Felix Weingartner, Josef Krips, Otto Klemperer, Erich Kleiber.

More Giants of the Keyboard: 5 Discographies: Claudio Arrau, Gyorgy Cziffra, Vladimir Horowitz, Dinu Lipatti, Artur Rubinstein.

More Musical Knights: 4 Discographies: Hamilton Harty, Charles Mackerras, Simon Rattle, John Pritchard.

Musical Knights: 6 Discographies: Henry Wood, Thomas Beecham, Adrian Boult, John Barbirolli, Reginald Goodall, Malcolm Sargent.

Philharmonic Autocrat 1: Discography of: Herbert Von Karajan [3rd Edition]

Philharmonic Autocrat 2: Concert Register of Herbert Von Karajan 2nd. Ed.

Philharmonic Autocrat: Discography of Herbert von Karajan (1908-1989). 4th Ed..

Philharmonisches Orchester Berlin, the historic years, 1913-1954

Philips Minigroove: Second Extended Version of the European Discography.

Pianists For The Connoisseur: 6 Discographies: Arturo Benedetti Michelangeli, Alfred Cortot, Alexis Weissenberg, Clifford Curzon, Solomon, Elly Ney.

Record Pioneers: Richard Strauss, Hans Pfitzner, Oskar Fried, Oswald Kabasta, Karl Muck, Franz Von Hoesslin, Karl Elmendorff.

Sächsische Staatskapelle Dresden: Complete Discography.

Singers of the Third Reich: 5 Discographies: Helge Roswaenge, Tiana Lemnitz, Franz Voelker, Maria Mueller, Max Lorenz.

Singers on the Yellow Label: 7 Discographies: Maria Stader, Elfriede Troetschel, Annelies Kupper, Wolfgang Windgassen, Ernst Haefliger, Josef Greindl, Kim Borg

Six Wagnerian Sopranos: 6 Discographies: Frieda Leider, Kirsten Flagstad, Astrid Varnay, Martha Moedl, Birgit Nilsson, Gwyneth Jones.

Staatskapelle Berlin. The shellac era 1916-1962.

Sviatoslav Richter: Pianist of the Century: Discography.

Teachers and Pupils: 7 Discographies: Elisabeth Schwarzkopf, Maria Ivoguen, Maria Cebotari, Meta Seinemeyer, Ljuba Welitsch, Rita Streich, Erna Berger

Tenors in a Lyric Tradition: 3 Discographies: Peter Anders, Walther Ludwig, Fritz Wunderlich.
The Art of the Diva: 3 Discographies: Claudia Muzio, Maria Callas, Magda Olivero.
The Furtwaengler Sound Sixth Edition: Discography and Concert Listing.
The Furtwängler Sound. Discography of Wilhelm Furtwängler. Seventh Edition.
The Great Dictators: 3 Discographies: Evgeny Mravinsky, Artur Rodzinski, Sergiu Celibidache.
The Lyric Baritone: 5 Discographies: Hans Reinmar, Gerhard Huesch, Josef Metternich, Hermann Uhde, Eberhard Waechter.
The Post-War German Tradition: 5 Discographies: Rudolf Kempe, Joseph Keilberth, Wolfgang Sawallisch, Rafael Kubelik, Andre Cluytens.
Wagner Im Festspielhaus: Discography of the Bayreuth Festival.
Wiener Philharmoniker 1 - Vienna Philharmonic and Vienna State Opera Orchestras: Discography Part 1 1905-1954.
Wiener Philharmoniker 2 - Vienna Philharmonic and Vienna State Opera Orchestras: Discography Part 2 1954-1989.
Wiener Staatsoper: 348 complete relays

Available from: Travis & Emery at 17 Cecil Court, London, UK.
(+44) (0) 20 7 240 2129. email on sales@travis-and-emery.com .

© Travis & Emery 2019

www.ingramcontent.com/pod-product-compliance
Lightning Source LLC
Chambersburg PA
CBHW070748230426
43665CB00017B/2286